THE PLOT TO OVERTHROW VENEZUELA

HOW THE US IS ORCHESTRATING A COUP FOR OIL

DAN KOVALIK

FOREWORD BY OLIVER STONE

HOT BOOKS
an imprint of Skyhorse Publishing, Inc.
New York, NY

Hot Books may be purchased in bulk at special discounts for sales promotion, corporate gifts, fund-raising, or educational purposes. Special editions can also be created to specifications. For details, contact the Special Sales Department, Arcade Publishing, 307 West 36th Street, 11th Floor, New York, NY 10018 or arcade@skyhorsepublishing.com.

Hot Books® is a registered trademark of Skyhorse Publishing, Inc.®, a Delaware corporation.

Visit our website at www.skyhorsepublishing.com.

10 9 8 7 6 5 4 3 2 1

Library of Congress Cataloging-in-Publication Data is available on file.

Cover design by Brian Peterson
Cover photos: Getty Images

Print ISBN: 978-1-5107-5072-2
Ebook ISBN: 978-1-5107-5073-9

Printed in the United States of America

This book is dedicated to my friend, Tibisay Lucena, a champion of democracy, women's rights and proud patriot of the Bolivarian Republic of Venezuela. She is also the bravest person I know.

CONTENTS

FOREWORD

IN A QUITE REVEALING STATEMENT, A senior Trump Administration official recently asserted that the cumulative effects of US sanctions against Venezuela are like Darth Vader's death grip upon that country. This, of course, is true. These sanctions are deadly, and they are killing Venezuelans. The US is attempting to starve out the people of Venezuela, as it has the peoples of so many other countries—e.g., Chile, Iran, Nicaragua—until they bend to its will. Meanwhile, the US and its compliant media blame Venezuela for starving.

What is most revealing about the Darth Vader quip, however, is that it is an inadvertent admission of a quite obvious truth which few are willing to acknowledge—that the US is the Empire in this saga unfolding, not just in Venezuela, but around the world. With its one thousand or so bases around the globe, the US is an empire dwarfing all others that preceded it by a huge magnitude, and yet, unlike all other empires, the US will never consciously admit to its imperial status.

And if the US is the Empire in this morality tale, then surely Venezuela and its people are the outgunned rebels. And yet, many Americans who should know better, including many liberals and self-proclaimed "leftists," find themselves rooting against them and for the Empire and its culture of death.

How befitting, meanwhile, that the US's imperial plans for Venezuela are being led by a real-life villain—Elliott Abrams—a convicted liar and an accomplice in some of the US's worst crimes in Latin America. These crimes include the genocide in Guatemala which claimed around 200,000, mostly Mayan, victims. Also included is an event which made such a horrifying impression on so many of us, myself included—the El Mozote massacre in El Salvador. While Abrams would do his best to cover up and deny this crime, it was impossible to keep it buried for long, for the brutal murder of 1000 people—mostly women and children—is not so easily concealed. Neither is it possible to conceal the guilt of the US, which trained and armed those who carried out this crime.

As Abrams was recently asked by courageous congresswoman Ilhan Omar, we must ask, is Abrams planning another massacre in Venezuela like that of El Mozote? And of course, the answer is a resounding yes. And yet, this horrifying possibility is greeted by our sniveling press with a shrug of the shoulders.

A recent article in *Foreign Affairs* tells us what lay in store for the long-suffering people of Venezuela should the US decide that it can only get what it wants (Venezuela's rich oil supply) by a military invasion. As *Foreign Affairs* explains, in a quite disturbingly dispassionate and clinical fashion, one possible scenario would be, and this is their words, "Death from Above."[1] And "Death from Above" could look something like this:

> In the worst-case scenario, a precision strike operation would last for months, killing possibly thousands of civilians, destroying much of what remains of Venezuela's economy, and wiping out the state security forces. The result would be anarchy. Militias and other armed criminal groups would roam the streets of major cities unchecked, wreaking havoc. More than eight million Venezuelans would likely flee. The chaos would likely lead the United States to send in ground troops in order either to finally dislodge the regime and its security forces or to provide security once the dictatorship had collapsed.

Foreign Affairs notes that we know this is a very real scenario, as we know from other US regime change operations such as the one that has left Libya a wasteland where slaves are now being sold openly in markets. In quite typical fashion, *Foreign Affairs* does not advocate such an operation, but only because it would have negative consequences for the US. The suffering of the Venezuelan people is at best an afterthought.

One might think that such a scenario is unthinkable and complete madness. I would agree, except for one thing—this country, and specifically its policy towards Venezuela, is being led by madmen. Does anyone truly believe that the likes of Trump, John Bolton, Mike Pompeo and Elliott Abrams—caricatures of villainy—can possibly bring about a humane end to the US's regime change operation in Venezuela? The answer should be a resounding "no," but incredibly, many who claim to be in the "resistance" against these thugs, believe that somehow they can and will pull off a "humanitarian intervention" in that country. Of course, such a belief also requires one to ignore the fact that one cannot point to even one intervention of the US in the Global South that has been humane.

Meanwhile, the inhumane consequences of the current US policies toward Venezuela are, as Kovalik details herein, already mounting. The US's theft—and that is what it is—of billions of dollars of Venezuela's oil revenues is already preventing the Venezuelan government from obtaining life-saving medicines for its people. Other US sanctions have already made it impossible for Venezuela to purchase food abroad, to buy necessary parts for its public transportation and electrical system and to generally keep up its civilian infrastructure. In a height of irony, the US sanctions—intended, the Administration claims, to bring democracy to Venezuela—are also preventing Venezuela's National Electoral Commission (CNE) from purchasing equipment necessary to keep up the country's voting machinery.

All of this imposed deprivation is, of course, by design. Indeed, the US's hand-picked puppet, Juan Guaido, has publically threatened the Venezuelan people that they will not have electricity or water until

President Maduro is gone. Mike Pompeo has made similar comments.

Somehow, this is what passes for "humanitarian" intervention in our Orwellian world. Thankfully, Kovalik helps to cut through the Orwellian lies and dissembling which make this intervention possible, and just when such truth-telling is so desperately needed.

—Oliver Stone

PREFACE

Another Regime Change,
Another Barrage of Lies and False Flags

AS I WRITE THESE WORDS, VENEZUELA is still struggling to get back on-line after five straight days without electricity in eighty percent of the country. I just returned from Venezuela where electricity was out about half the time I was there. And without electricity, there is no running water, internet, phone service or gasoline. In addition, without electricity, there is no refrigeration for food, and much food spoiled during the five-day outage, including 100 thousand liters of milk.[1]

Incredibly, though, the country was still amazingly calm, with people finding ways to adjust the best they can. Indeed, much to the chagrin of those in Washington hoping that such deprivations would lead to chaos and to people being at each other's throats, those on opposite sides of the political spectrum have been pulling together to help each other out through the periodic blackouts.

Meanwhile, three oil storage tanks at the Petro San Felix heavy oil processing plant in eastern Venezuela have just caught fire.[2]

So far, the blackout has cost the Venezuelan economy almost $3 billion (or 3% of GNP)[3] and it is considered the worst in Venezuelan history. It seems that officials in the Trump White House and that most media pundits could not be happier, for after all, this proves what everyone seems to know—that Venezuela is a country in need of saving from an inept and tyrannical government.

Venezuelan president Nicolas Maduro has claimed that the electrical outage, as well as other types of sabotage that followed, was the result of a cyberattack by the United States. He has also stated that the fire at the refinery at the oil processing plant was the result of intentional sabotage.

Predictably, Maduro's claims of sabotage have been met by laughter and ridicule in the United States. This reaction, of course, is quite predictable. Indeed, even when a video last summer clearly showed Maduro being attacked by drones as he delivered an address to the military, most of the media would not even give him the benefit of acknowledging that he survived an assassination attempt. Rather, even in the face of the video evidence, the media almost invariably talked about an "alleged" attempt on his life. Many months later, however, CNN has finally admitted that the assassination attempt was real, and it has released details about the planning of the attempt.[4]

And so, what about Maduro's claims about the sabotage of the electrical grid? There are indeed many indications that these claims are valid.

As an initial matter, just such a scenario was an explicit objective for gamers in the popular video game, "Call of Duty." Thus, as a producer for Telesur English explained on Twitter, complete with a clip from the game, "[i]n 2013, Call of Duty featured Caracas as the site of its war scene in Venezuela—a first-person shooter game which also depicted the Guri Hydroelectric Dam. Part of the 'mission' is to install a virus in the electrical system to generate a Blackout."[5] While obviously not conclusive, this certainly shows that people have been contemplating such sabotage for years, and as a worthy objective, including for gamers young and old.

In addition, former UN expert Dr. Albert de Zayas reminds us that the US, even back in 1973, managed to cause a blackout in Chile just weeks before it successfully overthrew President Salvador Allende in a coup, and he believes that the US is behind the blackout in Venezuela. Thus,

> de Zayas recounts that, four weeks before the coup d'etat of Augusto Pinochet against the Chilean president, "there was precisely a blackout." "Salvador Allende was in the middle of a speech when that happens, and evidently behind the blackout was sabotage," he said.
>
> The expert explains that the idea behind this type of act is to cause "anxiety" and "confusion", which in turn is combined with the sanctions of the North American country to generate "chaos" in Venezuela. "The United States, then, is causing this chaos. It wants to present itself as a good Samaritan," stressed De Zayas.
>
> The analyst, appointed by the United Nations for the promotion of a democratic and egalitarian international order (2012–2018), emphasizes that this US strategy "is not only illegal and not only violates customary international law," but also entails death.[6]

For its part, *Forbes* magazine printed a story explaining the very real possibility of a US cyberattack upon Venezuela's electrical system. Thus, as Kalev Lootaru, who specializes in the intersection of data and society, writes for *Forbes*:[7]

> In the case of Venezuela, the idea of a government like the United States remotely interfering with its power grid is actually quite realistic. Remote cyber operations rarely require a significant ground presence, making them the ideal deniable influence operation. Given the US government's longstanding concern with Venezuela's government, it is likely that the US already maintains a deep presence within the country's national infrastructure grid, making it relatively straightforward to interfere with grid operations. The country's outdated internet and power infrastructure present few formidable challenges to such operations and make it relatively easy to remove any traces of foreign intervention.

Widespread power and connectivity outages like the one Venezuela experienced last week are also straight from the modern cyber playbook. Cutting power at rush hour, ensuring maximal impact on civilian society and plenty of mediagenic post-apocalyptic imagery, fits squarely into the mold of a traditional influence operation. Timing such an outage to occur at a moment of societal upheaval in a way that delegitimizes the current government exactly as a government-in-waiting has presented itself as a ready alternative is actually one of the tactics outlined in my 2015 summary.

Similarly, journalist and author Steven Gowans opined[8],

Washington very likely has the cyberwarfare capability to cripple Venezuela's power grid. On November 12, 2018, David Sanger reported in the *New York Times* that,

> The United States had a secret program, code-named "Nitro Zeus," which called for turning off the power grid in much of Iran if the two countries had found themselves in a conflict over Iran's nuclear program. Such a use of cyberweapons is now a key element in war planning by all of the major world powers.

> If the United States can turn off the power grid in Iran, using a cyberweapon that is now a key element in war planning of all the major world powers, it's highly likely that it can do the same in Venezuela.

> What's more, the United States has on at least two occasions carried out cyberattacks against foreign states. Significantly, the attacks were unleashed against governments which, like Venezuela's, have refused to submit to US hegemony. US cyberattacks were used to cripple Iran's uranium enrichment program (now widely acknowledged) and to sabotage North Korea's rocket program, the latter revealed by various sources, including, again, by the *New York Time's* [sic] Sanger: "[F]or years . . . the United States has targeted the

North's missile program with cyberattacks," the reporter wrote in August, 2017.

As Gowans correctly concludes, "[t]he aforesaid, of course, is only evidence of capability, not of commission, but when placed within the context of Washington making clear its intention to topple the resource nationalist Maduro government, US capability, motivation, and practice, does very strongly cast suspicion on the US government." And indeed, there is even more to the story.

Thus, an electrical blackout was specifically listed as a potential catalyst for social unrest in a blueprint for regime change in Venezuela back in 2010. As journalist Max Blumenthal explains, "[a] September 2010 memo by a US-funded soft power organization that helped train Venezuelan coup leader Juan Guaido and his allies identifies the potential collapse of the country's electrical sector as 'a watershed event' that 'would likely have the impact of galvanizing public unrest in a way that no opposition group could ever hope to generate.'"[9]

Blumenthal further explains that the timing of the blackout, as well as the response of US officials to it—seemingly before it even happened—seems quite suspicious. Thus, Blumenthal relates, "[i]n a tweet on March 8, Secretary of State Mike Pompeo framed the electricity outage as a pivotal stage in US plans for regime change." Thus, Pompeo tweeted out, "'Maduro's policies bring nothing but darkness,'" and, "'No food. No medicine. Now, no power. Next, no Maduro.'" Meanwhile, as Blumenthal further explains,

> At noon on March 7, during a hearing on Venezuela at the Senate Foreign Relations Subcommittee, Sen. Marco Rubio explicitly called for the US to stir "widespread unrest," declaring that it "needs to happen" in order to achieve regime change.
>
> "Venezuela is going to enter a period of suffering no nation in our hemisphere has confronted in modern history," Rubio proclaimed.

Around 5 PM, the Simon Bolivar Hydroelectric Plant experienced a total and still unexplained collapse. Residents of Caracas and throughout Venezuela were immediately plunged into darkness.

At 5:18 PM, a clearly excited Rubio took to Twitter to announce the blackout and claim that "backup generators have failed." It was unclear how Rubio had obtained such specific information so soon after the outage occurred. According to Jorge Rodriguez, the communications minister of Venezuela, local authorities did not know if backup generators had failed at the time of Rubio's tweet.

Back in Caracas, Guaido immediately set out to exploit the situation, just as his CANVAS trainers had advised over eight years before. Taking to Twitter just over an hour after Rubio, Guaido declared, "the light will return when the usurpation [of Maduro] ends." Like Pompeo, the self-declared president framed the blackouts as part of a regime change strategy, not an accident or error.

Moreover, we have already witnessed other false flags unravel since the latest US push for regime change in Venezuela began, thus giving credence to those opposing regime change that the US may be lying again about what is truly happening in Venezuela.

Thus, as the *Miami Herald* explains[10], "widespread reports shared by [Senator Marco] Rubio, White House officials, and other prominent lawmakers that Maduro's security forces set fire to humanitarian aid at the Venezuela-Colombia border on Feb. 23" proved later to be false. Thus, "[v]ideo evidence analyzed by the *New York Times* showed that a Molotov cocktail thrown by an anti-Maduro protester was the likely culprit." This was a very revealing false flag, for it showed (1) the willingness of our government officials to spread untruths to justify intervention; (2) the eagerness of our press to spread such untruths uncritically; and (3) the fact that, as even the International Committee of the Red Cross and UN had already concluded[11], the aid being sent by the US is not so "humanitarian"; rather, it is simply a prop to be used, or simply lit on fire, as a Trojan Horse to attack the Venezuelan government.

The *Miami Herald* also reported that Senator Marco Rubio's retweeting of a report from Venezuela-based news outlet VPItv, which he translated into English on Sunday, also proved to be false. Here, the *Miami Herald* is referring to the following tweet of Rubio: "'[r]eport that at least 80 neonatal patients have died at University Hospital in Maracaibo, Zulia, since the blackout began on Thursday in Venezuela. Unimaginable tragedy. Heartbreaking.'" As the *Miami Herald* pointed out, however, "*Wall Street Journal* correspondent Juan Forero said the report was inaccurate. 'Actually, sources at the hospital said no neonatal deaths recorded as of this afternoon,' Forero tweeted in response." This particular bit of misinformation is reminiscent of one of the key lies used to justify the first Gulf War in 1990—the false claim that Iraqi forces invading Kuwait were killing babies by throwing them from their incubators onto the maternity ward floor.

As the attempted regime change continues, beware of more lies, half-truths and exaggerations to justify it. As Glenn Greenwald lamented shortly after the *New York Times* **quite belatedly** reported on what many independent reporters, such as Max Blumenthal, had revealed over two weeks before at the time it was actually happening— that is, that aid trucks were being lit ablaze by pro-Guaido forces and not by those loyal to Maduro:

> Every major US war of the last several decades has begun the same way: the US government fabricates an inflammatory, emotionally provocative lie which large US media outlets uncritically treat as truth while refusing at air questioning or dissent, thus inflaming primal anger against the country the US wants to attack. That's how we got the Vietnam War (North Vietnam attacks US ships in the Gulf of Tonkin); the Gulf War (Saddam ripped babies from incubators); and, of course, the war in Iraq (Saddam had WMDs and formed an alliance with Al Qaeda).

This was exactly the tactic used on February 23, when the narrative shifted radically in favor of those US officials who want regime change operations in Venezuela. That's because images were broadcast all over the world of trucks carrying humanitarian aid burning in Colombia on the Venezuela border. . . .

As it always does—*as it always has done from its inception when Wolf Blitzer embedded with US troops*—CNN led the way in not just spreading these government lies but independently purporting to vouch for their truth. On February 24, CNN told the world what we all now know is an absolute lie: that "a CNN team saw incendiary devices from police on the Venezuelan side of the border ignite the trucks," though it generously added that "the network's journalists are unsure if the trucks were burned on purpose."[12]

That lie—supported by incredibly powerful video images— changed everything. Ever since, that Maduro burned trucks filled with humanitarian aid was repeated over and over as proven fact on US news outlets. Immediately after it was claimed, politicians who had been silent on the issue of Venezuela or even reluctant to support regime change began issuing statements now supportive of it.

Similarly, a number of media outlets ran a story before the "aid" attempt showing a bridge between Venezuela and Colombia that was blocked with shipping containers, claiming that Maduro had blocked this bridge intentionally in order to stop aid from being delivered. As was revealed later, however, this was a lie. Instead, the photo was of a bridge between the two countries which had never been opened to traffic, and thus, that bridge had been blocked for years and the presence of the containers had nothing to do with any aid delivery.[13]

The stench of such lies still lingers in the air, giving oxygen to those who want regime change in Venezuela. And it still lingers, in large part, because few media outlets have even bothered to go back and explain to their readers and listeners that their original reportage was flawed; that it was indeed based on a complete lie. And so, for example, many still believe that Maduro is so evil and vicious that he would be willing to set aid trucks bound for his country on fire. Of course, what we know to be true is that it is the very forces the US is supporting to overthrow Maduro that are in fact the evil and vicious ones, but you will rarely hear them described this way.

Finally, there is the elephant in the living room which is rarely discussed—the effect that the US sanctions plays in all of this, including the blackout. Even if the US did not directly attack Venezuela's electric grid, it has attacked it just the same, as it has attacked all of Venezuela's infrastructure, with these sanctions. Indeed, this fact, which should be a quite obvious one, was buried near the end of a *New York Times* piece about the blackout—an article whose thrust was to blame President Maduro for the electric failure.

Near the top of the article, the *New York Times* explained in regard to the blackout:

> "It's further evidence of the government's lack of resources to maintain critical infrastructure," said Risa Grais-Targow, an analyst at Eurasia Group with expertise on Venezuela. "It seems to be a transmission issue at Guri, which would normally be offset by thermoelectric generation but in this case isn't, both because of the decay in that infrastructure and potentially due to lack of thermal inputs to fire those plants."[14]

Then, near the end of the article, the *Times* went on to relate, "[t]he sanctions have affected Venezuela's ability to import and produce the fuel required by the thermal power plants that could have backed up the Guri plant once it failed." And of course, the sanctions undoubtedly affected Venezuela's ability to maintain the Guri plant as well.

And this is all according to plan; this is all part of the strategy to undermine and overthrow the Venezuelan government. But it is a fact which one will rarely hear through the din of the calls to intervene to "save" Venezuela. The other reality that is rarely heard these days is the incredibly poor state of the electrical grid in US territory Puerto Rico. And certainly, no one has ever claimed that this reality presents a legitimate reason for regime change, either in San Juan or in Washington. As the *Miami Herald* reports in an article entitled, "Puerto Rico: The Forgotten Island,"[15]

> despite spending as much as $3.2 billion, the [US] federal effort over the past year to restore power to the island didn't build a better and more resilient system. In fact, the grid is more fragile. A severe new storm would put Puerto Rico's 3.3 million residents into deep trouble.
>
> "It's weaker today than before," said José F. Ortiz, chief executive of the Puerto Rico Electric Power Authority.

And as the *Miami Herald* explains, the already-weak state of Puerto Rico's electrical grid—a situation which already existed before the hurricane—has already proved deadly for the Puerto Rican people. As the *Herald* notes, the sorry state of the grid in Puerto Rico, which never gave Washington much concern, was a huge contributing factor in the deaths of nearly 3,000 Puerto Ricans which followed in the six months following the hurricane. Thus, the *Miami Herald* explains, "[d]uring that period, blackouts crippled hospitals, disrupted communications, impaired transport of the ill, hampered good hygiene practices and obstructed access to potable water—all problems that killed people."

But again, as the title of the *Miami Herald* article correctly reveals, all of this has largely been forgotten in the US press, and certainly has never elicited a call from US politicians or pundits for some sort of military intervention or regime change. To the contrary, in contrast to the situation in Venezuela which gets nearly daily news attention, the suffering and death of the Puerto Rican people—people the US is legally and morally charged with protecting—elicits a collective yawn from Washington and its compliant media.

* * *

Meanwhile, it has just been reported that US-led coalition forces killed 50 civilians, mostly women and children, through an indiscriminate bomb attack upon the al-Baghouz camp in the eastern Deir ez Zor province of Syria.[16] So far, the US-coalition forces have killed 3,222 civilians in prosecuting their war in Syria. But the US media, fixated on the US's "humanitarian"-motivated focus on "saving" Venezuela—the target *du jour*—seems to have little to no interest in such trifles.

1

THE US THREATENS TO "SAVE" VENEZUELA

The United States appear to be destined to plague America
with misery in the name of liberty.
—Simon Bolivar, 1829

As the old adage goes, "The Cavalry is coming!" And, this time it is coming to Venezuela; specifically, to save that country from a humanitarian disaster which includes a mass migration by Venezuelans fleeing a repressive and inept government—or at least, this is what we are told.

When most Americans hear the above adage, they are moved to believe that relief is in sight; that the cavalry has come to save and liberate those held captive by the bad guys. Those on the receiving end of the cavalry tend to feel differently.

As just one example, we learned nearly 50 years after the fact of possibly the worst US war crime of the 20th century—one committed by the US cavalry in Korea in 1950 to stop the flow of refugees from North Korea. As PRI explains:

> On the same day that the US Army delivered a stop refugee order in July 1950, around 400 South Korean civilians were killed in the town of No Gun Ri by US forces from the 7th Cavalry Regiment. The soldiers argued they thought the refugees could include disguised North Korean soldiers.

Many refugees were shot while on or under a stone bridge that ran through the town; others were attacked with bombs and machine-gun fire from US planes, the BBC reported. The ordeal lasted for three days, according to local survivors and members of the Cavalry.

"There was a lieutenant screaming like a madman, fire on everything, kill 'em all," veteran Joe Jackman recalled, according to the BBC. "I didn't know if they were soldiers or what. Kids, there was kids out there, it didn't matter what it was, 8 to 80, blind, crippled or crazy, they shot 'em all."

The Associated Press broke the news of the massacre in September 1999. It has come to be known as one of the largest single killings of civilians by American forces in the 20th century.[1]

As famed Latin American writer, Eduardo Galeano, once said, "Every time the US 'saves' a country, it converts it into either an insane asylum or a cemetery." And indeed, this assertion has been proven true time and time and time again.

For example, in the aftermath of the US invasion of Iraq in 2003—an invasion which many Iraqis believe left their country in the worst condition it has been since the Mongol invasion of 1258—there was much discussion in the media about the Bush Administration's goal for "nation-building" in that country. Of course, if there ever had been such a goal, it was quickly abandoned, with Secretary of State Rex Tillerson stating quite bluntly in 2017, "we are not in the business of nation-building or reconstruction."[2]

The stark truth is that the US is in fact in the business of nation destroying, and it has been in this business for some time.

Indeed, South Korean human rights scholar Dong Choon Kim, writing of the US war in Korea (1950–1953)—a war which he opines was at least arguably genocidal—explains that even back then, the nation-building of Third World peoples was viewed as an act of subversion which had to be snuffed out. As he explained, "[t]he American government interpreted the aspiration for building an independent nation as an exclusive 'communist conspiracy,' and thus took responsibility for killing innocent people, as in the case of [the] My Lai incident in Vietnam."[3] Thanks to the US war on Korea, Korea to this day remains a country divided in half, with no prospects for unification anytime soon. Kim explains that the Korean War "was a bridge to connect the old type of massacres under colonialism and the new types of state terrorism and political massacre during the Cold War. . . . And the mass killings committed by US soldiers in the Korean War marked the inception of military interventions by the US in the Third World at the cost of enormous civilian deaths."

Similarly, the US objective in Vietnam was the destruction of any prospect of an intact, independent state from being created. As Jean-Paul Sartre wrote as part of the International War Crimes Tribunal that he and Bertrand Russell chaired after the war, the US gave the Vietnamese a stark choice: either accept capitulation in which the country would be severed in half, with one half run by a US client, or be subjected to near total annihilation. Sartre wrote that, even in the former case, in which there would be a "cutting in two of a sovereign state . . . [t]he national unit of 'Vietnam' would not be physically eliminated, but it would no longer exist economically, politically or culturally."[4] Of course, in the latter case, Vietnam would suffer physical elimination; bombed "'back to the Stone Age'" as the US threatened. As we know, the Vietnamese did not capitulate, and therefore suffered near-total destruction of their country at the hands of the United States. Meanwhile, for good measure, the US simultaneously bombed both Cambodia and Laos back to the Stone Age as well.

To understand the purpose behind such violent and destructive actions, we need look no further than the US's own post-WWII policy statements, as well articulated by George Kennan serving as the State Department's Director of Policy Planning in 1948:

We must be very careful when we speak of exercising "leadership" in Asia. We are deceiving ourselves and others when we pretend to have answers to the problems, which agitate many of these Asiatic peoples. Furthermore, we have about 50% of the world's wealth but only 6.3 of its population. This disparity is particularly great as between ourselves and the peoples of Asia. In this situation, we cannot fail to be the object of envy and resentment. Our real task in the coming period is to devise a pattern of relationships, which will permit us to maintain this position of disparity without positive detriment to our national security. To do so we will have to dispense with all sentimentality and daydreaming; and our attention will have to be concentrated everywhere on our immediate national objectives. We need not deceive ourselves that we can afford today the luxury of altruism and world benefaction . . .

In the face of this situation we would be better off to dispense now with a number of the concepts which have underlined our thinking with regard to the Far East. We should dispense with the aspiration to "be liked" or to be regarded as the repository of a high-minded international altruism. We should stop putting ourselves in the position of being our brothers' keeper and refrain from offering moral and ideological advice. We should cease to talk about vague—and for the Far East—unreal objectives such as human rights, the raising of the living standards, and democratization. The day is not far off when we are going to have to deal in straight power concepts. The less we are hampered by idealistic slogans, the better.[5]

While it would have been impossible for the US to continue to monopolize a full half of the world's wealth after Europe, Japan, China and the USSR inevitably got up on their feet after WWII, the US has nonetheless done an amazing job of controlling an unjustifiable and disproportionate amount of the world's resources.

Thus, currently, the US has about 5% of the world's population, and consumes about 25% of its resources. An article in *Scientific American,* citing the Sierra Club's Dave Tilford, explains that,"[w]ith less than 5 percent of world population, the US uses one-third of the world's paper, a quarter of the world's oil, 23 percent of the coal, 27 percent of the aluminum, and 19 percent of the copper. . . . Our per capita use of energy, metals, minerals, forest products, fish, grains, meat, and even fresh water dwarfs that of people living in the developing world."[6]

The only way the US has been able to achieve this impressive, though morally reprehensible, feat has been to undermine, many times fatally, the ability of independent states to exist, defend themselves and to protect their own resources from foreign plunder. This is why the US has teamed up with the world's most deplorable forces in destroying independent states around the globe.

Just to name a few examples, since 1996, the US has supported Rwandan and Ugandan forces in invading the Democratic Republic of Congo, making that country ungovernable and plundering its incredible natural resources. The fact that around 6 million innocents have been murdered in the process is of no matter, and certainly not to the mainstream press which rarely mentions the DRC. In Colombia, the US has backed a repressive military and right-wing paramilitaries for decades in destabilizing whole swaths of the Colombian countryside, and in assisting multinational corporations, and especially extractive industries, in displacing around 8 million people from their homes and land, all in order to exploit Colombia's vast oil, coal and gold reserves. Again, this receives barely a word in the mainstream press.

Of course, in the Middle East, Northern Africa and Afghanistan, the US has been teaming up with Saudi Arabia and radical Islamist forces—forces the US itself has dubbed "terrorist"—in undermining and destroying secular states.

As far back as the 1970s, the US began supporting the mujahidin in attacking the secular, Marxist state of Afghanistan in order to destroy that state and also to fatally weaken the Soviet state by, in the words of Zbigniew Brzezinski, "drawing the Russians into the Afghan trap . . . [and] giving to the USSR its Vietnam war." Afghanistan may never recover from the devastation wrought by that fateful decision of the US and of its subsequent intervention which is now well into its

18th year and counting. As we know full well, the USSR never recovered either, and the US is trying mightily to prevent post-Soviet Russia from becoming a strong rival state again.

In addition, as we learned from Seymour Hersh back in 2007, the US began at that time to try to weaken Iran and Syria by supporting Sunni extremist groups to subvert those countries. As Hersh explained:

> To undermine Iran, which is predominantly Shiite, the Bush Administration has decided, in effect, to reconfigure its priorities in the Middle East. In Lebanon, the Administration has cooperated with Saudi Arabia's government, which is Sunni, in clandestine operations that are intended to weaken Hezbollah, the Shiite organization that is backed by Iran. The US has also taken part in clandestine operations aimed at Iran and its ally Syria. A by-product of these activities has been the bolstering of Sunni extremist groups that espouse a militant vision of Islam and are hostile to America and sympathetic to Al Qaeda.
>
> One contradictory aspect of the new strategy is that, in Iraq, most of the insurgent violence directed at the American military has come from Sunni forces, and not from Shiites.[7]

The US continues to intervene in Syria in a way that prevents the Syrian state from achieving a decisive victory against the various militant groups it is fighting—some of which the US itself admits are terrorists—while at the same time targeting some of these same militant groups themselves, thereby preventing either side of the conflict from coming out on top. Indeed, as we have learned, the CIA and the Pentagon have even been backing opposing militant groups that are fighting each other.[8] The result is a drawn-out war which threatens to leave Syria in chaos and ruins for the foreseeable future.

This would seem to be an insane course of action for the US to take, and indeed it is, but there is method to the madness. The US appears to be intentionally spreading chaos throughout strategic portions of the world, leaving virtually no independent state standing to protect their resources, especially oil, from Western exploitation. And, this goal is being achieved with resounding success, while also achieving the subsidiary goal of enriching the behemoth military-industrial complex.

Meanwhile, in Libya, the US again partnered with jihadists in 2011 in overthrowing and indeed smashing a state that used its oil wealth to guarantee the best living standards of any country in Africa while assisting independence struggles around the world. In this way, Libya, which under Qaddafi also happened to be one of the staunchest enemies of Al-Qaeda in the world, presented a double threat to US foreign policy aims. Post-intervention Libya is now a failed state with little prospects of being able to secure its oil wealth for its own people again, much less for any other peoples in the Third World.

Indeed, slaves are being openly marketed on the streets of Libya after being "saved" by Obama and his humanitarian interventionist ideologues, including Samantha Power.

I mention Samantha Power because, quite ironically, she won a Pulitzer Prize for her book decrying genocide. Of course, the book, entitled *A Problem from Hell*,[9] decried only other peoples' genocides, and none of those committed by the US. Meanwhile, Power would go on as Obama's UN ambassador to run interference at the Security Council to make sure that the US-backed genocide in Yemen, still ongoing, be permitted to continue without pause and without any pesky war crimes investigations getting in the way.[10] Millions will certainly die in Yemen as a result of the US-backed campaign of the Saudis, as even Power recognized at the time, but neither she nor any other US official will ever view this as a "problem from hell."

Meanwhile, despite these obvious truths, there appears to be no diminishment in fervor for another US intervention which purports to bring democracy and freedom to other peoples. Of course, in the case of Venezuela, the "humanitarian" part of the intervention is now barely a fig leaf for the real, and usual intention—the control of another country's oil supplies. Retread neo-con, John Bolton, recently made this clear, saying that "we're in conversation with major American companies now. . . . It would make a difference if we could have American companies produce the oil in Venezuela. We both have a lot at stake here."[11]

Despite Bolton's candor in this regard, the fact that convicted Iran-Contra spook Elliott Abrams has been tasked to oversee the Venezuela operations, and despite the fact that all of this is being led by a president who liberals otherwise, and quite rightly, view as unintelligent and mean-spirited, there is nearly unanimous, bi-partisan support for the US's dangerous game of regime change in Venezuela.

The irony in all of this seems lost in the seemingly ecstatic push for another US-backed coup in Latin America. Thus, we have Donald J. Trump—an individual who became president after losing to his opponent by nearly 3 million votes (that's 10% of Venezuela's entire population), and after around one million voters had been wrongly purged from the voter rolls—trying to unseat Nicolas Maduro who was duly elected president last May with over 67% of the votes cast in his favor and with 46% of the electorate voting.[12]

This may be a time, indeed, for one to cry out, "Doctor, heal thyself," but that never seems to be the prescription for the US's own great democracy deficit. Rather, instead of fixing our own problems, we project them onto others who we then invariably destroy in the name of freedom.

Moreover, while Trump, his cronies, and the media constantly talk about Maduro wrecking the Venezuelan economy and causing deprivation amongst the Venezuelan population, few will point out the obvious fact that it is the US which has helped bring Venezuela's economy to ruin through five years of illegal and deadly sanctions that cost Venezuela $20 billion just last year. Meanwhile, the Bank of England refuses to turn over $1.5 billion in gold deposited there by Venezuela, and President Trump just announced that we will now refuse to allow Venezuela's oil company, Citgo, to return any of its profits to Venezuela from the US. In short, as the US has done so many times before, including in Chile in the early 1970s which brought General Pinochet to power, it starves a country into submission and then blames it for starving.

The truth is that, prior to 2014 when the US and Saudi Arabia intentionally depressed oil prices to undermine countries like Venezuela,[13] Venezuela had been successfully eradicating poverty year after year since Hugo Chavez first became president in 1999. And, even despite this, and despite crippling US sanctions which began in 2015, Venezuela continues to build subsidized housing for the poor, having built around 2.5 million such homes.[14]

This is a pretty amazing feat when one considers the fact that the Red Cross, with $500 million in donations and without any sanctions to overcome, was only able to build 6 homes in total in Haiti after the 2010 earthquake.[15] At the same time, Venezuela partnered with Cuba in providing real aid to Haiti with medical teams which, as even the *New York Times* itself recognized, have been at the frontline of the battle against cholera.[16] As the UN explained:

> Cuban medical cooperation has saved thousands of lives in Haiti. Present in the country for the last 15 years and with over 700 people working closely with the Ministry of Health, the Cuban Medical Brigades have actively worked to fight cholera. The contingent has worked in 96 health care centers, 65 of which are part of a joint Cuban-Venezuelan program aimed at strengthening the health system in the country.[17]

One might recall that both Venezuela and Cuba offered to help the United States with relief assistance after Hurricane Katrina—a disaster famously mismanaged by the US and which was entirely preventable in any case through the proper fortification of the levees—but that the US refused these offers.[18]

Despite the tense relations between the US and Venezuela at the time, the Venezuelan government sent the following cordial message to the US:

The Ministry of Foreign Affairs would like to communicate to the Honorable Embassy of the United States that the Bolivarian Republic of Venezuela has offered the Governor of the State of Louisiana, Ms. Kathleen Babineaux Blanco, immediate aid of $1 million; 120 specialists in First Aid and search and rescue, part of the "Simon Bolivar" Humanitarian Response Team, an internationally recognized disaster relief unit; two mobile hospitals with a capacity of 150 people each at a time; ten water purification stations; eight electric generators, each with a capacity of 850 kilowatts; 20 tons of drinking water; 50 tons of canned food; and 5,000 blankets. The offer will be made available in immediate fashion, should the Government of the United States choose to accept it, through the CITGO Corporation.

The Ministry of Foreign Affairs takes the opportunity to reiterate to the Honorable Embassy of the United States of America its considerations of the highest esteem and regard.[19]

As one commentator wrote specifically regarding the Cuban offer:

Cuban leader Fidel Castro offered to ship over 1,600 doctors and dozens of tons of medical supplies to the US's affected areas. Considering the decades-long terrorist attacks perpetrated against Cuba by US governments, in addition to a crippling embargo, it was a noble gesture by the Castro government.

* * *

In the affected areas in the wake of Hurricane Katrina, the greatest problem was a lack of medical needs—"only a small portion of those seeking medical assistance were receiving care due to a shortage of medical personnel and supplies". The world's richest country did not have enough doctors when it mattered most.

Later, a bemused Castro responded to the rejection of his offer by saying that, "the American government's pride dictated that their own citizens had to die on the roofs of their houses, or on the roofs of hospitals from which no-one evacuated them, or in stadiums, or in nursing homes where some of them were given euthanasia in order to prevent a horrible death by drowning. That's the country that portrays itself as 'a defender of human rights'."[20]

Though "bemused," neither Castro nor Chavez threatened to storm the gates of the US to deliver the much-needed aid, and the press corps did not treat the US's refusal as some high crime. On the contrary, most pundits simply scoffed at the idea of Castro and Chavez offering aid to the mighty United States. And, 1,800 or so Katrina-related deaths later,[21] few remember that these offers were ever made.

With regard to Haiti, it should be pointed out that cholera was brought into that country by UN forces which intervened in Haiti after the earthquake and which remain there today much to the chagrin of many Haitians who see them as an occupying force. This resentment is not all too surprising given the fact that UN "peacekeepers," in addition to spreading cholera, raped untold numbers of Haitian women and children, and even ran child sex rings there in which they would pass children around like candy to scores of soldiers who would have their way with them.[22]

As I write these words, Haitians, upset by such indignities, are now engaged in a mass uprising against their government—a government of course backed by the US after it colluded with Canada and France in ousting and forcing into exile their duly-elected president, Jean Bertrand Aristide, in 2004. One of the big issues behind the current protests is the Haitian government's misuse of much-needed aid, including a loan from Venezuela, to line the coffers of corrupt officials.[23] Still, neither the US government nor press are calling for intervention to assist in this uprising.

And, while Haiti, post-earthquake, had the world's largest cholera outbreak, it is now Yemen, due to the US-backed war there, that has this dubious distinction. Indeed, Yemen's cholera outbreak is now the largest in recorded world history.[24] All of this is worth considering in evaluating the bona fides of US "humanitarian" concerns and the real results of "humanitarian interventionism."

Meanwhile, the US, the richest country on earth, has more people living in poverty (around 40 million) than Venezuela has people, and tent cities for the homeless have now popped up in almost every major US urban center. Again, instead of worrying about Venezuela's humanitarian problems—problems which the US has played a key role in creating to begin with—the US would do well to try to work on fixing its own, and quite preventable humanitarian crisis.

But that is not what is happening. Instead, the US continues to cut off its nose, and the nose of others, out of pure spite, self-inflicting an economic downturn for the sake of a useless wall to keep out Central American immigrants fleeing countries the US has destroyed, and spending trillions of desperately-needed dollars on wars which have only brought more terror to the world. Now, the US is courting civil war in Venezuela, and, in the process, will surely bring more misery and suffering to that country. Still, we will continue to pretend we are acting out of good intention, rather than greed, when all the while the world begs us to please stop "saving" everyone. The world simply cannot endure one more country "saved" into oblivion.

2

THE HISTORY OF US SUPPORT FOR DEMOCRACY IN VENEZUELA

I spent 33 years and four months in active military service and during that period I spent most of my time as a high class muscle man for Big Business, for Wall Street and the bankers. In short, I was a racketeer, a gangster for capitalism. I helped make Mexico and especially Tampico safe for American oil interests in 1914. I helped make Haiti and Cuba a decent place for the National City Bank boys to collect revenues in. I helped in the raping of half a dozen Central American republics for the benefit of Wall Street. I helped purify Nicaragua for the International Banking House of Brown Brothers in 1902–1912. I brought light to the Dominican Republic for the American sugar interests in 1916. I helped make Honduras right for the American fruit companies in 1903. In China in 1927 I helped see to it that Standard Oil went on its way unmolested. Looking back on it, I might have given Al Capone a few hints. The best he could do was to operate his racket in three districts. I operated on three continents.

—US Marine General Smedley D. Butler, *War Is Racket: The Antiwar Classic by America's Most Decorated Soldier*

THIS COULD BE A VERY SHORT chapter, indeed, for the US has never supported democracy in Venezuela, or anywhere else in Latin America. Rather, the history of US policy towards Venezuela has been invariably that of supporting one brutal dictator after another to ensure that Venezuela's rich oil reserves were in the right hands—meaning US hands of course.

Of course, all of Latin America has been brutally treated by the Western powers—first Spain, Portugal, France and Great Britain, and then the US—for over 500 years; that is, since Columbus sailed the ocean blue in 1492. The peoples and the resources of Latin America have been treated as existing, at best, for the benefit of the Western powers. At worst, the peoples of Latin America have been seen as impediments to Western expansion and domination, and, consequently have suffered mass slaughter when such a fate was deemed necessary or even simply convenient.

In *The Open Veins of Latin America: Five Centuries of the Pillage of a Continent*—a book from 1973 which became popular again after Hugo Chavez famously gave a copy of it to President Obama at the Summit of the Americas in 2009—legendary Uruguayan writer, Eduardo Galeano, eloquently summarizes this history:

> Latin America is the region of open veins. Everything, from the discovery [of Columbus] until our times, has always been transmuted into European—or later United States—capital, and as such has accumulated in distant centers of power. Everything: the soil, its fruits, and its mineral-rich depths, the people and their capacity to work and to consume, natural resources and human recourses. Production methods and class structure have been successively determined from outside for each area by meshing it into the universal gearbox of capitalism. To each area has been assigned a function, always for the benefit of the foreign metropolis of the moment, and the endless chain of dependency has been endlessly extended. . . .
>
> For those who see history as a competition, Latin America's

backwardness and poverty are merely the result of its failure. We lost; others won. But the winners happened to have won thanks to our losing: the history of Latin America's underdevelopment is, as someone has said, an integral part of the history of world capitalism's development. *Our defeat is always implicit in the victory of others; our wealth has always generated our poverty by nourishing the prosperity of others—the empire and their native overseers. In the colonial and neocolonial alchemy, gold changes into scrap metal and food into poison.* Potosi, Zacatecas, Ouro Preto became desolate warrens of deep, empty tunnels from which precious metals had been taken; ruin was the fate of Chile's nitrate pampas and Amazonia's rubber forests. Northeast Brazil's sugar and Argentina's quebracho belts, and communities around oil-rich Lake Maracaibo [Venezuela], have become painfully aware of the mortality of wealth which nature bestows and imperialism appropriates.

Of course, since the dawn of the 20th century and the widespread use of the gas-guzzling automobile, Venezuela has been assigned the function in the global capitalist world as a supplier of one chief raw material—oil. While Britain initially had a share in Venezuela's oil wealth, the US, which has viewed Latin America as its domain to rule exclusively ever since the Monroe Doctrine was announced in 1823, moved in swiftly to control this much-coveted resource. It should be noted that, lest one believe that the Monroe Doctrine is some relic of the past, National Security Adviser John Bolton just invoked this doctrine as justification for the US's current operations in Venezuela.[1]

Meanwhile, to advance what it saw as its exclusive interests in Venezuela, the US cozied up to Venezuelan dictator Vicente Gomez, who ruled Venezuela as an "oil Republic" (as opposed to a "banana Republic," a role assigned to other nations) from 1908 to 1935.

As Galeano explains,

While the black geysers spouted on all sides, Gomez took petroleum shares from his bursting pockets to reward his friends, relations, and courtiers, the doctors who look after his prostate, the generals who served as his bodyguard, the poets who sang his praises, and the archbishop who gave him a special dispensation to eat meat on Good Friday. The great powers covered Gomez's breast with gleaming decorations: the automobiles invading the world's highways needed food. The dictator's favorites sold concessions to Shell or Standard Oil or Gulf; the traffic in influence and bribes provoked speculation and set mouths watering for subsoil. Native communities were robbed of their lands and many farm families lost their holdings in one way or another. The petroleum law of 1922 was drafted by representatives from three US firms.

Gomez was known as "The Catfish," a reference to his brutality. American journalist John Gunther described this brutality: "The Catfish was—let us not gloss over the fact—a murderous blackguard. He made use of tortures of inconceivable brutality; political prisoners, of which there were thousands, dragged out their lives bearing leg irons (*grillos*) that made them permanent cripples, if they were not hung upside down—by the testicles—until they died. Others became human slime, literally. Gómez was quite capable of choosing one out of every ten by lot, and hanging them—*by meat hooks through their throats!*" (emphasis in original).[2] But given that Gomez continued the oil flowing to US companies, such tactics were fine with Uncle Sam.

As Noam Chomsky (whose 2003 book *Hegemony or Survival* went to number 1 after Hugo Chavez mentioned it at the UN in 2006), explains in another, quite aptly named book, *Year 501: The Conquest Continues*, "[b]y 1928, Venezuela had become the world's leading oil exporter, with US companies in charge." And this would not have been possible without "'the vicious and venal regime of Juan Vicente Gomez,' who opened the country wide to foreign exploration." As Chomsky explains, US control over Venezuela's one key resource only accelerated after WWII:

In a major scholarly study of US-Venezuelan relations, Stephen Rabe writes that after World War II, the US . . . State Department shelved the "Open Door" policy in the usual way, recognizing the possibility of "US economic hegemony in Venezuela," hence pressuring its government to bar British concessions . . . During World War II, the US agreed to a Venezuelan demand for 50–50 profit-sharing. The effect, as predicted, was a vast expansion of oil production and "substantial profits for the [US] oil industry," which took control over the country's economy and "major economic decisions" in all areas.

Then, "[d]uring the 1949–1958 dictatorship of the murderous thug Pérez Jiménez, 'US relations with Venezuela were harmonious and economically beneficial to US businessmen'; torture, terror, and general repression passed without notice on the usual Cold War pretexts. In 1954, the dictator was awarded the Legion of Merit by President Eisenhower. The citation noted 'his wholesome policy in economic and financial matters has facilitated the expansion of foreign investment, his Administration thus contributing to the greater well-being of the country and the rapid development of its immense natural resources'—and, incidentally, huge profits for the US corporations that ran the country, including by then steel companies and others. About half of Standard Oil of New Jersey's profits came from its Venezuelan subsidiary, to cite just one example."

As Eduardo Galeano relates, "When dictator Marcos Perez Jimenez was overthrown in 1958, Venezuela was one huge oil well, surrounded by jails and torture chambers and importing everything from the United States: cars, refrigerators, condensed milk, eggs, lettuce, *laws and decrees*" (emphasis added). And Venezuela's enduring poverty made it certain that Venezuela would continue to be dependent to its detriment upon imports rather than domestic production.

By the early 1970s, Galeano continues, Venezuela's industrial development showed "visible signs of exhaustion, of an impotence that is all too familiar in Latin America: the internal market, limited by the poverty of the masses, cannot sustain the development of manufactures beyond certain limits." And of course, that is exactly how the US likes it—to keep countries like Venezuela suppliers of raw materials for the United States which can then be sold back to the country as manufactured goods. While Hugo Chavez would later try to break this exploitative system which continued to keep Venezuela poor, this proved quite challenging, and Venezuela's dependence on imports from the US would make it vulnerable to the US's economic war against that country.

Meanwhile, after World War II, the US, in order to protect its interests in Venezuelan oil against pesky Venezuelans demanding that this resource be used for their benefit, heavily militarized the country for purposes of domestic social control. Thus, as Chomsky writes

> From World War II, in Venezuela the US followed the standard policy of taking total control of the military "to expand US political and military influence in the Western Hemisphere and perhaps help keep the US arms industry vigorous" . . . As later explained by Kennedy's Ambassador Allan Stewart, 'US-oriented and anti-Communist armed forces are vital instruments to maintain our security interests.' . . . The Kennedy Administration increased its assistance to the Venezuelan security forces for "internal security and counterinsurgency operations against the political left," . . . also assigning personnel to advise in combat operations, as in Vietnam. Stewart urged the government to "dramatize" its arrests of radicals, which would make a good impression in Washington as well as among Venezuelans (those who matter, that is).

While the US government lauded the Venezuelan government as an exemplary model of democracy in the region, claiming in reports that it had a stellar human rights record—and even going so far as to say that "TORTURE IS NOT PRACTICED" in Venezuela[3]—domestic and international human rights groups told a different story.

For example, in a revealing 1993 report entitled, "Venezuela: Eclipse of Human Rights," Amnesty International explained that things in Venezuela were not as the US was leading us to believe:

> Venezuela stands out in Latin America as one of the few countries which has been ruled by democratically elected civilian governments without interruption for over 35 years. What is less well known, particularly outside the region, is the extent to which the human rights of an increasing number of its 20 million citizens have been persistently and seriously violated over the years.
>
> To the outside world, Venezuelan governments have increasingly expressed their commitment to defending human rights. Inside the country, however, state officials have been allowed to violate those rights with virtual impunity.
>
> As this report shows, torture and other cruel, inhuman and degrading treatment or punishment are frequently reported. Criminal suspects, especially those living in poor neighbourhoods (barrios), are routinely tortured to extract confessions. Political, student and grass-roots activists are also targeted. Moreover, during periods of heightened political tension leading to disturbances, which have been growing in frequency in recent years, the security forces have carried out extrajudicial executions with little fear of being brought to account for their actions. . . .[4]

As for torture specifically, Amnesty International gives a detailed account about the grisly techniques regularly used to coerce confessions and to generally stifle dissent. As AI explains, "[t]orture and ill-treatment are widespread in Venezuela, in some cases resulting in death. Most reports concern law-enforcement agents during criminal investigations. The main purpose of torture and ill-treatment of prisoners appears to be to intimidate detainees and obtain confessions of guilt." AI explains that authorities generally target people in poor neighborhoods as well as "political, student and grass-roots activists" for torture. And, as AI relates,

Beating is the most common method reported, often starting at the moment of arrest or during initial phases of interrogation in police custody.

Beatings are also reported to be a common practice in prisons throughout the country. This method includes slaps, punches, kicks and blows with batons to sensitive parts of the body such as the abdomen, genitals and head.

One variation consists of simultaneous blows to both ears, which produces excruciating pain and often ruptures the ear-drums. Another variation is *"peinillazos"*, blows with *peinillas*, sabres without a cutting edge, which are commonly used by members of the police and prison warders.

Near-asphyxiation is also commonly reported. A plastic bag is put over the victim's head to cause suffocation. Irritants such as ammonia, powdered soap and insecticide aerosol are often added to the bag to increase the distress of the victim.

In some cases, victims are asphyxiated by having their heads forced into water, which frequently contains debris or faeces and urine when toilets are used.

Other commonly cited methods are electric torture with cattle prods applied to sensitive parts of the body, and suspending victims for prolonged periods by the wrists, so that the feet barely touch the ground.

These torture methods are often used in combination, most frequently by subjecting the victims to beatings during or after near-asphyxiation with a plastic bag.[5]

Indeed, as one will find, the reality of Venezuela and of Latin America generally, and of the role of the US therein, is much different from what we have been led to believe. The fear of our government and "free" press, of course, is that if we knew this awful reality, we might be moved to try to change it.

3

1989—THE YEAR OF HISTORIC MASSACRES YOU'VE NEVER HEARD OF

IN TERMS OF "PERIODS OF HEIGHTENED political tension leading to disturbances" and increased human rights abuses, Amnesty International describes one key one that continues to reverberate to this day in Venezuela but which is little known or totally forgotten outside that country—that is, the Caracazo which began on February 27, 1989. The Caracazo—which is really a misnomer because it suggests events limited to Caracas when in fact the events took place throughout Venezuela—refers to the massive uprising amongst poor and working class Venezuelans in response to the increase in oil and public transportation prices, and to the violent crackdown by state forces against the protesters which quickly followed.

As AI explains,

The human rights situation in Venezuela has markedly deteriorated in the context of rising social and political tensions, particularly since 1989. On 27 February that year widespread protests broke out following the introduction of austerity measures by the new government of President Carlos Andrés Pérez. People poured into the streets and there was extensive looting and violence. The government suspended a wide range of constitutional guarantees, imposed a curfew and transferred responsibility for law and order to the armed forces.

In the days that followed, several hundred people were killed. Some died in the general violence, but many were the victims of deliberate or indiscriminate shootings by the police or military personnel.

Since then, there have been frequent mass and occasionally violent demonstrations protesting against worsening economic conditions. The security forces have often responded with excessive and arbitrary force, including using live ammunition against unarmed civilians. Students have numbered heavily among the victims as they have been at the forefront of many of the protests.[1]

My Venezuelan friend Tulio Virguez, who has lived in a working class neighborhood of Caracas his whole life, recently told me that he was ten years old during the Caracazo, and that he saw military forces loading up scores of dead bodies in his neighborhood—bodies which most likely ended up in mass graves. A soldier shot at him during this time as he was walking by himself with his dog. He was lucky that the bullet missed.

The Caracazo marked a titanic turning point in the history of Venezuela, leading to the rise of Hugo Chavez, and to a leftward shift throughout Latin America generally. As AI explains, "several hundred people were killed" in the course of this event. The exact numbers are not known because the security forces "disappeared" people during this time without a trace—a common tactic of US-backed right-wing regimes in Latin America—and while mass graves of victims were discovered later, it is not certain that all such graves have been uncovered.[2] There are claims of as many as 3,000 killed by security forces, an astronomical figure.[3]

Meanwhile, the historic importance of the Caracazo is well explained by author George Ciccariello-Maher, who goes so far as to describe this as the beginning of a new world war.[4] Ciccariello points out that "this singularly important but oft-overlooked event . . . has been described . . . as 'the largest and most violently repressed revolt against austerity measures in Latin American history.'"

The Caracazo arose out of the Venezuelan population's angry reaction to the announcement by newly-elected President Carlos Andres Perez of austerity measures shortly after his inauguration, despite the fact that he had run on a campaign opposing these very measures. As Ciccariello relates:

Carlos Andrés Pérez was inaugurated on February 2nd 1989 for his second (but non-consecutive) term, after a markedly anti-neoliberal campaign during the course of which he had demonized the IMF as a "bomb that only kills people." In what has since become a notorious example of "bait-and-switch" reform, Pérez proceeded to implement the recently-formulated Washington Consensus to the letter. . .

In a Letter of Intention signed with the IMF on February 28th, while most large Venezuelan cities were in the throes of generalized rioting and looting, the basic premises of the Pérez plan were laid out as follows: government spending and salaries were to be restricted, exchange rates and interest rates were to be deregulated (thereby eliminating what were essentially interest rate subsidies for farmers), price controls were to be relaxed, subsidies were to be reduced, sales tax was to be introduced, prices of state-provided goods and services (including petroleum) were to be liberalized, tariffs were to be eliminated and imports liberalized, and in general, foreign transactions in Venezuela were to be facilitated.

In brief, this plan meant a potent cocktail of stagnating incomes in the face of skyrocketing prices and monetary devaluation. As might be expected, poverty reached a peak in 1989, claiming 44% of households (a figure which had doubled in absolute terms during the course of five years), with 20% of the population in extreme poverty.

The truth is that Pérez may have sincerely wanted to reject IMF austerity measures, just as he promised the electorate, but that he had little choice in the matter. An interesting document recently highlighted by Wikileaks in light of recent events in Venezuela, and entitled, "Field Manual (FM) 3–05.130, Army Special Operations Forces Unconventional Warfare" explains how foreign leaders such as Perez are disciplined and brought into line with US economic goals through institutions such as the IMF.

In particular, a section of this document entitled, "Financial Instrument of US National Power and Unconventional Warfare," explains

> that the US government applies "unilateral and indirect financial power through persuasive influence to international and domestic financial institutions regarding availability and terms of loans, grants, or other financial assistance to foreign state and nonstate actors," and specifically names the World Bank, IMF and The Organisation for Economic Co-operation and Development (OECD) . . . as "US diplomatic-financial venues to accomplish" such goals. . . .
>
> The role of these "independent" international financial institutions as extensions of US imperial power is elaborated elsewhere in the manual and several of these institutions are described in detail in an appendix. . . . Notably, the World Bank and the IMF are listed as both Financial Instruments and Diplomatic Instruments of US National Power as well as integral parts of what the manual calls the "current global governance system." . . .
>
> As a consequence of the lopsided influence of the US on these institutions' behavior, these organizations have used their loans and grants to "trap" nations in debt and have imposed "structural adjustment" programs on these debt-saddled governments that result in the

mass privatization of state assets, deregulation, and austerity that routinely benefit foreign corporations over local economies. Frequently, these very institutions—by pressuring countries to deregulate their financial sector and through corrupt dealings with state actors—bring about the very economic problems that they then swoop in to "fix."[5]

In the end, the IMF, exerting its various forms of pressure, may have simply made Perez an offer he could not refuse, and so he didn't. The results, however, were catastrophic.

Thus, on February 27, when the doubling of oil prices under the newly-announced austerity measures took effect, with the resultant rise in public transportation fares, people rose up *en masse* throughout the country in protest. And, while these protests sometimes turned violent, it was the Venezuelan security forces, freed from all restraint by Perez's suspension of Constitutional rights, who did the killing, and many times indiscriminately. Again, Ciccariello writes:

Repression was worst in Caracas' largest barrios: Catia in the west and Petare in the east. Police directed their attention to the former, and especially the neighborhood of 23 de Enero, as the organizational brain of the rebellion. Known organizers were dragged from their homes and either executed or "disappeared," and when security forces met resistance from snipers, they opened fire on the apartment blocks themselves (the bullet holes are visible to this day). In Petare, the largest and most violent of Caracas' slums, up to twenty were killed in a single incident, when on March 1st the army opened fire on the Mesuca stairway.

Much of the country was "pacified" within three days, while Caracas saw rioting for more than five days. The human toll of the rebellion has never been entirely clear, especially since the Pérez government obstructed any and all efforts to investigate the events. Subsequent government investigations set the number killed around

300, while the popular imagination places it around 3,000. Rumors of mass killings led to the 1990 excavation of a mass grave in a sector of the public cemetery called, perhaps not coincidentally, "The New Plague." There, 68 bodies in plastic bags were unearthed, and no one knows how many more deaths were concealed by government forces. . . .

Internationally, the democratic façade that had obscured Venezuelan reality for decades was shattered in a single blow.

In my own view, the last sentence of the above-quoted passage would be more accurate if it read, "[i]internationally, the democratic façade that had obscured Venezuelan reality for decades *should have been* shattered in a single blow." The truth is, of course, that few in the US knew that these events were taking place. This was simply business as usual in a US client state which was dutifully carrying out the US's retrograde economic policies.

Compare this to the Tiananmen Square massacre in China the same year in which a similar number of protesters were estimated to have been killed. This event, in contrast to the obscure Caracazo, was covered closely at the time, is etched in our collective memory, and continues to be commemorated to this day. (Quite tellingly, my spell check recognizes "Tiananmen," but not "Caracazo.") This proves once again that it is only the crimes of our ostensible enemies that matter to our government and our so-called "free press," and not those of ourselves or our allies.

A revealing account of the Caracazo, and of life in the poor barrios at the time, is given by Charlie Hardy, a former Catholic priest who I met in Venezuela while observing elections. Charlie explained to me that he had lived for eight years as a Maryknoll missionary in a cardboard hut in Terrace B of the barrio Nueva Tacagua, beginning in 1985.

As Charlie recounted to me, and as he explains in his book, *Cowboy in Caracas*[6], his first introduction to barrio life was stepping into "a mountain of fecal matter." As Charlie relates in his book, "I don't think there was a square inch of Terrace B that had not been tainted by human or animal excrement at some time. The problem was threefold: lack of running water, lack of toilets, and lack of enclosed sewers. In front of my door, a stream of black water carried the sewage from my neighbors' dwelling to the miniature black river behind my house. Soon I would cease to notice the stench. That day I did."

Charlie, a native of Wyoming (thus the cowboy part), explains, life in the barrio was hard and inevitably ground people down—even driving some to the point of insanity. Basic necessities, like water, were hard to come by, and were expensive. As Charlie explains in his book, "[w]ater arrived on Terrace B in tank trucks with the words 'DRINKING WATER' painted on their sides. They were old and dirty and the hoses that carried the water to our barrels were equally disgusting. The price was much, much higher than what the wealthy in other parts of town paid for the same quantity, which they received through their faucets. . . . We never knew when the trucks would return. Sometimes more than a month passed without water."

My favorite story of Charlie's is one he read to me on a long bus ride in Venezuela. It is entitled "Angels and Shepherds." As Charlie relates,

One Christmas Eve, before I had ever heard the name of Hugo Chavez, I was visiting families. I stopped for a moment at the home of Angelica. She told me she was taking care of a little baby who was sick and wondered if I could do her a favor. That afternoon she had gone with the baby's mother to see a doctor who had given them a prescription for medicine. The doctor's advice was free. The medicine was not, and they didn't have enough money to buy it. Her question was: could I get it for her?

It was probably about 9 p.m. and I asked her if she needed it right away. No, in the morning would be ok.

I assisted at midnight Mass in the neighboring barrio and then shared a meal with the local priest and the religious sisters. When I returned to my neighborhood at about 2 a.m., some young people stopped me. "Charlie, a baby just died." "Where," I asked. "In Angelica's house."

* * *

When I returned to my shack, I couldn't help but reflect on the incident. Two thousand years ago, it is reported that angels announced to shepherds and to the world the birth of a child. After two centuries of "civilization," a woman with the name of an angel had to announce to the world the death of a child.

Charlie explains how the grinding poverty in the barrios, combined with the rising price of basic foodstuffs and gasoline—which resulted in the jump in the cost of transportation—led to the spontaneous barrio uprisings of the Caracazo. As Charlie writes, during this uprising, the police "became assassins, firing indiscriminately into crowds running away from them. . . . The situation became worse when the president ordered the army into the streets." According to Charlie:

> No one knows the number of deaths that occurred in Venezuela during the tumultuous days of February and March, 1989. I would not be surprised if the number surpassed that of the massacre in Tiananmen Square in China three months later. The China event received extensive press coverage, and the date is still remembered every year. But what happened in Caracas received little coverage and was quickly forgotten. . . .
>
> Thousands of people had lost family members. Every barrio of Caracas had felt the repression of the police and the armed forces. Many of those living in the wealthier parts of the city had their business establishments destroyed, but the deaths they witnessed were

mostly on television, and they cheered the police who were chasing the barrio dwellers.

Alluding to the ahistorical coverage given to Venezuela and to Hugo Chavez, Charlie writes that "[t]he economic injustices and racial divisions that had existed for years in Caracas and in Venezuela as a whole had surfaced. Ten years later, political opponents of President Hugo Chavez would accuse him of dividing the country. But in 1989 Chavez was just another soldier. Like many Venezuelans, he probably wondered why soldiers should kill hungry people for stealing spaghetti."

Charlie witnessed the massive military incursion into and repression of his own barrio during the Caracazo, seeing soldiers shoot a man and then throw him down the mountainside. As Charlie explains, "[i]t was like a war movie, a horror show." Charlie himself confronted a soldier posted in the barrio, telling him,

> "My name is Charlie. I am the priest here. The people here are good people." I asked him if he was from a barrio, and he replied that he was from the countryside and had been called into action the day before.
>
> I could see tears in his eyes as he looked at us. My neighbors began to gather behind me. . . . Here he was, faced with men, women, and children who probably looked like his own family. But I also knew that if someone threw a rock, he had the power to kill us all.
>
> A lay missionary later wrote to a priest in the United States that she didn't think I was ever more a priest than that day when I stood between the automatic weapons and the people of the barrio.

Sadly, the Caracazo was not the only transformative, and largely forgotten, massacre in Latin America in 1989.

Another such massacre, possibly the largest of all those discussed here, was the US's attack upon the civilian, working-class neighborhoods in Panama City, Panama in December of 1989. This attack was carried out unilaterally and illegally, without UN Security Council authorization. And this attack, ostensibly carried out to capture one man—Panamanian leader Manuel Noriega, an ally of the US and CIA asset who then fell out of favor when he refused to allow Panama to be used as a staging ground for the Nicaraguan Contras—claimed the lives of hundreds, if not thousands of civilian lives.[7] As author Matt Peppe explains,[8]

> Twenty five years ago, before dawn on December 20, 1989, US forces descended on Panama City and unleashed one of the most violent, destructive terror attacks of the century. US soldiers killed more people than were killed on 9/11. They systematically burned apartment buildings and shot people indiscriminately in the streets. Dead bodies were piled on top of each other; many were burned before identification. The aggression was condemned internationally, but the message was clear: the United States military was free to do whatever it wanted, whenever it wanted, and they would not be bound by ethics or laws.
>
> The invasion and ensuing occupation produced gruesome scenes: "People burning to death in the incinerated dwellings, leaping from windows, running in panic through the streets, cut down in cross fire, crushed by tanks, human fragments everywhere," writes William Blum.

Again, this massacre, carried out by the US against a defenseless people, is barely remembered today here in the United States. And indeed, when George H.W. Bush was eulogized, and indeed lionized, upon his death in 2018, few would even bother to mention this episode in the list of his handiwork.

Another massacre, in El Salvador (literally, "The Savior," referring to Jesus Christ) though not large in terms of the numbers killed, was significant because of who was killed—6 well-known Jesuit priests along with their housekeeper and the housekeeper's daughter. As the

Center for Justice & Accountability, which has been seeking legal redress for these crimes, explains:

> On the morning of November 16, 1989, an elite battalion of the Salvadoran Army entered the grounds of the Jesuit University of Central America, with orders to kill Father Ignacio Ellacuría—an outspoken critic of the Salvadoran military dictatorship—and leave no witnesses. When it was all over, the soldiers had killed six Jesuit priests, a housekeeper and her daughter in cold blood. The Jesuits Massacre is one of most notorious crimes of El Salvador's 12-year civil war, which left over 75,000 people dead.[9]

Of course, the US was funding the Salvadoran Army at that time, and so the victims were not deemed worthy of noting, much less remembering. The murder of the 6 Jesuits in 1989 marked not only the culmination of the brutal Salvadoran civil war, but also the quite successful culmination of the US's decades-long war against liberation theology in Latin America—a war won by the murder of Catholic bishops, priests, nuns and religious laity by forces armed and trained by the United States.[10]

In their landmark book, *Manufacturing Consent*,[11] Noam Chomsky and Edward S. Herman devote a chapter to the media's unbalanced coverage of the murder of one priest in Poland in 1984 as compared to the coverage of the 72 religious killed throughout Latin America between 1964 and 1978, the killing of 23 religious in Guatemala between 1980 and 1985, the murder of Archbishop Oscar Romero of San Salvador in 1980, and the rape and murder of the 4 US Church women in El Salvador in 1980. In short, the murder of the one Polish priest—the perpetrators of which were actually tried, convicted and sentenced to prison—received significantly more coverage than all of the latter killings, which largely remain unsolved and unpunished, *combined*.

Of course, the reason for the disparity in coverage is that the

Western media invariably fixates on the crimes of others while ignoring our own crimes. In this case, the media focused on the murder of one priest in then-Communist Poland while largely ignoring the scores of priests killed by right-wing governments aligned with and supported by the United States.

Fast forward to the present when the *National Catholic Reporter* (NCR) reported on the extradition order for Col. Inocente Orlando Montano to be tried for his role in the murder of six Jesuit priests.[12] Montano is being extradited to Spain from the US where he has been comfortably sheltered for years. As the NCR reported:

> In her 23-page ruling, [Judge] Swank said the evidence shows that Montano participated in the "terrorist" murders and attended the key meetings where the high command plotted the assassination of Jesuit Father Ignacio Ellacuría, the rector of the University of Central America.
>
> Ellacuría was also serving as a key negotiator trying to mediate a peace between the US-backed Salvadoran government and the Farabundo Martí National Liberation Front (FMLN.) The peace talks included discussions about purging the military of those officers linked to atrocities.
>
> The operation to eliminate Ellacuría and all witnesses was carried out Nov. 16, 1989 **by a US-trained anti-terrorist unit**, which stormed the Central American University in San Salvador and blew out the brains of the Jesuits with high-powered weapons. The assassins then executed their housekeeper, Julia Elba Ramos, and her daughter Celina (emphasis added).[13]

The NCR notes that **Montano "was also trained at the US Army School of the Americas (SOA)** at Fort Benning, Ga., now known as the Western Hemisphere Institute for Security Cooperation" (emphasis added).

That Montano, a murderer of Catholic priests, was trained at the

SOA makes perfect sense, for the SOA—which continues to train thousands of repressive Latin American military forces—has itself bragged about its role in destroying liberation theology (the Christian philosophy which advocates "the preferential option for the poor") in Latin America. As Noam Chomsky has explained, "[o]ne of its advertising points is that the US Army [School of the Americas] helped defeat liberation theology, which was a dominant force, and it was an enemy for the same reason that secular nationalism in the Arab world was an enemy—it was working for the poor."[14]

And, the SOA specifically encouraged the violent assault on priests, as Jack Nelson-Pallmeyer notes in his book, *School of Assassins*.[15] Thus, as he explains, 75 percent of the training exercises at the SOA ended with the priest or other religious figure (usually played by a US army chaplain) either killed or wounded.

As Noam Chomsky has noted elsewhere, the US's military campaign in Latin America since 1962

was in substantial measure a war against the Church. It was more than symbolic that it culminated in the assassination of six leading Latin American intellectuals, Jesuit priests, in November 1989, a few days after the fall of the Berlin wall. They were murdered by an elite Salvadoran battalion, fresh from renewed training at the John F. Kennedy Special Forces School in North Carolina. As was learned last November, but apparently aroused no interest, the order for the assassination was signed by the chief of staff and his associates, all of them so closely connected to the Pentagon and the US Embassy that it becomes even harder to imagine that Washington was unaware of the plans of its model battalion. This elite force had already left a trail of blood of the usual victims through the hideous decade of the 1980s in El Salvador, which opened with the assassination of Archbishop Romero, "the voice of the voiceless," by much the same hands.

The murder of the Jesuit priests was a crushing blow to liberation theology, the remarkable revival of Christianity initiated by

Pope John XXIII at Vatican II, which he opened in 1962, an event that "ushered in a new era in the history of the Catholic Church," in the words of the distinguished theologian and historian of Christianity Hans KŸng. Inspired by Vatican II, Latin American Bishops adopted "the preferential option for the poor," renewing the radical pacifism of the Gospels that had been put to rest when the Emperor Constantine established Christianity as the religion of the Roman Empire—"a revolution" that converted "the persecuted church" to a "persecuting church," in KŸng's words. In the post-Vatican II attempt to revive the Christianity of the pre-Constantine period, priests, nuns, and laypersons took the message of the Gospels to the poor and the persecuted, brought them together in "base communities," and encouraged them to take their fate into their own hands and to work together to overcome the misery of survival in brutal realms of US power.[16]

A September 27, 2005 cable emanating from the US Embassy in San Salvador, entitled "El Salvador: The Declining Influence of The Roman Catholic Church," confirms Chomsky's analysis about the historic import of liberation theology and the historic import of the US's successful effort to wipe it out. Thus, the embassy states that

> [i]n 1977, former Archbishop Oscar Arnulfo Romero adopted an outspoken stance in favor of "liberation theology" that alienated many of the church's most influential members. Archbishop Arturo Rivera y Damas followed Romero's example during his 1983–1994 tenure. Much changed in the years following the 1992 Peace Accords, which ended repression and violence on the part of government forces and guerrillas. With the selection of Fernando Saenz Lacalle as Archbishop of San Salvador in 1995, the Catholic Church entered a new era during which it withdrew its support for "liberation theology"; Saenz-Lacalle has placed a renewed emphasis on individual

salvation and morality. However, an underlying division still exists within the Salvadoran Catholic Church vis–vis such political issues.[17]

The embassy later on explains that, with its withdrawal from Liberation Theology, "[t]he Salvadoran Catholic Church has in effect been 're-Romanized'. . . ."

As is true so often, what is not said in the foregoing passage is what is most illuminating. First, the embassy simply remains silent about the murder of the six Jesuits in 1989 which was the coup de grâce against the Liberation Church in El Salvador. In addition, the embassy skirts over the opening salvo against the Liberation Church there—the death in 1980 of Archbishop Romero—an individual the Vatican just canonized as a saint in October of 2018.

Thus, the embassy refers to Oscar Romero as the "former Archbishop" who embraced liberation theology. But what the embassy does not say is that Romero is the "former" Archbishop because he was murdered while saying Mass by forces trained, funded and armed by the US. The embassy, wanting to avoid these inconvenient facts, simply sloughs him off as the "former Archbishop," as if he were simply retired. And, what is left unspoken is that it was the murder of good people like Archbishop Romero, and the 6 Jesuits in 1989, that led to the Church "re-Romanizing"—a term with a double meaning, for it can properly mean that the Church is again in line with the Vatican in Rome (the intended meaning), but also that it has returned to the pro-Empire stance the Church has maintained (with limited interruption after the second Vatican Council in 1962) since 324 A.D. In other words, mission accomplished for both the Vatican and the US.

In short, the massacre which took place in El Salvador in November of 1989 may have been one of the most significant world events in many decades, for it marked the end of the radical transformation of the Catholic Church, and quite possibly humanity with it. But few will know of this event, or its import, or what the world could have been had the "preferential option for the poor" survived as a philosophy.

In the end, because the foregoing events went according to plan—to the US plan of continuing to bend the world to its will and to transform it for its sole benefit—the events were not worth noting. While President George H.W. Bush would not officially announce his "New World Order" until September of 1990, this Order was already being ushered in with the end of the Cold War and the rise of the US as the world's sole hegemon. The murder of the 6 Jesuits carried out just one month after the fall of the Berlin Wall as a fatal blow against liberation theology; the unilateral invasion of Panama, carried out in part just to show that the US could act unilaterally as it pleased; and the violent imposition of neo-liberal economic policies in Venezuela were all part of the birth of this new Order. Because this was all taking place according to plan, there was no need for any hand-wringing by the US's captive press.

4

THE BOLIVARIAN REVOLUTION

The Rise of Hugo Chavez

Meanwhile, the Venezuelan government continued down the neo-liberal economic path prescribed by Washington. The results were predictably disastrous for the vast majority of Venezuelan people who would not be put down so easily. Indeed, the Caracazo only inspired more protests and greater political organization among the poor and working class. Thus,

[t]hough rarely reported in the US, protests continued along with strike waves severe enough to lead to fear that the country was headed towards "anarchy." Among other cases, three students were killed by police who attacked peaceful demonstrations in late November 1991; and two weeks later, police used tear gas to break up a peaceful march of 15,000 people in Caracas protesting Pérez's economic policies. In January 1992, the main trade union confederation predicted serious difficulties and conflicts as a result of the neoliberal programs, which had caused "massive impoverishment" including a 60 percent drop in workers' buying power in 3 years, while enriching financial groups and transnational corporations. . . .

Other flaws were to come to light (in the US) a few weeks later after a coup attempt, among them, the government's admission that only 57 percent of Venezuelans could afford more than one meal a day in this country of enormous wealth. Other flaws in the miracle had been revealed in the report of an August 1991 Presidential Commission for the Rights of Children, not previously noticed, which found that "critical poverty, defined as the inability to meet at least one half of basic nutritional requirements," had tripled from 11 percent of the population in 1984 to 33 percent in 1991; and that real per capita income fell 55 percent from 1988 to 1991, falling at double the rate of 1980–1988.[1]

Then, on February 4, 1992, 200 members of the Venezuelan military, led by a young officer named Hugo Chavez, attempted a coup to overthrow the now much hated regime of President Carlos Andres Perez. The group Chavez led was known as the Revolutionary Bolivarian Movement-200. The coup failed, and Hugo Chavez, once arrested, publicly urged forces loyal to him to give up in the interest of preventing further bloodshed.[2]

Hugo Chavez would spend the next two years in jail until he was eventually pardoned. Others, including many who had nothing to do with the coup, suffered worse fates at the hand of state forces for merely being suspected of supporting the coup. As the *Guardian* reported at the time, "[t]he cabinet passed a decree suspending the constitution, enabling it to search homes and detain people without warrants. Strikes and public gatherings have been banned."[3]

Amnesty International reported that, in the wake of the coup, "the security forces carried out widespread raids in many cities. They arbitrarily arrested a number of people, including student leaders, members of political parties and community activists. Most of those detained were later released without charge. Dozens, however, were tortured. Complaints were submitted to the authorities, but by July 1993 none of those responsible for illegal arrests, torture or ill-treatment had reportedly been brought to justice, and the victims had not received any compensation."[4]

However, the genie of popular revolution against regressive economic policies and repression had now been released from the bottle, and the security crackdown after the coup only sparked greater popular resentment. As Noam Chomsky explains:

> On February 4, 1992, an attempted military coup was crushed. "There was little jubilation," AP reported. "The coup attempt caps a crescendo of anger and frustration over the economic reforms that have written such a macroeconomic success story but have failed to benefit the lives of most Venezuelans and have embittered many" (*Financial Times*). It "was met by silent cheers from a large part of the population," Brooke reported, particularly in poor and working-class areas. Like the Brazilian technocrats, Pérez had done everything right, "cutting subsidies, privatizing state companies and opening a closed economy to competition." But something had unaccountably gone wrong. True, the growth rate was impressive, "but most economic analysts agree that the high price of oil in 1991 fueled Venezuela's growth more than Pérez's austerity moves," Stan Yarbro reported, and none can fail to see that "the new wealth has failed to trickle down to Venezuela's middle and lower classes, whose standard of living has fallen dramatically." Infant deaths "have soared in the past two years as a result of worsening malnutrition and other health problems in the shantytowns," a priest who had worked in poor neighborhoods for 16 years said.[5]

There would be another coup attempt in November of 1992, again by military personnel of the Bolivarian Revolutionary Movement-200 loyal to Hugo Chavez, who was then sitting in jail.

The foment in Venezuela took the world by surprise. Indeed, Venezuela was the last country in Latin America most people suspected would have a popular revolution. The *Guardian* explained this surprise, stating that, "[a]fter all, the country is one of the most stable democracies in Latin America. It was not affected by the flurry of military coups that swept across South America in the late 1960s and early 1970s. Indeed, the last coup was in 1958, when a popular uprising overthrew the dictator Marcos Pérez Jimenez and restored civilian rule."[6]

But Perez had betrayed the people by embracing with great enthusiasm the IMF-demanded austerity measures he had promised to resist. And by doing so, Perez awakened 500 years of resentment of a people violently prevented from deciding their own fate. Even some mainstream newspapers acknowledged this. The *Guardian*, for example, related that:

> The underlying cause of the military unrest is undoubtedly the widespread social discontent. When he came back to power three years ago, President Pérez was expected to repeat the expansionist policies of his first term of office in the late 1970s when Venezuela was one of the richest countries in the developing world, enjoying the easy wealth brought by its huge oil reserves.
>
> But Mr Pérez overnight adopted the liberal economic policies dominant in most of the Western world. He cut back heavily on government spending, opening up the economy to market forces and international competition.
>
> His reforms were in some ways even more radical than the similar changes in Mexico at the same time. And the social cost was high.
>
> Thousands lost their jobs. . . .

The *Guardian* ended this piece by a quite prescient statement: "As Latin America commemorates the 500th anniversary of Columbus's voyage with growing Indian nationalism, 1992 could also mark the discovery that neo-liberalism is not the answer to all their problems." Certainly, this was how Chavez and his supporters saw their struggle. Invoking the memory of "The Great Liberator," Bolivar, they believed themselves to be at the forefront of a Continental movement to free Latin America of foreign control and intervention. And ultimately, they would achieve this feat. Thus, in the words of Noam Chomsky upon Hugo Chavez's death, Chavez led "the historic liberation of Latin America" from the over 500 years of subjugation it had suffered since the time of the Conquistadors.

Revolution for Continental Independence and Dignity

Hugo Chavez was elected president of Venezuela in 1998, and was inaugurated on February 2, 1999. It is important to point out the fact that he was duly elected because one will still sometimes see in the press references to Chavez allegedly coming to power through a coup.

Chavez termed the revolution he led "The Bolivarian Revolution" after Simon Bolivar. Eventually, as per the 1999 Constitution which was drafted by constituent assembly meetings throughout the country and approved by a referendum of the Venezuelan people, Venezuela was in fact renamed "The Bolivarian Republic of Venezuela." Caracas's international airport is named after Bolivar, and Simon Bolivar's image is ubiquitous throughout Venezuela.

Given the foregoing, it is important to remember who Simon Bolivar was. Bolivar was known as "The Liberator" because he led the successful revolutionary military campaign to liberate six Latin American countries (Venezuela, Colombia, Panama, Peru, Ecuador and Bolivia) from Spanish imperial rule.[7] The successful liberation of all six of these countries, which he designated "Gran Colombia," was finally successful, against great military odds, in 1825.[8] Bolivar ruled the fragile and short-lived Gran Colombia until shortly before his death in 1830, and, among other things, instituted a land reform program to distribute land to the poor and dispossessed.

Of great relevance, Bolivar, while an admirer of the American Revolution and George Washington, was greatly disturbed by the slave market (the largest in the US) he witnessed in Charleston, South Carolina, while visiting there.[9] He decided, given what he saw there, that which should have been apparent to our own Founding Fathers— that one could not fight for liberty and maintain slavery at the same time. This is a lesson, I would submit, that the US has never fully acknowledged or understood.

And so, Hugo Chavez's goal as president was a quite lofty one: liberating Venezuela and the rest of Latin America from the domination of the new empire, the United States, and liberating Venezuela's poor from the domination of the wealthy elite, through which the United States has governed Venezuela. In many ways, Chavez was quite successful at this. As even the BBC acknowledged upon his death in 2013,[10] Chavez's

> most important goal was the building of an alliance among the countries of Latin America and the Caribbean that would fulfil the frustrated dream of his great hero, South American independence leader Simon Bolivar, two centuries before.
>
> The first step towards the Bolivarian dream had been Petrocaribe—a scheme to provide cheap oil to the countries of Central America and the Caribbean that depend on imports.
>
> It was hugely popular, with only Barbados refusing to take part.

As the *Haitian Times* relates about Petrocaribe, "[i]n 2005, when oil prices began to creep upwards and when the Bolivarian socialists led by Hugo Chávez were at their peak, 14 countries from the Caribbean met in Puerto La Cruz, Venezuela, to launch the Petrocaribe scheme. The idea was elegant. Venezuela, with one of the world's largest oil reserves, would sell oil to the struggling Caribbean islands through a very lucrative deal. Part of the oil price was paid up front, and the rest was to be paid back over the years at a ridiculously low interest rate (1 percent)."[11] Haiti and Nicaragua would join this group of 14 in 2007. And, in 2010, after the earthquake in Haiti, Hugo Chavez forgave Haiti the $4 billion in debt it owed Venezuela for the oil. As the *Haitian Times* notes, this is in contrast to France which never forgave Haiti the "debt" France claimed Haiti owed it after the Haitian revolution of 1804 when

Haiti freed the slaves France claimed to own. Haiti would ultimately pay off this $21 billion debt in 1947.

Meanwhile, the Petrocaribe pact

> was followed by Alba, a regional integration scheme that would grow to include Cuba, Bolivia, Ecuador, Honduras (until 2009) and Nicaragua, as well as a few small independent Caribbean states.
>
> Venezuela under Mr Chavez, along with Brazil under President Luiz Inacio Lula da Silva, also promoted a new regional architecture designed to embrace all American states except the US and Canada.
>
> This led to Unasur, the Union of South American countries, and a proposed Community of Latin American and Caribbean nations (Celac).
>
> It also led to a development bank designed to counter the influence of the IMF.[12]

I had the pleasure of meeting Hugo Chavez and hearing him speak at an international trade union conference in Caracas in the summer of 2010. Chavez made the profound observation that the 20th century had not been the "American Century" after all, as so many have trumpeted, but that it indeed had been the "Century of Revolution," seeing socialist revolutions most notably in Mexico, Russia, China, Cuba, Vietnam and Nicaragua—revolutions which succeeded in varying degrees in throwing off the chains of domination by the capitalist Western powers, most notably the US.

Chavez explained that when he became president of Venezuela in 1999, there was only "one light left on in the home," and that was Cuba—a socialist island in a sea of capitalism just barely managing to hang on.

With Chavez's election to the presidency, and the mutual support Venezuela and Cuba then gave to each other, Cuba was not only able to thrive but was able to expand its international medical solidarity even further, most notably in Haiti where Cuban doctors have been at the front line against post-earthquake cholera in that country.

In addition, Venezuela and Cuba joined forces to create Operation Miracle, a medical program which has given sight to over 3 million (or about 10% of the total) of the world's blind persons, including, in a great act of forgiveness, to the man who shot and killed Che Guevara.[13] One might recall that, in another act of altruism, Chavez provided low-cost heating oil to poor residents of Boston and New York City through Citgo, Venezuela's state-owned oil company.[14]

In addition to buoying Cuba, Venezuela under Chavez's leadership helped give rise and support to other progressive, anti-imperialist governments in Latin America—for example, in Nicaragua, Brazil, Ecuador, Honduras, Bolivia, and Paraguay. Therefore, it was no exaggeration for Noam Chomsky to say in an interview shortly after the death of Hugo Chavez that he had led "the historic liberation of Latin America" from the over 500 years of subjugation it had suffered since the time of the conquistadors—again, much to the chagrin of the United States.[15] Indeed, Chomsky, agreeing with the interviewer that Chavez was a "damaging figure," explained that Chavez was indeed "destructive to the rich oligarchy, to US power."

Moreover, Chavez, in addition to playing a uniting role for the countries of Latin America, was one of the most important voices for peace in Colombia—a country ravaged by over 50 years of civil war. Indeed, Colombia's current peace deal between the Colombian government and left-wing FARC guerillas was accomplished largely due to Chavez's unflagging efforts in coordination with that of Fidel Castro. Both Chavez and Fidel prevailed upon the FARC to give up their many years of armed struggle, and all of the Colombian peace talks were held in Havana, Cuba.

As the US is wont to do, it has exploited Venezuela's magnanimity in helping broker the Colombian peace accords, and used the resulting disarmament of the once-powerful FARC guerillas as an occasion to accelerate its offensive against Venezuela. In short, if the FARC still existed, the US's ability to use Colombia as a staging ground against

Venezuela, as it currently is, would have been incredibly difficult, if not impossible, for the FARC would have aggressively resisted this.

Preferential Option for the Poor

One of the few honest commentators, Sylvia Brodzinsky, wrote the following the day before the 2015 Venezuelan legislative elections in a story entitled "Venezuela's High-Life Elite Hope Hard-Hit Poor Will Abandon Chavez's Legacy":

> [S]ince the late Hugo Chávez began what he called his "Bolivarian revolution" in 1998, that elite has been derisively termed *los escualidos*, the squalid ones, and they have been the object of government scorn.
>
> Fed up with corrupt politics and neoliberal economic policies that the poor felt left them unprotected, Venezuelans swept Chávez into power hoping for change. With an economy buoyed by sky-high oil prices, Chávez set up social welfare programmes to benefit the poor in education, health and housing, winning him the gratitude and loyalty of millions.

In these few sentences, Brodzinsky captures the essence of the Bolivarian Revolution—a revolution of the poor, for the poor, and in conflict with the wealthy who had hitherto governed Venezuela, with US support.

Hugo Chavez himself was a poor man, having been famously raised in a mud hut. And, he was a deeply religious man as well, a devout Roman Catholic who, in addition to receiving inspiration from the example of Simon Bolivar, was moved by The Gospels and Jesus's call to feed and clothe the poor. And, as discussed above, he followed Jesus' example in giving sight to the blind—to millions of the blind.

The Bolivarian government did a laudable job until Chavez's death in 2013 in greatly reducing poverty and in reducing economic inequality.

Chavez wasted no time in his offensive against poverty. Thus, beginning on February 27, 1999, the tenth anniversary of the Caracazo massacre, Chávez set into motion a huge social welfare program called Plan Bolívar 2000 which involved sending thousands of military personnel from each branch of the Venezuelan Armed Forces to engage in public works programs, including rebuilding roads, bridges and hospitals; draining stagnant water that offered breeding areas for disease-carrying mosquitoes; and offering free medical care and vaccinations. As Gregory Wilpert describes, each branch of the Armed Forces developed its own projects.[16] Thus,

> The Air Force developed a plan to transport people who could not afford to travel but urgently needed to, for free, to different parts of the country. The Navy developed *Plan Pescar* (fishing) 2000, which involved repairing refrigerators, organizing cooperatives, giving courses. The National Guard became involved in police activity, particularly in areas where the state's presence was minimal. Another program was *Plan Avispa*, also organized by the National Guard, to build homes for the poor. *Plan Reviba* was similar, except instead of building new homes from scratch, involved rebuilding old homes. Other aspects of Plan Bolivar 2000 involved distributing food to remote areas of the country.

The other purpose of this program was to transform the military into a force for good in the country rather than a force for repression as it had been for so long.

Even the World Bank acknowledged the success of Chavez's anti-poverty programs, explaining:

> Among the most important programs that oil resources have helped to finance are the broad-based social programs called Misiones. Economic growth and the redistribution of resources associated with these missions have led to an important decline in moderate poverty,

from 50% in 1998 to approximately 30% in 2012. Likewise, inequality has decreased, reducing the Gini Index from 0.49 in 1998 to 0.39 in 2012, which is among the lowest in the region.[17]

As Greg Shupak of Fairness and Accuracy In Reporting (FAIR) recently wrote,[18]

Under Chávez, poverty in Venezuela was cut by more than a third, and extreme poverty by 57 percent (CEPR, 3/7/13). (These declines were even steeper if measured from the depths of the opposition-led oil strike, designed to force Chávez out by wrecking the economy.)

In June 2013, the UN's Food and Agriculture Organization (FAO) included Venezuela in a group of 18 nations that had cut their number of hungry people by half in the preceding 20 years, 14 of which were governed by Chavismo: The FAO said that Venezuela reduced the number of people suffering from malnutrition from 13.5 percent of the population in 1990–92 to less than 5 percent of the population in 2010–12; the FAO credited government-run supermarket networks and nutrition programs created by Chávez.

Three months later, the UN Committee on the Elimination of Racial Discrimination . . . noted that it welcomes the progress made by the [Venezuelan government] in the area of education and its efforts to reduce illiteracy, as a result of which it was declared an "illiteracy-free territory" by the United Nations Educational, Scientific and Cultural Organization (UNESCO) in October 2005.

In 2014, Niky Fabiancic, resident UN coordinator for Venezuela, called the country "one of the leading countries in Latin America and the Caribbean in reducing inequality," according to *Venezuela Analysis* (5/9/14). The website also quoted UNICEF representative Kiyomi Kawaguchi as saying that from 2009–10, 7.7 million students attended school, an increase of 24 percent over ten years previously.

Thus, in the Bolivarian Revolution's 14th and 15th year, multiple UN organs highlighted how Chavismo had improved the lives of Venezuela's poor majority.

As Shupak notes, even the *Wall Street Journal* begrudgingly acknowledged in a recent 2019 article that during the period 2003 to 2012, "Mr. Chávez expropriates farms and businesses, and uses oil revenue to build homes, distribute food and upgrade healthcare. The programs reduce poverty and make him popular."[19]

In addition, Chavez, and then Maduro, who was a union bus driver for many years, have done much for workers' rights and organized labor in Venezuela. As explained to me by my union friends in Venezuela, Jacobo Torres and Carlos Lopez, both leaders of the Central Socialista Bolivariana de Trabajadores (CSBT), through the efforts of the two-million-member CSBT union in dialogue with President Hugo Chavez, the Venezuelan workers are now receiving the benefit of one of the most far-reaching and progressive labor laws in the world. This labor law, which was signed on May 1, 2012, was the product of a convention of 4500 worker delegates who made 19,000 proposals to President Chavez for the new law which, they explained, had the purpose of "overcoming the capitalist weaknesses in the Venezuela law" which had governed labor relations in the past.

Amongst other things, the new law[20]

- forbids employers from firing any worker (including non-union) without just cause;
- requires businesses to share at least 15 percent of their profits with the workers;
- requires employers to pay workers severance if they lose their job for any reason;
- gives workers the right to continue running factories which employers may decide to stop operating;

- limits the work week to 40 hours and requires that workers be given two successive days off from work a week;
- grants 6 months of parental leave to mothers and 15 days to fathers, gives mothers who return to work 1.5 hours per day to breast feed and gives new fathers and mothers absolute protection from discharge for the first 2 years after the birth of their child;
- forbids all sub-contracting as of 2017.

And, on several occasions, when businesses have attempted to close and layoff employees, the Venezuelan government has backed workers' demands to take over the business. A dramatic example of this took place in 2016 when US company Kimberly Clark, which produces many necessary household paper products, including toilet paper, announced it was shuttering its Venezuelan operations. In this instance, the Venezuelan government supported the nearly 1000 workers in taking over and running the factory, and they have been successful in doing so to capacity.[21]

As Jacobo and Carlos explained, the destiny of the Venezuelan workers and unions are intimately tied to that of the revolution and Nicolas Maduro—the first "worker president" of Venezuela. And that is why you will see nearly no support amongst union workers in Venezuela for the ongoing coup attempt against Maduro.

Meanwhile, the *Guardian* wrote in 2013,[22] "[l]ast month marked the second anniversary of Venezuela's great housing mission, started by the late Hugo Chavez, to tackle the country's massive housing deficit. The mission was to start by building 350,000 houses in 2011 and 2012 combined—a target exceeded by nearly 25,000. . . . From now on the annual targets are much tougher—over 300,000 a year." As the same article notes, Venezuela "has had three years of steady growth and a longer period of growth in real incomes. Poverty has been halved and the gap between rich and poor is now one of the lowest in Latin America. At 50% of GDP, government debt is high but less than half the level in the UK. Public spending doubled under Chávez, but is still only just over 20% of GDP."

In addition, if one looks at the UN's Human Development Index, which measures several key indicators of the health of a country's citizenry (e.g., life expectancy, income, education, equality), one sees that Venezuela experienced a steady growth in such human development indicators from the time Chavez took office to the time of his death, with a total Human Rights Index score of .662 in 2000, and rising to .748 in 2012.[23] Significantly, Venezuela had a huge relative increase in this index during that time, jumping nine rankings in the HDI chart from 80 to number 71 in the world. (If one compares this to Venezuela's neighbor, and chief US ally in this hemisphere, Colombia, that country was stuck at position 91 in the world during that same time period.)

However, such statistics do not give the full story of the accomplishments of the Bolivarian Revolution. One emblematic accomplishment has been the rebuilding of Vargas state, which was devastated by historic rains and mud slides in 1999, just after Chavez became president. Because of the poor infrastructure of the poor barrios straddling the mountains surrounding Vargas, untold numbers of families lost their homes in these mud slides, and it is estimated that 30,000 people lost their lives in them, having been buried alive in the mud.

In 2018, I was part of a delegation that was given a tour of Vargas by its current, and quite popular governor, Jorge Garcia Carneiro. Carneiro is a Chavez loyalist who had been a general in the Venezuelan military and later minister of defense after helping to bring Chavez back to power after the 2002 coup. While driving through Vargas, with the rebuilt homes of the poor on one side, and the ocean on the other, what struck me was how different this reconstruction had taken place than it would have in the United States, or in any other Western country for that matter. Recall, for example, how New Orleans was transformed after Katrina. That disaster was used to gentrify that city. A discriminatory rebuilding finance program, the mass firing of thousands of teachers which disproportionately affected African Americans and rising rents combined to prevent 100,000 African-Americans who fled after the hurricane—many who had lived in New Orleans for generations—from returning.[24] In the end, New Orleans is now "a smaller, whiter city" with a new "start-up" economy which provides less and lower-paying job opportunities to those African-Americans who remain.[25]

But the Bolivarian government did not, as certainly would have been done almost anywhere else, use the tragedy of 1999 as an opportunity to rebuild Vargas as a beach-front playground for rich Venezuelans and tourists. Rather, the government rebuilt the homes for the poor just where they had been, along the oceanfront. And so, instead of seeing new hotels and condos along the shore, I witnessed kids playing soccer in their front yards overlooking the sea. This is the Bolivarian Revolution for me.

I've also had a few opportunities to visit Ciudad Caribia, the giant socialist city that Chavez had dreamed of years before and which, as most other public housing projects, bears Chavez's giant signature. On one occasion, when I was travelling with Charlie Hardy, the former priest who ministered to the poor in Caracas, we visited his old neighbor from the barrio, Luz, a name which means "light" in Spanish. Luz had lived in the barrio for 40 years without sewage and running water. Her 16-year-old son had been murdered by the police in 1990 (eight years before Chavez was elected president), and she just received some justice with the policeman responsible for the killing receiving a sentence of 12 years in prison for the crime.

The barrio which was Luz's home for 4 decades was recently condemned because, as many of the hill-side barrios lining Caracas, it was built on a landfill and is now sliding down the hill. However, she and her family received four fully furnished apartments in the spanking brand new Ciudad Caribia—they had all shared one tiny dwelling in the barrio. They now have running water, sewage and electricity. The city has its own health clinic and day care. She doesn't have to pay for the new apartment because she already paid the government for the old house. Her other family members have to pay the equivalent of eight to sixteen US dollars a month for 30 years.

Luz says thanks to the president for all of this. Luz explains that President Chavez now provides food in all the schools. Now children in Bolivarian schools receive breakfast and lunch, but "they call our President a terrorist in other countries." At the time, Ciudad Caribia, which already housed thousands of Venezuela's poor, was still under construction. All told, it will house a total of 88,000 people.

Meanwhile, in 2017, I had the pleasure of visiting the parish of San Agustin del Sur in Caracas, Venezuela, where I support a youth symphony with music supplies. San Agustin is well-marked by the red cable cars (the MetroCable) which President Chavez had built in 2010 to connect this poor parish, along with many other poor parishes, with the center city. Before Chavez, the sprawling poor barrios which ring the cities, including San Agustin, were literally not on any government maps, and they had no utilities and no election centers. After Chavez, the existence of these barrios was recognized for the first time, and they were provided with utilities, health service, election stations and, most important, dignity.

San Agustin is also world-renowned for its music, especially its salsa. And indeed, the community has been working hard to use music, and music training, as a means of fighting youth violence in the parish. What I witnessed in San Agustin was a vibrant community which was certainly not well-off by first world standards, but which seemed peaceful, content and resolute. I also did not see the starving people which I was told I would see in Venezuela. Instead, I saw fruit and vegetable stands lining the streets, a fully-stocked bread shop, and I witnessed the distribution of the government-subsidized food staples (e.g., rice, flour, milk, canned tuna) to those in need. This subsidized food program, organized through Local Provision and Production Committees (CLAPs), reaches around 6 million people in Venezuela.

This is the side of Venezuela rarely reported in the US media which, like vultures circling over their next meal, appear eager to witness what is being promised as Venezuela's imminent collapse.

And, while there is undoubtedly much want in Venezuela, there are also hungry people in the US where 41 million people live in poverty and struggle to put food on the table. If one wishes to read more on this, check out the recent article in the *Guardian* entitled, "A Journey Through the Land of Extreme Poverty: Welcome to America." As this article notes, the UN expert on deprivation, Philip Alston, wants to know why the US, the richest country on earth, has 41 million poor people (that is more than the entire population of Venezuela which has around 31 million people).

This is a very good question. That Venezuela—a developing country which has been devastated by a Saudi-imposed drop in oil prices (produced by the Saudis' pumping nearly 20 million more barrels of oil per day, a whopping 25% increase, into the world market)[26] as well as multiple rounds of US economic sanctions—has issues combating hunger should be much less news-worthy, and yet news outlets cannot seem to get enough one-sided stories about deprivation in Venezuela.

I am not the only observer disturbed by media distortions about Venezuela. One person who has been talking about these distortions to anyone who will listen—and this is rarely in the mainstream press—is Dr. Alfred de Zayas, who recently served as UN independent expert on the promotion of a democratic and equitable international order. Dr. de Zayas was in Venezuela in 2017 as well, studying the realities of Venezuela in his capacity as UN expert. As de Zayas stated at the time,

> There is a worrying media campaign to force observers into a preconceived view, e.g., that there is a "humanitarian crisis" in Venezuela. We should be wary of hyperbole and exaggeration, bearing in mind that "humanitarian crisis" is a *terminus technicus and could be misused as a pretext for military intervention and regime change.*

Of course, there should be free flow of food and medicines into Venezuela in order to alleviate the current scarcity of food and medicines. But such help should be truly humanitarian and should not have ulterior political purposes. . . .

The situation in Venezuela definitely does not reach the threshold of humanitarian crisis, even though there is suffering caused by internal and external reasons. Any observer will recognize that there is scarcity in sectors, malnutrition, insecurity, anguish. When in Venezuela I inquired from many stakeholders about the reasons and I also learned of the measures taken by the government to address these problems. . . .[27]

Dr. de Zayas applauded, for example, the Venezuelan government's "program of building low-cost housing [which] has proven a good thing and has saved millions of persons from poverty and homelessness." This building continues, I might add, even now during this quite difficult economic period in Venezuela, with the government recently celebrating the building of its 2.5 millionth housing unit.

Dr. de Zayas also singled out the CLAP program, which, he commented, "provide[s] needy Venezuelans with 16kg packages containing sugar, flour, dried milk, oil etc., as the independent expert was able to verify at the Urbanización Nelson Mandela."

In addition, the reduction of extreme poverty, which the Chavista revolution has been known for, has also continued during the crisis, at least until recently.

Other progress of the Bolivarian Revolution continues to hold, though this is increasingly difficult because of the Western sanctions. Again, Greg Shupak from FAIR explains[28]:

One widely used measure of a country or territory's overall well-being is the UN's Human Development Index (HDI), a statistical composite index of life expectancy, education and per capita income indicators. The most recent HDI report is the one that was published in 2018, based on 2017 data.

The 2018 report put Venezuela in the category of countries or territories that have "High Human Development," the second best of the HDI's four rankings, and 78th of the 189 countries and territories examined.

Quite tellingly, Shupak points out that, in terms of HDI, Venezuela outranks the majority of countries making up the so-called "Lima Group"—the 14 countries which the US, unable to gain the support of a sufficient number of countries of the Organization of American States (OAS), has assembled as a regional "coalition of the willing" to try to bring down Venezuela's government. Specifically, Venezuela outranks "Lima Group" countries Brazil, Colombia, Guatemala, Guyana, Honduras, Paraguay, Peru and Saint Lucia, with "Guatemala, Guyana and Honduras . . . categorized as 'Medium Human Development,' the group below the one to which Venezuela belongs and the second lowest HDI category."[29]

The other reality about Venezuela barely portrayed by the mainstream press is the incredible resiliency of the Venezuelan people. What I have been most struck by in my travels to Venezuela is not the lack of things Venezuelans possess, but their abundance of joy and human solidarity. Indeed, as I told the airline agent at the ticket desk who was grilling me about my travel to Venezuela, it is my sense that, "in the US, we have everything, but at the same time nothing; while in Venezuela, you have nothing, but at the same time everything." The woman, who was Venezuelan herself, then stopped her questioning, paused, and said, "yes, Venezuelans have a certain spirituality about them, don't they?" I answered in the affirmative, and she then took my hand and said, "I hope we meet again." This is the Venezuela I know.

One rarely hears such voices of hope from Venezuela, nor does one often hear from those who still support the Bolivarian Revolution because of such gains, though fragile as they are. A rare airing of such voices was in a recent, March 4, 2019, BBC article, entitled, "Venezuela Crisis: Why Chavez's Followers Are Standing By Maduro."[30] This article quotes Marcos Lobos, an Afro-Venezuelan photographed in front of a small hand-built shrine to Chavez:

> "He was more than an icon, he represented hope and still does because his ideas were revolutionary," Mr. Lobos says.
>
> "He was all about social equality and justice. He opened our eyes, created a national conscience about how to take Venezuelan politics to the people."
>
> His wife, Mirna, chimes in: "Before, it was all about the rich people, politically powerful people, and we had nothing," she says. "Chávez loved us. People thought that when Chávez died, we'd be buried with him but no," she says, adding that Nicolás Maduro is the "son" of Hugo Chávez so they are prepared to fight to keep him.

"It's not Maduro's fault," she says of the deep economic crisis Venezuela is facing. Instead she holds the "empire" responsible, a reference to the US, which the Maduro government says has ruined the economy through its sanctions and through its opposition to Mr. Maduro's socialist government. Meanwhile, judging from the US's most recent successful regime change operation against another leader who was using his nation's oil wealth for his own people—Libya's Muammar Qaddafi—we know that the US has no interest in rebuilding that which Chavez built up for the poor after its imperial demolition project is finished. Thus, at the time the US and NATO began its bombing campaign against Libya in 2011, Libya had the highest standard of living in Africa, with the highest GDP per capita, the highest life expectancy and with free health-care, education and electricity.[31] And now, post-invasion, Libya is a failed state, dominated by warring militia factions, and with the worst standard of living in the continent.[32]

This is a very likely scenario for Venezuela if the US gets its way there. And indeed, this was alluded to by Senator Marco Rubio, who recently threatened in a tweet that Maduro would meet the same fate as Qaddafi (who was sodomized and then killed) if he does not voluntarily step down.[33] Rubio included the a photo of the bloodied Gaddafi in his death throes in this tweet.

Democracy

While both Chavez and Maduro have incessantly been described by the Western press as "authoritarian," "tyrannical," and other such pejorative terms, one of the biggest feats of the Bolivarian Revolution was to democratize Venezuela. Indeed, Chavez was clear that he wanted to build socialism in a non-authoritarian way. He called this "21st Century Socialism," by which he meant to distinguish the Venezuelan project from the more statist, command-and-control forms of socialism built in the Soviet Union, China and to a lesser extent in Cuba.

And so, Chavez helped to create a government in Venezuela more accountable to the people and more thoroughly democratic, and this is reflected in the 1999 Bolivarian Constitution, which itself was the product of grass-roots constituent assembly meetings throughout the country and which was approved by a popular vote. In addition, this Constitution provides procedures for the recall of the president during his/her term, and indeed, Chavez, who was first elected president in 1998 and then re-elected in 2000, himself stood for recall in 2004 and 2006, winning both recall referendums.

Indeed, there have been numerous elections for various candidates and on various issues since the Bolivarian Revolution began. As Chilean writer Pedro Santander put it so well in 2014:

Regarding the supposed "democratic deficit of the Venezuelan regime", the facts speak for themselves. Since 1998 there have been four national plebiscites, four presidential elections, and eleven parliamentary, regional, and municipal elections. Venezuela is the Latin American country with the highest number of elections and it also has an automatic electoral system (much more modern than Chile's one). . . .[34]

Moreover, under the 1999 Constitution, Venezuela's National Election Commission (CNE), which runs and oversees elections, became one of five branches of the Venezuelan government. That is, unlike in the US, the electoral commission is not merely one of a number of regulatory bodies within the Executive Branch of government. Rather, it is its own, independent branch answering to no other, and its president is ultimately approved by a two-thirds vote of the National Assembly rather than being appointed by the president of the republic as is the case in the US. Since 2006, the elected president of the CNE has been a woman—Tibisay Lucena—who has successfully ensured that women are well-represented in the leadership and staff of the commission.

The CNE is in charge of elections throughout the country and ensures a uniform system of voting, again unlike the US which has 50 separate voting systems in the 50 separate states (e.g., remember Florida's "hanging chads" in 2000). And, the electoral system used throughout Venezuela guarantees a secure, reliable and verifiable voting process—a process I have observed in action on a number of occasions. The voting machine used in every polling location throughout the country—including in the poor barrios which, before the Bolivarian Revolution, rarely had their own polling places—is only turned on when a voter presents both a valid voter id card and places their finger on an electronic machine which reads and verifies their fingerprint.

Once this takes place, the voter walks to another machine, surrounded by a cardboard barrier which allows them a private, secret vote, and casts an electronic vote. When they are finished, the machine prints out a paper receipt of the votes cast which the voter then places in a box which is sealed at the end of the voting day. By the end of the night, witnesses from all the parties involved in the election audit around 54% of the total ballots cast to validate that the vote tallies reflected in the paper receipts match up with the electronic vote count.

All of the paper receipts and electronic machines are then brought to a central location in Caracas where an audit of 100% of the votes can take place if necessary.

Indeed, in 2013, I was able to observe just such a post-election audit of the vote count at the invitation of the CNE (the National Electoral Council). The audit, known as the Citizens' Verification process, is impressive in its scope and thoroughness.

From eight in the morning until noon every day, a team of professors, their students and CNE support staff, operating out of the CNE warehouse in the Mariches barrio of Caracas, randomly select 350 boxes containing paper vote receipts to audit. They then count each receipt in these boxes to verify whether they match up with the electronic vote count from the machines linked to each box. Demonstrating the amazing transparency of this process, this auditing is being broadcast by live webcam on the CNE website.

By the time I left Caracas, 81 percent of all the paper receipts had been audited, and this audit has shown the original vote count to be 99.8 percent accurate. And, in the following weeks, the CNE finished auditing each and every box of receipts—each box having been brought to the Mariches center from the thousands of voting locations throughout Venezuela, some being brought from the Amazon by canoe.

As the Center for Economic and Policy Research explained at the time, the original audit on election day—in which witnesses from the various parties, including the opposition MUD party, reviewed at least 53 percent of the voting receipts right there in the polling places—was more than statistically significant to verify the results of the election.[35] But alas, as one sociology professor who was witnessing the audit told us with an impish grin, "the Venezuelan people are a kind people, and we readily give in to the caprices of others."

Former US president Jimmy Carter said the following about this electoral system: **"As a matter of fact, of the 92 elections that we've monitored, I would say the election process in Venezuela is the best in the world."**[36] Jimmy Carter made a point to say that Venezuela's electoral system is better than that of the United States, which he has found to be deeply flawed. More recently, Carter has gone so far as to say that the US "has no functioning democracy."[37]

In the same vein, Mark Weisbrot of the Center for Economic Policy Research (CEPR) observed:

> Unlike in the US, where in a close vote we really have no idea who won (see Bush v Gore), Venezuelans can be sure that their vote counts. And also unlike the US, where as many as 90 million eligible voters will not vote in November, the government in Venezuela has done everything to increase voter registration (now at a record of about 97%) and participation.[38]

Moreover, and quite ironically, it is the US which has, time and again since 1999, interfered in Venezuela's elections in significant ways which have made these elections unfair. For example, in the most recent Venezuelan presidential elections in May of 2018—elections I myself observed—the Trump Administration, with the intent to delegitimize the results of the vote, actually attempted to prevail upon the opposition candidate, Henri Falcon, to drop out of the election.[39] President Trump went so far as to threaten Falcon, who comes out of the Venezuelan business community, with sanctions if he went ahead and ran in the election.

In addition, as the US has done on a number of occasions, Trump threatened the Venezuelan electorate with reprisals—in this case, increased economic sanctions, including a possible oil embargo—if they voted for Nicolas Maduro.[40] It is worth noting that Falcon's own economic adviser, Francisco Rodríguez, a Venezuelan economist at Torino Capital, a brokerage firm, has been extremely critical of Trump's sanctions against Venezuela, saying of those that had been implemented in 2017 that they were destroying the economy and were likely to cause starvation.[41]

And Trump threatened even more pain if Venezuelans voted the wrong way in the 2018 elections. Trump, true to his word, announced new sanctions against Venezuela the day after the elections which Nicolas Maduro won handily.

Civil Rights and Racial Equality

In April of 2013, I served as an election observer in Venezuela. I was one of 170 international election observers from around the world, including India, Brazil, Great Britain, Argentina, South Korea and France. Among the observers were two former presidents (of Guatemala and the Dominican Republic), judges, lawyers and high-ranking officials of national electoral councils.

This was a very emotional time in Venezuela, for Hugo Chavez had just passed away from cancer on March 5, 2013. For many, particularly the poor of Venezuela, this was like losing a father. And now, as per the 1999 Constitution, the government was holding a new election for president. That is, Maduro, who was vice president at the time, could not just serve out the remainder of Chavez's term as would be the case in the United States. Rather, because Chavez had not yet served fifty percent of this term, new elections were constitutionally required. And so, during this time of mourning, parties were campaigning and the election was being organized.

On April 11, 2013, I witnessed a campaign rally for Maduro, and what occurred to me was that nearly everyone I saw at the rally was black. That is, they were of African descent. I had not thought much about the racial composition of and divisions within Venezuela, but this cannot be overlooked when thinking of that country and of the Bolivarian Revolution. But strangely, as journalist John Pilger has noted,[42] such issues are almost totally ignored by the Western press, and even by the liberal punditry who otherwise seems obsessed with identity politics issues.

Compare what I saw at the pro-Maduro rally with this observation of an anti-Maduro rally made by former UK ambassador Craig Murray[43]:

But I ask you to look at this photo of supporters of CIA poster-boy, the West's puppet unelected "President" Juan Guaido, taken at a Guaido rally in Caracas two days ago and published yesterday in security services house journal *The Guardian*. . . .

These are not the poor and most certainly not the starving. As it chances I have a great deal of life experience working amongst seriously deprived, hungry and despairing people. I know the gaunt face of want and the desperate glance of need. . . . This designer spectacled, well-coiffed, elegantly dressed, sleekly jowled group does not know hunger. This group does not know want. This is a proper right wing gathering, a gathering of the nicely off section of society. This is a group of those who have corruptly been siphoning Venezuela's great wealth for decades and who want to make sure the gravy train flows properly in their direction again. It is, in short, a group of exactly the kind of people you would expect to support a CIA coup.

The other notable thing about the pro-Guaido rally is that the participants tend to have lighter skin than those attending the pro-government rallies. And this is so because the struggle going on in Venezuela is one as much about race as it is about class: it is the darker-skinned poor versus the lighter-skinned well-to-do, and the US is backing the latter against the former.

As journalist Greg Palast recently colorfully explains[44]:

And who is this guy Juan Guaido that Trump has said he's recognized as president? He's not someone who said, "Oh, the election was stolen from me." He literally never ran for president. He's just a 35-year old white guy—and that's really at the heart of it. That's something that Trump likes. He speaks good English, he hung out with the Right Wing think tanks in Washington, went to George Washington University. He's a rich, white guy. That's really, really important. And in a Mestizo nation, which is made up of about 70% Mestizos, that is people, as Chavez told me, who are a combination of "Negro e Indio," as he said, black and indigenous, that's the majority of the people in Venezuela, but they're finding a white guy to run it.

And make no mistake about it, US policy is often about race. Most notably, the US has always resented Haiti for being the first country in the hemisphere to throw off the bonds of slavery through a slave revolt. Indeed, "when the slaves in the country fought for independence in the late 18th century, the US provided aid to the French colonists in an effort to stop the rebellion, fearful that the revolt would spread to the US."[45] And, when the independence movement in Haiti finally succeeded, in spite of the US's best efforts, the US withheld recognition of the new Haitian government for 60 years in retaliation for its premature outlawing of slavery.[46]

Then, in 1915, the great promoter of democracy and international law, President Woodrow Wilson—after whom Princeton's world-renowned international diplomacy school is still named—ordered the invasion of Haiti. Through the 1915 invasion, the US brought liberty to the people of Haiti by re-establishing forced labor, putting them on chain gangs to build roads and infrastructure to support US business concerns, looting the Haitian bank of all its cash and gold reserves and dissolving its democratically-elected legislature for refusing to adopt a constitution allowing for foreign land ownership.[47] The US would not withdraw its troops until 1934. All told, about 15,000 Haitians were killed in the first three years of the resistance to the invasion in which, according to one of the leaders of the US campaign, General Smedley Butler, the rebels were "'hunted down . . . like pigs.'"[48]

And note with what type of urgency the US is pursuing its regime change program in Venezuela on behalf of the white ruling class compared to the lack of urgency it showed in helping the people of Puerto Rico after the recent hurricane—a lack of urgency which cost the lives of around 3,000 Puerto Ricans.[49] The very same comparison can be made to the US's lackluster preparation for and reaction to the hurricane which destroyed large swaths of the African-American community in New Orleans.

Meanwhile, in Venezuela, a little-told story is that the Chavista government has worked hard to address the legacy of slavery in that country and to help lift up Afro-Venezuelans—a community largely forgotten and ignored before Chavez came to power in 1999. As one Venezuelan commentator, Jesús Chucho García who himself is Afro-Venezuelan, wrote in explaining why Afro-Venezuelan communities were largely absent from the violent protests against the government in 2014[50]:

> In these 15 years of the Bolivarian process, afro-descendant Venezuelans have been dignified in an unprecedented way in Venezuelan history. . . . Before, the land of afro communities was in the hands of latifundistas and agrarian bourgeoisie. One the worst cases of discrimination was reflected in the Farriar municipality, where Cuban supporters of Batista, with the help of the [pre-Chavez] government, dispossessed thousands of hectares of ancestral land, including Cañizos, Palo Quemao, Farriar, Palmarejo, and El Chino. Numerous witnesses tell of how the Batista supporters hired armed bands to assault community inhabitants at night, threatening them and burning their cane crops. This lead to persecutions, and a youth was murdered when people protested these events. When Chavez arrived, on an episode of "Alo, President" filmed in Palmarejo, he declared himself afro-descendant, and handed over 11 thousand hectares along with agriculture credits, and decreed the land communal property of the afro-descendants of Yaracuy. . . .

Jesús Chucho García goes on to explain how Chavez returned thousands of hectares of land to Afro-Venezuelans in other regions, such as Barlovento. I had the pleasure of meeting with the Afro-descendant community in Barlovento back in 2010. This community continues to maintain a lot of the cultural traditions from Africa, including clothing and music. One such tradition is that of women gathering in the river to drum on the water; this is an amazing sight to behold.

The Bolivarian government is quite proud of this water drumming tradition. Indeed, I later saw a movie about it at the Bolivarian Hall of the Venezuelan Embassy in Washington, DC. Just last night, I received a call from the former chargé d'affaires of this embassy, Carlos Ron, who told me that Guaido loyalists have now moved in to the embassy and taken it over. I guarantee you that these folks will never be showing films about Afro-descendant water drumming . . .

Similarly, Chavez and the Bolivarian Revolution has done much to advance the rights of Venezuela's indigenous peoples. For starters, Article 9 of the 1999 Constitution

> proclaims that while Spanish is the official language of Venezuela, "Indigenous languages are also for official use for Indigenous peoples and must be respected throughout the Republic's territory for being part of the nation's and humanity's patrimonial culture." In chapter eight of the constitution, the state recognizes the social, political, and economic organization within indigenous communities, in addition to their cultures, languages, rights, and lands. What is more, in a critical provision the government recognizes land rights as collective, inalienable, and non-transferable. Later articles declare the government's pledge not to engage in extraction of natural resources without prior consultation with indigenous groups. Three long time indigenous activists have been elected to the Venezuelan National Assembly, and prominent leaders hold positions in government. In a novel move, Chávez has even had the constitution translated into all of Venezuela's languages.

In 2014, I interviewed Flor Angela Palmar de Hernandez, a professor of intercultural bilingual education in Venezuela and current member of the Organization of Indigenous Educators of Zulia.[51] Professor Palmar is a member of Venezuela's largest indigenous group, the

Wayuu, who live in Zulia—a territory in the northwestern corner of Venezuela between Lake Maracaibo and the Colombian border. At the time of my interview, Venezuela was being rocked by violent, anti-government protests.

I asked Professor Palmar specifically about how these protests were being viewed in the Indigenous communities. Professor Palmar answered emphatically,

> We refuse to call the actions earlier this year, "protests." Instead, we referred to them as "guarimbas"; as actions intended to create chaos. While the opposition would like the Indigenous to participate in these actions, that will never happen. Indeed, the "guarimbas" did not take place in Indigenous lands. We are not a shameless people, and we will not legitimize the "guarimbas" which have a hidden agenda.

This statement is supported by the Minorities at Risk (MAR) Project[52]—a university-based research project that monitors and analyzes the status and conflicts of politically-active communal groups in all countries. As the MAR Project concluded:

> The indigenous of Venezuela have few of the risk factors for rebellion. They are minimally cohesive and have restricted their activities largely to nonviolent protests in the recent past. Venezuela is also one of the longest established democracies in Latin America. Furthermore, under the 1999 constitution passed under the leadership of President Hugo Chavez, both political and economic remedial policies are in place to address indigenous concerns.
>
> Indigenous are likely to continue low to moderate levels of protest. While protests have been directed at the government as groups struggle for the implementation of their constitutional rights, almost all indigenous groups are very clear that they support President Chavez.

According to Professor Palmar, there have been positive changes for Indigenous peoples since Chavez came to power in 1999. For one, she explained that, for the first time ever, the rights of Indigenous peoples have been enshrined in the popularly-approved Constitution of 1999, a Constitution which also guarantees Indigenous representation at the national, state and local levels.

Professor Donna Lee Van Cott, in her article "Andean Indigenous Movements and Constitutional Transformation: Venezuela in Comparative Perspective,"[53] echoes this view. As Van Cott relates, under Chavez, Venezuela went from being one of the most backwards countries in terms of Indigenous rights to one of the most progressive ones. She explains that the changes brought on by the Chavez revolution

> enabled Venezuelan Indians to obtain a constitution containing the region's most progressive indigenous rights regime. Venezuelan constitution-makers incorporated most of the symbolic and programmatic rights that neighboring constitutions recognize . . . , while making several interesting innovations—such as guaranteeing political representation at all levels of government (Art. 125) and prohibiting the registration of patents related to indigenous genetic resources or intellectual property associated with indigenous knowledge (Art. 124). . . . Symbolic achievements—rhetorical recognition of Venezuela as a "multiethnic and pluricultural state," and recognition of their special status by dint of including a separate chapter on "Rights of the Indigenous Peoples"—may be enjoyed immediately. As in the other Andean cases, however, most programmatic rights require future legislation.

Professor Palmar told me that, indeed, further legislation on Indigenous rights has been forthcoming, including on her most cherished issue—that of the protection and fortification of Indigenous languages. For example, the Law of Indigenous Languages, which expressly calls for the preservation of Indigenous languages, was passed in 2008.

And, Professor Palmar herself, along with other Indigenous lead-ers, has been working with the government on the creation of an Institute of Indigenous Languages to help with the codification of Indigenous language alphabets and dictionaries. This project came to fruition in 2014 when President Nicolas Maduro formally announced, on the Day of Indigenous Resistance, the creation of this institute to "register, rescue and revive all indigenous languages that exist within the Venezuelan territory."[54]

Moreover, for the first time in its history, Venezuela now has a Ministry of Indigenous Peoples as well as a Vice Minister of Education for Indigenous Peoples to ensure the protection of Indigenous rights, including the right to a multilingual education and for the Indigenous to create their own school curriculum.

Still, there is much to be done. As Professor Palmar explained, they are still working on an Indigenous land law and on the process of demarcation of Indigenous lands. This is a continuing struggle largely due to the resistance of powerful economic elites—particu-larly in mining, ranching and agribusiness—which covet Indigenous land for exploitation. In addition, as Professor Palmar also explained, though with some obvious trepidation, there is the very real threat of violence by Colombian paramilitary groups which cross into areas like Zulia and engage in "social cleansing." It is believed that the Colombian paramilitaries have also been engaged in assassina-tions of key Venezuelan leaders, such as left-wing legislator Robert Serra.[55]

Since 1999, the Indigenous Peoples have largely found their sup-port from the Venezuelan government in their struggles, receiving thousands of hectares of land from the government and protection from the Venezuelan military.[56] As one commentator notes, "Chávez has lived up to the constitution by awarding communal land titles to six Kariña indigenous communities. The land titles will be handed out to 4,000 people and encompass 317,000 acres in the Venezuelan states of Monagas and Anzoategui. The land transfers form part of Mission

Guaicaipuro, a plan to provide land titles to all of Venezuela's 28 indigenous peoples."[57]

The UN Committee on the Elimination of Racial Discrimination has applauded these efforts of the Bolivarian government, saying that it "welcomes the social development measures, programs and plans that include indigenous peoples and people of African descent, which have helped to combat structural racial discrimination" in the country.[58]

However, the white elite of Venezuela has not been applauding these measures, and they want the country back firmly in their hands. They resented the very fact that Chavez was, in their view, a black man, and they made fun of his physical attributes, sometimes likening him to an ape. They have done the same to Maduro.

A very striking example of the racism of much of the opposition occurred during an April 2019 delegation to Venezuela in which I participated. A co-delegate of mine, Ajit Singh, a man of Indian descent, received violent and racist messages from opposition supporters in response to his tweets about Venezuela.[59] He was even threatened with being lynched.

Even the US Embassy has engaged in such race baiting. As Nikolas Kozloff writes, "[t]he Venezuelan elite has used racial slurs to taint Chávez, denouncing him as a black monkey. . . . 'A puppet show to this effect with a monkey playing Chávez was even organized at the US Embassy in Caracas.'"[60]

I would suspect that there are many in the US who would be sympathetic to the gains the Bolivarian Revolution has made in advancing the rights of oppressed racial groups, if they only knew about these gains. Many might also take umbrage at the fact that the US is backing an opposition which desperately wants to roll these gains back.

* * *

Meanwhile, the April 2013 elections I was observing went forward. With an impressive 79 percent of registered voters going to the polls,

Nicolas Maduro, heir to Hugo Chavez, won by more than 260,000 votes—or, by 1.8 percent of the total vote—over opposition leader Henrique Capriles. A fellow election observer and former president of Guatemala, Alvaro Colom, called the vote "secure" and easily verifiable.

However, because the "wrong" candidate won, the US refused to honor the results of this election. Indeed, they have never recognized Nicolas Maduro as the duly-elected president of Venezuela. And, the results of this failure to recognize the election results had immediately devastating effects. Thus, the opposition forces, emboldened by this refusal, immediately began burning down health clinics, attacking Cuban doctors and destroying ruling-party buildings, reasonably believing themselves to have the backing of the US government and military. At least nine Venezuelans died in this opposition violence.

5

A TALE OF TWO COUNTRIES—COLOMBIA AND VENEZUELA

AND SO, HOW HAS COLOMBIA, VENEZUELA'S next door neighbor and closest regional ally of the US, been faring these past 20 years by comparison? I would submit that if a country in this hemisphere is suffering a humanitarian and human rights crisis, it is indeed Colombia, but you would never know this from the press, which stays relatively quiet about that country except to talk about its role as a staging ground for the operations against Venezuela.

By any measure, Colombia, despite the billions of dollars of assistance it has received from the US over the years (or more precisely, because of this assistance) is one of the worst human rights disasters on this planet. The numbers speak for themselves.

Colombia has more internally displaced people (IDPs) than any other country on earth (including Syria) at nearly 8 million, and most of these IDPs were forcibly displaced by right-wing paramilitary death squads aligned with the Colombian military which the US backs.[1] Moreover, a disproportionate number of these IDPs are Afro-Colombians and indigenous who are faring particularly badly in that country.

And it is state actors who are largely responsible for these displacements. Thus, as Amnesty International has recently reported, "[m]ost forced displacement has been carried out by paramilitaries and the security forces, either acting alone or in collusion with each other," and, what's more, these forced displacements are often-times accompanied by grisly crimes such as "the forced recruitment of children and youth, sexual and gender-based violence (SGBV), threats, disappearances and murders. . . ."[2]

Moreover, the figure of nearly 8 million IDPs is on top of the 5.6 million who have fled to and are currently living in, yes, you guessed it, Venezuela![3] And so, while we hear about all of the people from Venezuela who are fleeing to neighboring countries like Colombia, we never hear about these millions who have been thriving in Venezuela as citizens with full rights and social benefits.[4] Moreover, we rarely hear of the fact that, as noted by the World Bank, nearly twenty-five percent of the people migrating from Venezuela to Colombia are indeed Colombians returning home.[5]

Meanwhile, according to the International Committee of the Red Cross, over 92,000 individuals (a hemisphere record) have been forcibly disappeared in Colombia.[6]

And, between 2002 and 2010, the height of Plan Colombia, the US's $10 billion counter-insurgency military aid package to Colombia, around 10,000 youths were killed in cold blood by the US-backed military and then dressed up to appear as guerillas killed in combat.[7] The military carried out these killings to justify military assistance from the US. This is known as the "false positive" scandal, and is being investigated, quite rightly, as a war crime by the International Criminal Court. For its part, "[t]he UN called the[se] extrajudicial killings "widespread" and "systematic" and figures showed the practice occurred in 30 of Colombia's 32 provinces by the majority of military brigades."[8]

In addition, social leaders—such as trade unionists, indigenous and Afro-Colombian leaders, environmental activists and human rights defenders, and priests who advocate for the poor—continue to be killed at a rate of more than one every three days by paramilitary death squads working hand-in-glove with the Colombian military.

As for the priests advocating for the poor—that is, liberation theologians—the Colombian Catholic Bishops Conference reports that "more than 80 priests have been killed in the last three decades, along with five religious sisters, three religious brothers, three seminarians, one bishop and one archbishop. In the same period of time, 17 bishops and 52 priests have received death threats."[9] This, of course, is all according to plan, and is really your tax money at work!

Since 2016 when the peace process between the Colombian government and the left-wing FARC guerillas was signed, 430 social leaders have been killed in Colombia.[10] The mass murder of social leaders has also been referred to the International Criminal Court.[11]

In its most recent, 2018 report, Frontline Defenders, which monitors world-wide violence against human rights defenders (HRDs)—a term which appears can be used interchangeably with "social leaders"—explains the dire situation of HRDs in Colombia since the peace accords were signed:

> While the pattern of violence and killings documented in 2016 continued into 2017, the drop in the general level of violence brought about by the peace process seemed to offer cautious grounds for optimism. However, with regard to the situation of HRDs, the implementation of the peace agreements with the FARC has been a bittersweet experience. While it is very important to recognize that the silence of the guns brought with it the lowest rate of killings among the general population in the last 30 years, the number of killings of HRDs increased dramatically. According to figures from *Programa Somos Defensores*, there has been a general increase in killings of HRDs since the beginning of the peace process: 2013—78 cases, 2014—55 cases, 2015—63 cases, 2016—80 cases, and in 2017, this figure rose to 121 cases.[12]

And, the reason that deaths of HRDs, or social leaders, has increased since the signing of the peace accords is because the disarming of the left-wing FARC has allowed the Colombian right-wing paramilitaries to do what they are meant to do—to destroy the peaceful social movements in Colombia, and to thereby pave the way for maximum exploitation of Colombia's rich land resources by domestic and transnational corporations.

A little history is in order. As Human Rights Watch has explained, the paramilitary death squads of Colombia, and other Latin American countries as well, trace their roots back to the early 1960s when US general William P. Yarborough first conceived of them as an instrument to advance US economic interests by violently destroying progressive social movements.[13] The idea was that because the paramilitaries are not official military forces, the US and its allies would have plausible deniability for their conduct. In other words, they would be a "*hidden weapon . . .* of hired killers" which carry out the dirty war which the regular troops "cannot do officially"[14] (emphasis added).

As *Telesur* explained in a recent article,[15] the paramilitaries continue to serve such functions:

> Paramilitary groups in Colombia are typically linked to powerful oligarchs within Colombia as well as multinational companies seeking to secure economic interests in resource-rich Colombian land. Many of these armed right-wing civilian groups also stocked their arsenals thanks to Plan Colombia, a 1999 counterinsurgency initiative that saw the US pour billions of dollars into the country for the purpose of further militarizing the region. The year 2016 witnessed the blossoming of such far-right paramilitary and narco-paramilitary groups, who extended their regional presence and visibility.
>
> The Colombian government, however, has largely denied the existence of such armed groups, even when the groups post videos of themselves training in the rural countryside.

And, of course, the mainstream US press is complicit in covering up the very existence of these paramilitary groups by giving them zero media coverage. In this case, the paramilitaries are able to repeat the devil's greatest trick—that of convincing the world that he does not exist—with great help from our "free press."

Once in a while, however, the truth does come to light. For example, the *New York Times* reported a quite embarrassing episode regarding the Colombian paramilitaries in a 2018 article entitled, "The Secret History of Colombia's Paramilitaries & the US War on Drugs."[16]

As the *Times* related, beginning in 2008, the US has extradited "several dozen" top paramilitary leaders, thereby helping them to evade a transitional justice process which would have held them accountable for their war crimes and crimes against humanity. They have been brought to the US where they have been tried for drug-related offenses only and given cushy sentences of 10 years in prison on average. And, even more incredibly, "for some, there is a special dividend at the end of their incarceration. Though wanted by Colombian authorities, two have won permission to stay in the United States, and their families have joined them. There are more seeking the same haven, and still others are expected to follow suit."

That these paramilitaries—40 in all that the *Times* investigated—are being given such preferential treatment is shocking given the magnitude of their crimes. For example, paramilitary leader Salvatore Mancuso, "who the government said 'may well be one of the most prolific cocaine traffickers ever prosecuted in a United States District Court,'" has been found by Colombian courts to be "responsible for the death or disappearance of more than 1,000 people." Yet, as a result of his cooperation with US authorities Mr. Mancuso "will spend little more than 12 years behind bars in the US."

Another paramilitary, the one the *Times* article focuses on most, is Hernan Giraldo Serna, and he committed "1,800 serious human rights violations with over 4,000 victims. . . ." Mr. Giraldo was known as "The Drill" because of his penchant for raping young girls, some as young as 9 years old. Indeed, he has been "labeled . . . 'the biggest sexual predator of paramilitarism.'" While being prosecuted in the US for drug-related crimes only, Mr. Giraldo too is being shielded by the US from prosecution back in Colombia for his most atrocious crimes.

The *Times* gives a couple reasons for why the US would protect such "designated terrorists responsible for massacres, forced disappearances and the displacement of entire villages," and give them "relatively lenient treatment." First, it correctly explains that former president Alvaro Uribe, the most prominent and outspoken opponent of the peace deal between the Colombian government and the FARC guerillas, asked the US to extradite these paramilitary leaders because, back home in Colombia, they had begun "confessing not only their war crimes but also their ties to his allies and relatives."

The *Times* also writes off the US treatment of these paramilitaries as the US giving priority to its war on drugs "over Colombia's efforts to confront crimes against humanity that had scarred a generation." It must be noted that another country where this balancing act between the war on drugs (an abysmally unsuccessful war, by the way, which has never meant to be won in the first place) and human rights is in Mexico. As the high commissioner of the United Nations Organization for Human Rights, Michelle Bachelet, the former president of Chile, has just reported, over 250,000 Mexicans were killed in 2006 in the so-called US-backed drug war. Ms. Bachelet "told reporters that the stories of anguish she heard from families of victims [of the Mexican drug war] reminded her of the darkest days of the police state that Chilean Dictator Augusto Pinochet oversaw during the 1970s and 1980s."[17] Further, "Bachelet cited other 'terrifying figures,' including 26,000 bodies that Mexican officials have not been able to identify and 850 mass graves that have been dug up." But again, for much of the press, there is nothing to see here, and certainly no cause for concern or for another humanitarian intervention. Rather, if the Trump Administration gets its way, we will simply wall up Mexico and its very real humanitarian crisis with it.

Meanwhile, the explanations given for the US tolerance and even support of the Colombian paramilitaries (e.g., allegedly fighting drugs) let the US off the hook too easily, for they do not tell the whole story behind the US's relationship with Colombia and its death squads.

First of all, let's start with former president Alvaro Uribe, who the *Times* states has a "'shared ideology'" with these paramilitaries and their leaders. This is of course true. But what does this say about the United States, which gave billions of dollars of military assistance to Colombia when Uribe was president, all the while knowing that he had a long history of paramilitary ties and drug trafficking and that his military was working alongside the paramilitaries in carrying out abuses on a massive scale? And, how about the fact that Uribe was also awarded the Presidential Medal of Freedom by President George W. Bush, who considered Uribe his best friend in the region?

The answer is that the US also shares an ideology with both Uribe and his paramilitary friends, and that it has wanted to prevent the paramilitaries from not only confessing to their links with Uribe, but also from confessing their links to the US military, intelligence and corporations.

The *Times*, while ultimately pulling its punches here, at least touches upon this issue when it states that "the paramilitaries, while opponents in the war on drugs, were technically on the same side as the Colombian and American governments in the civil war." But "technically" is not *le mot juste*; rather, it is an imprecise and mushy term used to understate the true relationship of the paramilitaries with the US. The paramilitaries have not just been "technically" on the side of the US and Colombian governments; rather, they have been objectively and subjectively on their side, and indeed an integral part of the US/Colombia counter-insurgency program in Colombia for decades.

Indeed, the paramilitaries were the invention of the United States back in 1962, even before the FARC itself was formed (in 1964) and before the civil war there began in earnest. Thus, as Noam Chomsky explains:

The president of the Colombian Permanent Committee for Human Rights, former Minister of Foreign Affairs Alfredo Vasquez Carrizosa, writes that it is "poverty and insufficient land reform" that "have made Colombia one of the most tragic countries of Latin America," though as elsewhere, "violence has been exacerbated by external factors," primarily the initiatives of the Kennedy Administration, which "took great pains to transform our regular armies into counterinsurgency brigades," ushering in "what is known in Latin America as the National Security Doctrine," which is not concerned with "defense against an external enemy" but rather "the internal enemy." The new "strategy of the death squads" accords the military "the right to fight and to exterminate social workers, trade unionists, men and women who are not supportive of the establishment, and who are assumed to be communist extremists."

As part of its strategy of converting the Latin American military from "hemispheric defense" to "internal security"—meaning war against the domestic population—Kennedy dispatched a military mission to Colombia in 1962 headed by Special Forces General William Yarborough. He proposed "reforms" to enable the security forces to "as necessary execute paramilitary, sabotage and/or terrorist activities against known communist proponents"—the "communist extremists" to whom Vasquez Carrizosa alludes.[18]

While the paramilitaries have been ever-evolving, taking different forms over the years and receiving legal imprimatur at some times and not at others, they have remained until this day, carrying out the same essential functions enumerated by Chomsky above while giving plausible deniability to both the US and Colombian governments.

The potential confession of paramilitary leaders to their links with the US and Colombia, as well as to US multinationals, was as much of a threat to the US as their confessions were to Colombian president Alvaro Uribe. And that is why the US extradited the top paramilitary leaders and treated them with kid gloves.

As just one example, paramilitary leader Salvatore Mancuso told investigators nearly 10 years ago that it was not only Chiquita that provided financial support to the paramilitaries (this is already known because Chiquita pled guilty to such conduct and received a small, $25 million fine for doing so), but also companies like Del Monte and Dole.[19] However, given that Mancuso was never put on trial (the *Times* notes that none of the paramilitary leaders have) but instead was given a light sentence based upon a plea deal, such statements have never gone on the court record, were never pursued by authorities, and have largely been forgotten.

For its part, Frontline Defenders explains that the paramilitaries continue to be the greatest threat to HRDs in Colombia. Thus, it relates that

> the studies and organisations consulted identify the presence of paramilitary groups, including drug dealers or people close to them, such as the Autodefensas Campesinas de Colombia [Colombian Peasant Self-Defence Forces], as the main source of violence against defenders. The Human Rights Ombudsman, Carlos Alfonso Negret Mosquera, recently pointed out that "one of the main causes of this phenomenon is the attempt by illegal armed groups to occupy the territory from which the FARC have withdrawn". At the same time, several cases of collusion between state officials and paramilitary groups have been documented in different parts of the country such as Norte de Santander or Antioquia. In the cases documented between 2009–2016, where state forces were allegedly responsible for the death of community leaders, there is a consistent pattern in the circumstances of the killings: "HRDs are killed more frequently in the mornings or late at night, in rural areas, inside or in the vicinity of their homes or when travelling. And finally, the murder of these activists is carried out in most cases with the use of firearms."[20]

Meanwhile, in 2018, out of the 321 HRDs murdered world-wide, a whopping 126 were killed in Colombia, making Colombia by far the most dangerous country in the world to be a Human Rights Defender.[21]

The next countries in line for this dubious distinction were as follows: Mexico, with 48 HRDs killed; The Philippines with 39 killed; Guatemala with 26; and Brazil with 23. All of these countries, moreover, are close US allies, and Colombia and Brazil are the US's key partners in its allegedly "humanitarian" regime change war against Venezuela.

And what about the "Troika of Tyranny" (John Bolton's words)—Venezuela, Cuba and Nicaragua? As for Venezuela, 5 HRDs were killed in 2018, and 0 HRDs were killed in Cuba and Nicaragua. And, as for Venezuela, it appears that many of these killings can be ascribed to large landowners who use their own private security forces to attack land rights activists; that, is, not to the Venezuelan government.[22] Not so "tyrannical," certainly when compared to Colombia, which has been by far the largest US military aid recipient in Latin America over the past 17 years.[23] Mexico, with its 48 HRD murders is second, and Guatemala is in the top five of US military aid recipients in Latin America.[24]

But of course, all of this stands to reason, for the US consistently supports the most right-wing, repressive countries around the globe, and particularly in Latin America. As Noam Chomsky has explained:[25]

> The "prevailing orthodoxy" has occasionally been submitted to tests beyond the record of history. Lars Schoultz, the leading academic specialist on human rights in Latin America, found that US aid "has tended to flow disproportionately to Latin American governments which torture their citizens, . . . to the hemisphere's relatively egregious violators of fundamental human rights."
>
> That includes military aid, is independent of need, and runs through the Carter period. More wide-ranging studies by economist Edward Herman found a similar correlation world-wide, also suggesting a plausible reason: aid is correlated with improvement in the investment climate, often achieved by murdering priests and union leaders, massacring peasants trying to organize, blowing up the independent press, and so on.

The result is a secondary correlation between aid and egregious violation of human rights. It is not that US leaders prefer torture; rather, it has little weight in comparison with more important values.

While Chomsky wrote this back in 1998, the same holds true to this day, with the ongoing human rights nightmare in US-backed Colombia being a case in point. And, the reasons for the US-backed repression in such countries as Colombia remains the same as when Chomsky wrote this—the advancement of investment opportunities for multi-national corporations.

Thus, Frontline Defenders notes that the uniquely high murder rate of HRDs in Colombia is the result of "[t]he conflict between the exploitation of natural resources, including the capture of long-held indigenous or Afro-descendant land for private profit, and the efforts of defenders of land, environmental or indigenous peoples' rights to protect the environment and their communities—and to guarantee that legally-mandated consultations are implemented—resulted in systematic attempts to silence HRDs by both government and business."[26]

And, critical to the US's ability to get away with its backing of monstrous crimes is the Orwellian nature of US government rhetoric about "democracy" and "human rights," and the mainstream press's eagerness to parrot this rhetoric and selectively report upon human rights abuses. Again, Chomsky explains in words which again ring true today:

In his preface to *Animal Farm*, Orwell turned his attention to societies that are relatively free from state controls, unlike the totalitarian monster he was satirizing. "The sinister fact about literary censorship in England," he wrote, "is that it is largely voluntary. Unpopular ideas can be silenced, and inconvenient facts kept dark, without any need for any official ban."

He did not explore the reasons in any depth, merely noting the control of the press by "wealthy men who have every motive to be dishonest on certain important topics," reinforced by the "general tacit agreement," instilled by a good education, "that 'it wouldn't do' to mention that particular fact." As a result, "Anyone who challenges the prevailing orthodoxy finds himself silenced with surprising effectiveness."[27]

And so, today, we find a corporate-controlled press in the US which, in the interest of profit, "keeps dark" the massive crimes of such US client states as Colombia—which barely gets a mention in the news—while constantly vilifying such countries as Venezuela with comparatively cleaner human rights records.

Meanwhile, while Afro-descendants and indigenous people are receiving special, protected treatment from the Venezuelan government, they are the ones being disproportionately killed in Colombia.

As the Washington Office on Latin America explains, "[t]he assassinations have primarily targeted Afro-Colombian and indigenous rights activists, in addition to rural farmers and landowners in Valle del Cauca, Putumayo, and La Guajira."[28] For its part, Front Line Defenders explains that "[m]ost of the HRDs killed [in 2018] were working in defense of the right to land or to protect the territory of indigenous peoples. At particular risk are members of ethnic minorities, peasant communities, indigenous peoples, people of African descent or members of local community action boards in rural areas."[29]

Indeed, it is quite fair to say that Afro-Colombians and indigenous peoples are being subject to a genocidal war in Colombia, and the genocide is being carried out in order to advance the interests of transnational mining and oil companies, as well as big agribusiness—many of these from the US and Canada. Indeed, some of these (for example, Exxon) are the very players pushing for regime change in Venezuela.

As Arelis Maria Urinan Guariyu, the Councilor for Women of the National Indigenous Organization of Colombia (ONIC), and a member of the Wayuu tribe in Colombia's La Guajira Peninsula, reported at a meeting I attended in Washington, DC, 34 of the 102 indigenous tribes in Colombia are on the verge of extinction. According to the United Nations, this in fact may be an underestimate, with possibly over 40 tribes at risk of total annihilation.[30] In total, over 62% of all indigenous peoples in Colombia are at risk of extinction.

And, Arelis, CERAC and the UN agree on one thing: the main cause of the violence against and existential threat to Colombia's indigenous population, and to the Afro-Colombian community as well, is from mining operations in that country. Indeed, according to a report by ABColombia, a UK-based NGO coalition, "[s]ome 80% of human rights and international humanitarian law violations in the last 10 years have been carried out in mining and energy regions in Colombia. . . ."[31]

As Colombia Reports has explained quite well[32]:

Mining operations in Colombia have a notorious history when it comes to violence, displacement, and toxic exposure. In what became an internationally infamous case, the Cerrejon mine owned by Exxon-Mobil destroyed the entire [Afro-Colombian] village of Tabaco in 2001, and displaced all of its residents with the help of armed security forces. . . .

The Cerrejon mine, named for "a nearby mountain held sacred by the indigenous Wayuu people, who comprise 44% of La Guajira's population," is now owned by a joint venture of Glencore, Anglo American and BHP Billiton.[33]

As Arelis has explained to me, and as I myself witnessed upon my trip to the Wayuu community in La Guajira in 2017, this mine continues to pose a threat to the existence of the Wayuu people, as well as to Afro-Colombians living in La Guajira. This threat is in the form of both forced displacements as well as the ravaging of La Guajira's natural resources.[34]

Recall that Professor Flor Angela Palmar de Hernandez, a supporter of the Bolivarian Revolution in Venezuela, is a member of the Wayuu tribe as well. The Wayuu live in an area which straddles both Colombia and Venezuela. And so, their varying experiences in their two different countries give us an interesting comparison.

The Cerrejon mine utilizes 17 million liters of water per day, while each resident of the dry and arid La Guajira, Colombia, has access to less than one liter of water per day. The impact upon the Wayuu peoples is devastating, according to the Inter-American Human Rights Commission. Thus, as reported recently by *Telesur*,[35]

> The Inter-American Human Rights Commission (IAHRC) is demanding the Colombian state adopt measures to protect the children and teenagers of the Wayuu community after activists and indigenous leaders said that about 4,770 of them died over the eight past years as a result of malnutrition and lack of clean drinking water.
>
> The human rights body, part of the Organization of the American States (OAS), said the Wayuu people—"powerful humans" in the Arahuaca language—were suffering high levels of child mortality, putting in danger the survival of the group as a whole. . . .
>
> The Wayuu community, which represents almost half of the local population living in La Guajira, lost valuable hectares of land, as well as the access to the Rancheria River, as a result of mining exploitation that expanded in the area as result of it being home to the world's largest coal reserve, called El Cerrejón.

When I visited Colombia's La Guajira, I was taken to the Rancheria River where we stood right in the center of it. One can do this because there is absolutely no water in it; it is dry as a bone. And the Wayuu are dying as a result. Their crops were visibly dead, and the children were evidently malnourished as seen in their brittle, discolored hair and distended bellies. For their part, the Wayuu claim that over 14,000 children have died as a result of this man-made drought.

I have not yet heard of a benefit concert being organized by Richard Branson or anyone else for the thousands of dying children of La Guajira just across from Venezuela's border. Apparently, they just don't rate.

The above-described phenomenon is being played out throughout Colombia, particularly in the rich and coveted lands of the Pacific and northwest Caribbean coasts to which the indigenous peoples and Afro-Colombians hold title. And, those who actively resist such mining interests are at risk of assassination by paramilitary groups that work hand-in-glove with a number of mining companies and which, in some cases, even own mining operations themselves.

For example, in 2015, I travelled to Colombia with a delegation of the Coalition of Black Trade Unionists (CBTU), a delegation which included US congressman Hank Johnson from Atlanta, Georgia. We travelled to Cali, Quibdó (in the Choco Department) and Bogota to hear from numerous representatives of the Afro-Colombian community about the grave civil, human and labor rights situation confronting them, and their demand to have a say in what then were the ongoing peace talks in Havana, Cuba, in order to find redress for their concerns.[36]

As our delegation observed, Colombia is at least fifty to 75 years behind the US in terms of race relations. Incredibly, there are no laws which protect Afro-Colombians from racial discrimination in employment or services. As a consequence, Afro-descendants, who officially make up 10 percent of the Colombian population, though in reality up to 25 percent, have no presence in high-level positions in the State, or in the private sector, media, industry or financial market. In addition, 80 percent of Afro-Colombians live under the poverty line, over 30 percent have no water and sanitation services, their infant mortality rate is over three times the national average, and their life expectancy is also well below the national average at around 65 years.[37]

Yet, these statistics do not begin to capture the depths of the crisis confronting the Afro-Colombian people. While there are nearly 8 million people in Colombia who are internally displaced, over 2 million, are Afro-descendant. And, as many of us who opposed the US-Colombia Free Trade Agreement (FTA) had predicted, such displacement has only accelerated after the 2011 passage of the FTA, which has allowed, and indeed encouraged, the penetration of the prized Afro-Colombian land on the Pacific coast by mining and agricultural companies which often utilize armed groups to forcibly remove Afro-Colombians from territorial lands—lands which are supposed to be protected by Colombia's Law 70.

As eloquently explained by one Afro-Colombian leader—a young, brave attorney named Francia Marquez who herself has been displaced, along with her two children, on at least two occasions—the Colombian government has itself recognized that their rights to the territory have been violated. As Ms. Marquez, who recently won the prestigious Goldman Environmental Prize (also known as the "Green Nobel")[38] noted, Afro-Colombians have won a number of court decisions under Law 70 which was passed to protect their territorial land, but none of these court decisions have been enforced. She said that "a slave-like system, a system of murder is instead being reinforced."

She explained that they are being targeted by a number of armed groups, especially right-wing paramilitaries who have bombed their homes and laid land mines around their communities. She further explains that the water that they depend on is being contaminated by mercury from illegal mining operations. She was interviewed by Reuters which writes, "Marquez says illegal mining is a scourge for Afro-Colombian communities whose ancestral lands are rich in gold reserves as it pollutes rivers with toxic mercury and cuts down forests."[39] But, she exclaimed, with righteous indignation, "who cares, we're black?!"

She asked how one can talk about a peace process when there are "chop houses" operating in Colombia—most famously in the port town of Buenaventura as documented by various human rights groups including Human Rights Watch[40]—where paramilitaries terrorize the community by dismembering social leaders while they are still alive. She related that 60 percent of the Afro-Colombian territory is being destroyed by mining operations. She emphasized that the US has financed this war in Colombia and that the US has a duty to construct the peace. She concluded by saying, "We Afro-Colombians gave birth to humanity, we must give birth to the peace."

Our trip was organized by my long-time friend Marino Cordoba, the founder of AFRODES, a group that advocates for the rights of displaced Afro-Colombians. Mr. Cordoba himself has been forcibly displaced on several occasions, beginning in 1997 when his town of Riosucio, in the largely Afro-Colombian Choco Department, was famously invaded by a paramilitary group known as the Self-Defense Forces of Cordoba and Uraba (ACCU) with the active support of the US-backed Colombian military.

Quite frighteningly, similar operations are now being carried out in the same area by a paramilitary group known as the Self-Defense Forces of Colombia Gaitanistas' (AGC). As *Semana* magazine explains, "[o]ne of the similar aspects of this raid with that of the ACCU in 1997 is that the arrival of the AGC to the basins of the Lower Atrato had no restriction by the security forces. State reports outlined the presence of speed boats of the Navy that crossed the Atrato River from the town of Riosucio, as well as soldiers from Front 54."

"For this reason, communities feel a deep mistrust because there is no explanation as to how this illegal armed group reached Truandó without an effective reaction" by the state security forces. Moreover, some of the paramilitaries entering the area are wearing official "uniforms with insignia of the Marine Corps, but identified as 'Self-Defense Forces of Colombia Gaitanistas,'" again showing the continuing links between the paramilitaries and the US-backed Colombian military.

Not surprisingly, both the US and Colombian governments are vigorously denying the very existence of the paramilitary forces. US Ambassador Kevin Whitaker indeed engaged in such denials in our meeting with him at the US Embassy in Bogota. The denial of the existence of the paramilitaries serves quite well the purposes of the US in creating them back in the early 1960s—that is, in order to give plausible deniability to the US and its Colombian military surrogates for their war against those who would challenge the unjust social order which continues to reign in that country.

But again, as Front Line Defenders explains, "[t]he continued frequent and severe threats and attacks against HRDs around the country contradict government claims of paramilitary demobilisation."[41]

Meanwhile, there is no doubt that these brutal paramilitaries are a part and parcel of the US's regime plans for Colombia. Indeed, as discussed above, these paramilitaries have been engaging in cross-border terrorist attacks in Venezuela with increasing frequency over the years, even killing at least one left-wing Venezuelan politician, just as they are wont to do back home in Colombia.[42] Let me submit that nothing "humanitarian" can come out of an operation against Venezuela which involves these death squad forces, but that is exactly what is in the works.

HOW TO MAKE REGIME CHANGE: "MAKE THE ECONOMY SCREAM," ADD CHAOS AND STIR

No Food. No medicine. Now, no power. Next, no Maduro.
—Tweet by Secretary of State Mike Pompeo, March 7, 2019

FOR YEARS NOW, WE HAVE BEEN told on a regular basis about the deprivations facing the Venezuelan people. While some of what we are told is exaggerated, there is no doubt that there are serious deprivations there, and that many Venezuelans have left their country because of them. The situation is certainly no laughing matter.

And yet, there is a sense that people in the US government and press corps are laughing; that they are taking glee in the suffering of the Venezuelan people, for this suffering seems to justify their view that the Venezuelan government is tyrannical and in need of changing, if even by force. Indeed, the foreign minister of Venezuela, Jorge Arreaza, criticized "'those close to Donald Trump have been celebrating [the recent power outage in Venezuela], enjoying the reckless distortion [of facts] despite what Venezuelans are going through.'"[1] Arreaza criticized Senator Marco Rubio in particular who, in mocking the Venezuelan government's claim that the US had sabotaged the hydro-electric dam, suggested, complete with a photo, that Godzilla had been behind the sabotage.

Even if the alleged incompetence of the Venezuelan government were to blame for this power outage as well as Venezuela's other ills, this would be no joking matter, and should not be wished upon them. And moreover, Venezuela's claims that it is the US which is sabotaging the country, its economy and its electric grid, are not at all fanciful. Indeed, as for the economy, it is demonstrably true that US actions, including sanctions, are behind much of the deprivation Venezuelans are suffering, and yet that connection is rarely made in the press. In order to assess this proposition, it is worth looking at other historical antecedents that such economic sabotage is indeed the proven means used by the US and its Western allies to overthrow governments which have found themselves out of favor with the West.

Cuba

In his book, *The Economic War Against Cuba*, author Salim Lamrani, a professor at the Sorbonne in Paris, explains that the US war against post-revolutionary Cuba began on March 17, 1960, one month before Cuba established relations with Moscow.[2] Lamrani relates that this war, declared by President Eisenhower, was "built on several pillars: the cancellation of the Cuban sugar quota, an end to the deliveries of energy resources such as oil, the continuation of the arms embargo imposed in March 1958, the establishment of a campaign of terrorism and sabotage, and the organization of a paramilitary force designed to invade the island overthrow [sic] Fidel Castro."

This war would then be expanded by President Kennedy in 1962 to include the unprecedented economic blockade against Cuba—a blockade which continues to this day, almost 30 years after the collapse of the Soviet Union.

This is important, for it demonstrates what Noam Chomsky has argued numerous times before: that during the Cold War the US intentionally pushed Third World countries guilty of declaring their independence from US hegemony towards the Soviet Union so as to manufacture a convenient pretext for US belligerence. And, the blockade initially imposed by Kennedy did just that. As Lamrani explains, "[o]n September 16, 1962, Kennedy developed a blacklist that included all ships having commercial relations with Cuba, regardless of their country of origin, and banned them from docking in a US port. These measures drastically reduced the links between Cuba and the Western World and increased the island's dependence upon the USSR."

The results of this relentless 50-year economic war has cost Cuba more than $751 billion, and has "affected all sectors of Cuban society and all categories of the population, especially the most vulnerable: children, the elderly, and women. Over 70 percent of all Cubans have lived in a climate of permanent economic hostility."

This economic war, moreover, has been combined with decades of violent, terrorist attacks by the United States—attacks intentionally devised to provoke a violent response by Cuba which could justify a full-scale invasion, but that violent response never came due to the incredible restraint of the Cuban government and people.[3]

As Noam Chomsky details, these attacks came very shortly after the January 1, 1959 Cuban Revolution and with incessant frequency. As Chomsky relates, "[i]n May [1959], the CIA began to arm guerrillas inside Cuba. 'During the winter of 1959–1960, there was a significant increase in CIA-supervised bombing and incendiary raids piloted by exiled Cubans' based in the US."[4]

These assaults against Cuba continued for decades. In addition to the infamous 1961 Bay of Pigs invasion, these attacks included: "the speedboat strafing attacks on a Cuban seaside hotel 'where Soviet military technicians were known to congregate, killing a score of Russians and Cubans'; attacks on British and Cuban cargo ships; the contamination of sugar shipments"; a covert sabotage attack, organized in the US, which blew up a Cuban industrial facility, killing 400 workers; and attacks in the mid-1970s "on fishing boats, embassies, and Cuban offices overseas, and the bombing of a *Cubana* airliner, killing all seventy-three passengers"; and a machine-gun attack against a Spanish-Cuban tourist hotel in 1989, on the 30th anniversary of the Revolution.[5]

There were more attacks into the 1990s with lessons for Venezuela. These attacks included a number of bombings in Cuba organized by Luis Posada, who was being financed from Miami. Posada had escaped from a Venezuelan prison, where he had been held for the bombing of the *Cubana* airliner. As Chomsky relates, "Posada went from Venezuela to El Salvador, where he was put to work at the *Ilopango* military air base to help organize US terrorist attacks against Nicaragua under Oliver North's direction."[6]

US Lt. Col. Oliver North, one might recall, was a key figure in the Iran-Contra scandal—the Reagan Administration program to illegally fund the Nicaraguan Contras. One of North's associates in this scandal, moreover, was Elliott Abrams—the man currently in charge of the US's regime change operations against Venezuela.

Posada, and how he was treated by US law enforcement, gives one a good glimpse into how the US treats terrorists who commit crimes against our ostensible enemies. As Chomsky explains, Posada

> was a Bay of Pigs veteran, and his subsequent operations in the 1960s were directed by the CIA. When he later joined Venezuelan intelligence with CIA help, he was able to arrange for Orlando Bosch, an associate from his CIA days who had been convicted in the US for a bomb attack on a Cuba-bound freighter, to join him in Venezuela to organize further attacks against Cuba. An ex-CIA official familiar with the *Cubana* bombing identifies Posada and Bosch as the only suspects in the bombing, which Bosch defended as "a legitimate act of war." Generally considered the "mastermind" of the airline bombing, Bosch was responsible for thirty other acts of terrorism, according to the FBI. He was granted a presidential pardon in 1989 by the incoming Bush I administration after intense lobbying by Jeb Bush and South Florida Cuban-American leaders, overruling the Justice

Department, which had found the conclusion "inescapable that it would be prejudicial to the public interest for the United States to provide a safe haven for Bosch [because] the security of this nation is affected by its ability to urge credibly other nations to refuse aid and shelter to terrorists."[7]

In short, the US is quite fine with people it views to be "our terrorists," and Posada and Bosch certainly fit that category. And moreover, the US aided and abetted their terrorist attacks, as well as those of many others, against Cuba.

This gives credence to current claims by Venezuela and President Maduro that the US is currently working to organize terrorist attacks within Venezuela—attacks which look a lot like those carried out against Cuba over the years.

Thus, Venezuelan security forces have just arrested Roberto Marrero—the "chief of staff" of Juan Guaido, the individual the US has recently recognized as Venezuela's president—on charges of conspiracy to carry out terrorist attacks against the country.[8] According to Venezuelan authorities, Marrero and his accomplices have been using monies seized from Venezuela by the US to organize attacks which included paying hefty sums of between $500,000 to $700,000 a day to "eight to ten teams of assassins, brought from Nicaragua, Honduras and El Salvador, who were trained in Colombia to carry out terrorist acts in Venezuela. They planned selective assassinations of high-profile figures of the Venezuelan State and attacks on the country's public services. Half these groups had entered the country, while others were blocked by the shutdown of the borders."[9]

Specifically, they planned to carry out the following acts in pursuit of their plot known as "Operation Libertad":

- Selective killings of government officials
- New sabotage to the Caracas Metro, the Cable Car and the electric service

- False-positive operations or false flags by people disguised as military deserters
- A general strike, an assault on Miraflores [the Presidential Palace] and terrorist actions such as the assassination of President Maduro[10]

Just as with the multiple terrorist attacks against Cuba over the years, it is unlikely that the mainstream press will provide much, if any coverage, of this terrorist plot against Venezuela. And if it does, it is even more likely that it will give claims about this plot little to no credence. But the truth is that such terrorist plots and attacks are standard operating procedure of the US against its targets for regime change.

Meanwhile, the US assault against Venezuela is being expanded to include countries like Cuba. Thus, the US just announced sanctions upon Venezuelan and international companies involved in shipping oil to Cuba on a daily basis in order to stop those shipments.[11] The result, of course, will be more suffering for both the Venezuelan and Cuban people.

US sanctions have already affected shipments from Venezuela to Haiti, preventing Venezuela from providing Haiti with the subsidized oil it has been providing to Haiti for many years pursuant to Chavez's Petrocaribe program. As the *Haitian Times* explains, "[i]n the midst of the economic war against it, Venezuela has not been able to provide Haiti with subsidized fuel. Haiti's people had to now go to the US oil companies and pay US prices for fuel. This has created bottlenecks in the supply of fuel and frustration at the rising prices. Novum Energy—of the United States—kept ships sitting in Port-au-Prince harbor, waiting for the cash-strapped Haitian government to pay up before unloading 164,000 barrels of petrol and 205,000 barrels of kerosene."[12] Contrasting US oil company policies with those of the Bolivarian Venezuelan Republic's, the *Haitian Times* notes that, with the US companies, "there is no solidarity pricing here. . . . These firms want cash, and they want full price."

The other country which the US is attempting to cut off from Venezuelan oil support is Nicaragua.

Nicaragua

Very shortly after the Sandinista Triumph on July 19, 1979, the US began an all-out attack against that country which included an economic embargo, the bombing of Nicaragua's oil refineries and mining of its ports, and a 10-year military assault in the form of the Contras—a group formed from the ranks of the brutal National Guard of the former US-backed dictator Anastasio Somoza.

According to Contra leader Edgar Chamorro, the CIA trained the Contras in "guerilla warfare, sabotage, demolitions, and in the use of a variety of weapons. . . ." Chamorro described the CIA officials as more than advisers to the Contras. Rather, they were the leaders of the group, with Chamorro attributing "virtually a power of command to the CIA operatives."

The International Court of Justice (ICJ) would ultimately conclude that, under the CIA's direction and control, the Contras carried out numerous incidents of "kidnapping, assassinations, torture, rape, killing of prisoners, and killing of civilians not dictated by military necessity."[13]

In addition, the ICJ found that the United States violated international law norms through the CIA's *Psychological Operations in Guerilla Warfare* manual which, among other things, advised the Contra forces to organize people for public executions. Specifically, the manual called for "Selective Use of Violence for Propagandistic Effects" in which "selected and planned targets, such as court judges, *mesta* judges, police and State Security officials, CDS chiefs, etc." would be "neutralize[d]" by a particular population which "will be present, [and] take part in the act" of killing the target.

Meanwhile, the United States not only disregarded the ICJ's judgment—pursuant to which Nicaragua estimated it was owed nearly $400 million in compensation—but also declared that it was no longer subject to ICJ jurisdiction at all unless it explicitly consented to such for a particular case. Justice is, after all, to be administered against the weak, not the strong.

Moreover, the atrocities of the Contras became such a problem that the US Congress ended up cutting off their funding through legislation known as the Boland Amendment. Undeterred, the Reagan Administration found creative ways to continue arming and bankrolling the Contras, nonetheless.

Quite tellingly, one of the key figures in charge of this operation, later known as the Iran-Contra scandal, was Elliott Abrams, now the individual in charge of US policy towards Venezuela. This may be why, as the Venezuelan government is now alleging, the US is plotting a Contra-like military campaign against that Venezuela.[14]

In addition to funding the Contras through illicit sales of cocaine, with at least $14 million in drug sales being used as seed money to fund the post–Boland Amendment arms trade to the Contras,[15] the Reagan Administration would also turn to Iran to aid his scheme. The problem there was that the United States was then supporting Iraq in its war against Iran, and there was therefore an arms embargo against Iran at this time. Again, Reagan would find a way.

Nothing but total capitulation by the Sandinistas would suffice for Reagan. Thus, as the ICJ related, revolutionary leader and then Nicaraguan president, Daniel Ortega, made it clear that he would give into all of Reagan's stated demands (i.e., that he would send home the Cuban and Russian advisers and not support the FMLN guerillas in El Salvador) in return for only "one thing: that they don't attack us, that the United States stop arming and financing . . . the gangs that kill our people, burn our crops and force us to divert enormous human and economic resources into war when we desperately need them for development." But Reagan would not relent until the Sandinistas and Ortega were out of power altogether.

Meanwhile, even in the midst of Reagan's brutal Contra War, the Sandinistas created democracy in Nicaragua for the first time in its history. As Professor Ricardo Perez explains, "[t]he democracy that was built under the FSLN is a democracy for the great majority of Nicaraguans and not a democracy for a few. Under the low-intensity war promoted and sustained by the United States in 1984, the first multi-party elections outside the will of the United States took place for the first time in Nicaraguan history when they decided who would govern Nicaragua."[16]

And then, as Professor Perez further explains, it was Daniel Ortega who helped bring peace and reconciliation to the country through the Peace Agreements of Esquipulas and Sapoá, pursuant to which he stood for elections 9 months early, and stepped down when he lost the vote in 1989. As Perez explains, Ortega took such steps "to stop and put an end to the unjust war imposed by the United States and therefore to lead to the construction of peace and strengthen democracy, which until then lacked a culture of peace and democracy in Nicaragua."

The US actually ramped up the Contra terror war against Nicaragua until the eve of the 1990 election, and it made it clear to the Nicaraguan people that the war would continue unless the elections went the right way—that is, if Ortega were voted out of office. However, the US did not stop with this blatant extortion to secure the election outcome it so desired.

The US's machinations were well-explained by a group of US military veterans, turned peace activists, who went to Nicaragua to observe the run-up to the elections and their aftermath. In their report, they detailed the three pillars of the US's election meddling campaign:

> President Bush continued the US economic embargo against Nicaragua by again declaring on October 25, 1989, that Nicaragua posed an "unusual and extraordinary threat to the national security and foreign policy of the United States." The economic situation throughout Nicaragua continues to force the majority of people to live in painful depravity.
>
> The US Congress and the CIA have combined to finance, with what are believed to be unprecedented amounts of money, the

so-called opposition political parties in an effort to defeat the majority Sandinista Party in the February 1990 elections.

In effect, the US orchestrated and financed 3-pronged attack
through use of "low intensity" warfare against Nicaragua is in full
force: (1) continued Contra terrorism throughout Nicaragua's rural
areas, (2) continued economic strangulation, and (3) unprecedented
efforts to purchase the internal political process and elections.[17]

As for the first prong of the US campaign, the report explains that
Congress appropriated new funding for the Contras in April of 1989,
and the funding was authorized at least until just after the February
1990 elections—again, this would depend on the outcome. Lest, there
were any doubt as to the intentions of the timing of this aid package,
"[t]he Contras are communicating to virtually all rural campesinos,
through word of mouth, distribution of US funded leaflets, and direct
threats, that they will 'make the war worse than ever if the FSLN wins
the elections.' Dr. Summerfield [an English psychiatrist studying the
effects of the Contra war on the Nicaraguan population] suggested
that a lot of people may not vote because of the fear of terrorist reprisals, like murder and maiming."

As for the second prong of the election intervention, President
Bush went "on record saying he would lift the embargo if Violeta
Chomorro, Presidential candidate for UNO, is elected" over Daniel
Ortega.

Finally, as for the actual purchasing of the election, S. Brian
Willson—the Vietnam veteran who famously lost his legs sitting on
train tracks to stop armaments from being shipped from the US to the
war in Central America and who currently lives in Grenada,
Nicaragua—wrote that the CIA and NED combined to provide nearly
$50 million, or around $14 per each eligible voter in Nicaragua, to
support the opposition groups in Nicaragua.[18]

Not surprisingly, the Nicaraguans succumbed to this combination
of terror, economic pressure and direct interference in the political

process, and voted out Daniel Ortega in the 1990 elections. Ironically, the 1990 Nicaraguan elections are widely considered in the US to be Nicaragua's first democratic elections, when they were anything but. However, notwithstanding the blatant interference of the US on the side opposing him, Daniel Ortega willingly stepped down as president, allowing peace, if an uneasy one, to finally come to Nicaragua after 10 years of US-sponsored war.[19]

The US has continued its interference in Nicaragua's elections and political life. For example, in the 2001 elections—elections in which I served as an international observer—the US blatantly threatened again that a Sandinista victory could lead to both a cessation of US aid to Nicaragua as well as a return to the US's "oppositional policies" of the 1980s, a not-so-veiled threat of the restart of the Contra War.[20]

The US ambassador, Oliver Garza, even went so far as to join right-wing candidate Enrique Bolaños on the campaign trail where he proceeded to give out food to those attending Bolaños' events. As historian and author William Blum explains, "The US ambassador literally campaigned for Ortega's opponent, Enrique Bolaños. A senior analyst in Nicaragua for Gallup, the international pollsters, was moved to declare: '[n]ever in my whole life have I seen a sitting ambassador get publicly involved in a sovereign country's electoral process, nor have I ever heard of it.'"[21]

With such help, Bolaños came out on top, despite the fact that the Sandinistas were ahead in the polls leading up to the time of the election.[22]

Iran

The first country targeted with intentional economic sabotage in the post-WWII period was Iran, and specifically the government of Prime Minister Mohammad Mossadegh, who had committed the grave sin of nationalizing Iran's own oil fields which, since 1919, had been controlled by Great Britain for the latter's own benefit and profit.

While Great Britain had profited greatly from Iran's oil, the people of Iran were kept "in a state of squalor unequaled in the world." According to historian D. F. Fleming, in *The Origins of the Cold War*, "[i]n some villages 90 percent of the people had malaria, and infant mortality exceeded 50 percent." Iran, according to Fleming, was truly "'a nation in rags.' Abject misery was graven on most faces. Even in Teheran anyone standing on the street would be approached by a beggar every five minutes."

It was against this backdrop that, in the early 1950s, the people of Iran united around a talented, nationalist politician to try to gain true independence—independence that necessarily included more Iranian control over its precious oil resources. The politician's name was Mohammed Mossadegh.

Mossadegh, upon being elected to the Majlis' oil committee, and suspecting that the British were short-changing the Iranians on the oil royalties owed them, initially made the quite reasonable request for the British to open Anglo Persian's financial books. The British refused this request as well as Mossadegh's request to train Iranians in technical jobs of the oil industry. When Mossadegh was elected head of the Majlis' oil committee, he then demanded that Iran receive half the profits of the Anglo Persian Oil Company. Again, Britain refused.

It was only after the British refusals of these reasonable requests that the Majlis, under the leadership of Mossadegh who was elected prime minister by overwhelming vote of the Majilis on April 28, 1951, finally decided to nationalize Iran's oil industry on May 1, 1951.

In retaliation, the British stopped exporting refined oil from the Abbadan refinery, and Iran, without tankers or oil technicians of its own, could neither run the refinery nor export any oil. And once Winston Churchill returned as UK prime minister in October of 1951, Britain took even more aggressive action against Mossadegh, buying off Iranian media and undermining the country's economy.[23] And in short order, Churchill would prevail upon the US to lead the overthrow effort against Mossadegh. This would be the CIA's first such regime change operation.

The US joined Britain in starving Iran's economy in the interest of regime change, and this worked like a charm. Thus, Iran was prevented from receiving any revenue from its oil as a consequence of a world-wide embargo and blockade against Iranian oil which was enforced by the British Navy. Meanwhile, the US itself, in support of Britain, refused to buy Iranian oil. The result was that "the country's main source of income was gone. Iran had earned $45 million from oil exports in 1950, more than 70 percent of its total earnings. That sum dropped by half in 1951 and then to almost zero in 1952."[24]

As a May 30, 1953 "Memorandum of Conversation" between the Shah and US Ambassador Loy W. Henderson reflects, even the Shah, the US's hand-picked successor to Mossadegh and soon-to-be tyrannical dictator, was alarmed at the situation.[25] As the memo relates, "Shah told by Henderson that US would not buy Iranian oil for the foreseeable future unless dispute with Britain was resolved, nor would it give financial or economic aid." It should be noted that, as reflected in the 2017 released documents, the resolution of the oil dispute, at least on the surface, now came down to the question of how much Iran would pay Great Britain as compensation for the nationalization of the oil fields.

And, the Shah—Mohammad Reza Pahlavi of the Pahlavi monarchial dynasty who the US sought to reinstall as the top leader of Iran in the place of Mossadegh and the parliamentary government which had sidelined the monarchy—gave his opinion that the best chance for settlement was actually under Mossadegh. He further "said that the present economic position of Iran is so dangerous that he would like to see the US give financial and economic assistance to the country even though Dr. Mossadegh was still in power and even though the extension of that assistance might make it appear that the US was supporting Mossadegh."[26]

The US was unmoved by the Shah's plea. As a later, June 19, 1953 Memorandum of Conversation relates, it was agreed by the major US decision-makers, including President Eisenhower himself, that

Mossadegh would be told that the US is refusing to give him any economic aid, as "it would be unfortunate at this time to give Mossadegh any ammunition which would strengthen his political position."[27]

Early on, as initial preparations were being made for the overthrow, the CIA laid out a list of the assets which it had had in Iran for some time, even before the coup plans had been formulated and greenlighted by Eisenhower. A March 3, 1953 CIA Memo lists the following: "*Mass Propaganda means* (press, etc.): CIA controls a network with numerous press, political, and clerical contacts which has proven itself capable of disseminating large-scale . . . propaganda . . . ; *Poison Pen, personal denunciations, rumor spreading, etc.:* CIA has means of making fairly effective personal attacks against any political figure in Iran, including Mossadegh. . . . ; *Street Riots, demonstrations, mobs, etc.:* CIA [*less than 1 line not declassified*]. . . .[28] The CIA also explains that it "has one group in Iran which, it is believed, may be fairly effective in carrying on morale sabotage within the country and stimulating various types of small scale resistance."

Similarly, in but another CIA Memo, dated April 16, 1953, the CIA, under a heading entitled, "Activist Assets," discusses the fact that "[less than 1 line not declassified] have the capabilities of bringing out gangs of street fighters."[29]

As one author puts it succinctly, the CIA's "agents in Tehran bought off secular politicians, religious leaders and key military officers. They hired thugs to run rampant through the street, sometimes pretending to be Mossadegh supporters, sometimes calling for his overthrow, anything to create a chaotic political situation. Money was spread around the offices of newspaper editors and radio station owners as well."[30]

The plan was to create chaos and confusion which would be blamed on Mossadegh, and then to move against Mossadegh by arresting him at his home in the middle of the night.

And, this attempt was made and succeeded in a most devious way.

Thus, while CIA Bureau Chief Kermit Roosevelt set plans into motion to cause street riots and other provocations, he needed one last ruse to pull off the coup plot, known by then as Operation AJAX. There is a reference to this in the CIA documents when Ambassador Henderson, in a telegram to the US State Department, explains how he went to see Mossadegh at his home.[31] He then told the unsuspecting Mossadegh that he was "particularly concerned [about] increasing attacks on Americans," and how every hour or two he was "receiving additional reports [of] attacks on American citizens not only in Tehran but also other localities." He pleaded with Mossadegh to call on law enforcement agencies to take affirmative action to protect Americans.

What is not said here is that Henderson was meeting with Mossadegh as part of Roosevelt's plans to create enough pressure for the lid to be blown off the situation on the streets of Tehran. The problem, as Stephen Kinzer explains so well in his great *All the Shah's Men*, was that Mossadegh was too restrained in the face of the terrible violence being stoked by the CIA. As he relates:

> The riots that shook Tehran on Monday intensified on Tuesday. Thousands of demonstrators, unwittingly under CIA control, surged through the streets, looting shops, destroying pictures of the Shah, and ransacking the offices of royalist groups. Exuberant nationalists and communists joined in the mayhem. The police were still under orders from Mossadegh not to interfere. That allowed rioters to do their jobs, which was to give the impression that Iran was sliding towards anarchy. Roosevelt caught glimpses of them during his furtive trips around the city and said that they "scared the hell out of him."

The riots were working to a point, but now Roosevelt needed an overreaction by Mossadegh to justify what amounted to a military coup in the name of restoring order and democracy. This is where Ambassador Henderson comes in. Thus, as Kinzer explains, Henderson was told by Roosevelt to go to Mossadegh and to ask him for police to crack down on the rioters in Tehran in order to protect the lives of Americans who were allegedly under threat and attack.

In so doing, Roosevelt and Henderson were appealing to Mossadegh's better angels to undo him. As Kinzer puts it, "Roosevelt had perfectly analyzed his adversary's psyche. Mossadegh, steeped in a culture of courtliness and hospitality, found it shocking that guests in Iran were being mistreated. That shock overwhelmed his good judgment, and with Henderson still in the room, he picked up a telephone and called his police chief. Trouble in the streets had become intolerable, he said, and it was time for the police to put an end to it. With this order, Mossadegh sent the police out to attack a mob that included many of his own most fervent supporters."

The fuse had been lit, and Roosevelt was ecstatic. As he wrote in a telegram from the station in Iran to the Central Intelligence Agency, dated August 19, 1953, "Overthrow of Mossadegh appears on verge of success. Zahedi now at radio station."[32] By August 20, 1953, the coup had been successful, with Mossadegh's home being stormed and looted, and with Mossadegh taken away under arrest.[33] The Shah was then summoned back from his own self-imposed exile at the time prescribed by Kermit Roosevelt.

As planned, the Shah's monarchy was fully restored and the US's hand-picked successor, General Zahedi, was installed as prime minister in Mossadegh's stead. The coup government now installed, though still precariously, any pretenses to such lofty goals as democracy and freedom were quickly abandoned.

Meanwhile, the UK and the US both got what they wanted all along with the fall of Mossadegh. Thus, the Anglo Iranian Oil Company was reorganized into British Petroleum, or BP for short.[34] And, according to an appendix in the newly-released documents, it received 40% of the Iranian oil industry.[35] The US received another 40% of the industry, split between five companies—according to the appendix, Gulf-International Company (8%), Standard Oil Company of California (now, Chevron) (8%), Standard Oil of New Jersey (8%) (now, ExxonMobil), Texas Company (now, a subsidiary of Chevron) (8%) and Socony-Vacuum Overseas Supply Company (now, ExxonMobil) (8%). An additional 14% of Iran's industry went to Royal Dutch Shell, with the remaining 4% to a French company.

In 1979, Iran committed the unforgivable sin of ousting the US-installed Shah and US oil interests from the country. The US has been attempting to regain control over Iran and its oil ever since. And again, the US has turned to economic warfare (the US calls this "sanctions") to accomplish these ends. The goal, as usual, is to inflict as much suffering on the population as possible. As the *LA Times* explains,

> Economic analysts say the sanctions will spread misery across Iran's economy—worsening inflation, accelerating the decline of the currency, making imports scarcer and making medicine, in particular, more difficult to acquire. . . .
>
> As with the previous sanctions regime, these penalties are likely to hit working-class and low-income families the hardest, said Esfandyar Batmanghelidj, founder of Bourse & Bazaar, a publication that tracks Iran's economy. . . .
>
> Wealthier families will also struggle but are better able to weather the storm, drawing on savings and sourcing some scarce goods—such as medication—from overseas, Batmanghelidj said.[36]

So far, these sanctions do not appear to be working in terms of changing the government of Iran, but they are certainly working to undermine the well-being of the Iranian people.

Brazil

As Noam Chomsky and Edward S. Herman explained in their landmark book, *The Washington Connection and Third World Fascism*,[37] "[b]etween 1960 and 1969, 11 constitutionally elected governments [in Latin America] were displaced with military dictatorships," with varying degrees of assistance from the United States. One of the more tragic examples of such "displacements" was in Brazil in 1964.

Brazil was a particular problem for Washington given the rise of liberation theology in that country after the Second Vatican Council in 1962 which democratized the Church and encouraged its reaching out to the masses of poor in the world. Chomsky and Herman explain that, particularly in Brazil, the changes brought about by this new opening led the Church there to turn away from its old allegiances to elite and to the military, and to begin advocating for and ministering to the poor. That is, it began to advocate for "the preferential option for the poor"—the main tenet of liberation theology.

Even more troubling, the Brazilian Church began to criticize the role of the US itself in Latin America. As Chomsky and Herman explain, "[t]he church has also become more clear-eyed and explicit on the class bias and massive inhumanity of the development model of growth, and on the role of the US and its military and economic interests in bringing into existence and sustaining the subfascist state." Such a position was simply unacceptable to the US and its leaders.

The Church in Brazil found a friend for its emerging philosophy in Joao Goulart, who was elected president in 1961. Goulart himself, allied with the radical labor movement and left-wing parties, wanted an independent Brazil that would do more for the poor and working people and which would not be subject to the dictates of Washington's regressive economic model of development. As one account explains, "[t]he Goulart regime of 1961–1964 represented the 'fundamental contradiction between a government's responsibility to the citizens who elected it, and the obedience to the demands of foreign creditors expressed in the IMF stabilization program,'" which required austerity measures that squeezed the people economically to allow for the payment of the country's foreign debt.[38] And, "[a] government which refuses to make any gesture toward meeting their conditions frequently finds its international credit for imports cut off which, in turn, increases the likelihood of a CIA-induced right-wing coup."[39]

Because Goulart had inherited a massive foreign debt from prior administrations, this contradiction was particularly keen, and the danger of US meddling particularly great. One president, Getulio Vargas, had already committed suicide in 1954 under the strain of the unjust world economic system which simply made it impossible for Brazil to break out of its cycle of debt and impoverishment. Thus, in his suicide note, he wrote, "'[t]he foreign companies made profits of up to five hundred percent. They demonstrably deprived the state of more than a hundred million dollars by false evaluations of import goods.'"[40]

In truth, the US had already been meddling in Brazil's affairs for years, making the coup against Goulart a near-certainty. Thus, as it had been doing in many other countries after WWII to ensure compliance with the world order—a world order controlled by the US, which was the only major power in the world not devastated by the war and thus in control of 50% of the world's resources at its end—the US established "powerful, centralized police forces" that could be called into service against recalcitrant governments like Goulart's which decided to go their independent path.[41]

As explained in 1969 by *CounterSpy*—a publication founded by Phil Agee, a CIA agent who quit the agency over his disgust with its use of torture in countries like Uruguay where Agee had been stationed:

Since the end of World War II, Washington had used it role as policeman of the so-called Free World to justify expanding its influence in the Brazilian forces. Military planning between the two countries was coordinated by a Joint Brazil United States Military Commission (JBUSMC). In 1949, the Pentagon helped Brazil set up and staff the Escola Superior de Guerra (Advanced War College), a carbon copy of the US National War College.

The Advanced War College is responsible for national security studies, development of military strategy, and ideas on nation building. . . . To this day, the college has graduated over three thousand civilians and military managers indoctrinated in a right-wing military ideology and they believe that only the armed forces can lead Brazil to its proper destiny as the great power of Latin America.

In short, before Goulart was even elected, the US had already created a system in which the military would dominate over the civilian government, and ruthlessly at times. Brazil suffers from this system even still.

Meanwhile, "[i]n the fall of 1961, just as Joao Goulart was taking over the presidency, the United States began an expanded influx of CIA agents and AID officials into Brazil" to train Brazilian police forces in counterinsurgency techniques. The US began hatching plans to use these security forces and other groups in Brazil to destabilize and then overthrow Goulart shortly thereafter.

A very good summary of the US's game plan against Goulart, begun under John and Bobby Kennedy, and continued under Johnson, appeared recently in the magazine of the North American Congress on Latin America (NACLA):

> Washington's long-term efforts in Brazil and elsewhere to undermine movements springing from lower class aspirations and strengthen groups favorable to US investors were infused with a sense of urgency when João ("Jango") Goulart assumed the presidency of Brazil in 1961. Declassified documents released recently by the National Security Archive reveal that officials of the Kennedy Administration were perturbed by Goulart's proposed social reforms and contemplated promoting a military coup. . . .
>
> Accelerating under the Johnson Administration, destabilization of the Goulart government involved the concerted effort of US government agencies in collaboration with the multinational corporate community and international financial institutions. While banks withdrew investments and withheld credit, the CIA, the Agency for International Development, and US businesses channeled funds to

political candidates, state governors, police and paramilitary groups, labor unions, media companies, and others inclined to plot against the federal government. Supporters of the government faced an elaborate campaign of divide and suppress, co-opt or conquer.

US military attachés encouraged and coordinated factions of the Brazilian military in plotting a coup d'état. And in case Brazilian military conspirators should begin to falter, the United States had a naval carrier task force standing by.[42]

The CIA's efforts in Brazil during this period went beyond the mere funding of political candidates as above-described to actually hijacking vast swaths of the Brazilian government from top to bottom. Thus, "part of the CIA's effort to create anti-Goulart sentiment in Brazil was the rigging of elections. Working through a front group called the Instituto Brasileiro de Acao Democratica (IBAD), the CIA channeled money into local political campaigns. . . . In the 1962 elections, IBAD not only funded more than one thousand candidates but recruited them so that their first allegiance would be with IBAD and the CIA. At every level, from state deputies up to governorships, the CIA stacked the ballots in favor of candidates."[43]

So thoroughly did the CIA control the Brazilian government, even before Goulart was ousted, that a February 1964 Brazilian investigation into the CIA's election rigging (which the CIA spent $20 million on, that is, $160 million in today's dollars) was suppressed by the very committee doing the investigation. The committee did so because five of its nine members were on the CIA payroll.[44]

When Goulard was finally ousted according to plan by the military on March 31, 1964, "[t]he White House recognized the new government in Brazil with indecent haste, on 2 April 1964."[45] The coup brought much joy to Washington, including to Bobby Kennedy who was still angry with Goulard for refusing his demands in 1962 to remove leftists from his government, restructure the economy in the interest of foreign capital and relent from nationalizing businesses such as an ITT subsidiary. Kennedy responded upon hearing of the news of the coup, "[w]ell, Goulart got what was coming to him. . . ."[46]

The people of Brazil, however, were not so happy, as "[t]he subsequent militocracy saw many thousands exiled, purged, imprisoned, tortured, and/or murdered by death squads."[47] A recently declassified US Department of State document dated June 8, 1971, discusses the proliferation of death squads linked to the Brazilian police.[48] As the Department of State explained, press reports of these death squads (in Portuguese, *Esquadrão da Morte* [EM]), did not start appearing until 1964—that is, the year of the coup.

The State Department explained that the EM was an open secret to which the Brazilian authorities turned a blind eye. According to the State Department, by the writing of this document in 1971, about 800 people had been killed by the EM, and all of the killings had the following characteristics in common: "the victims are almost always *marginais* [marginals]"; they are shot multiple times and tied with nylon cords, "the bodies is left in deserted places in the early morning"; a sign with the EM symbol is left with the corpse; calls are made to the press telling where the body may be found; and "the police don't question any suspects and the case is closed for lack of evidence." As the State Department explained, "the vast majority of the victims . . . have been from the poorest classes, those with the least ability or predilection to protest." In short, the death squads carried out a war against the poor.

The military dictatorship, which the US helped bring to power in 1964 and then backed till its bitter end, lasted until 1985, and continues to haunt Brazil to this day. As far as the US was concerned, it was an unmitigated success as it successfully protected the interests of the elite and foreign corporations to the great detriment of the masses. As Chomsky and Herman explain:

> The military regime has encouraged and subsidized the shift to export crops such soybeans and cattle, without the slightest concern,

provision, or consideration for the (non-existent) opportunities for the millions of dispossessed:

> Their lands, houses and crops are wiped out by the savage growth of latifundia and big agribusiness. Their living and working conditions are becoming more difficult. In a tragic contradiction, in which the government economic favors multiply herd of cattle and enlarge plantations, the small laborer sees his family's food supply diminishing.
>
> Volkswagon, Rio Tinto Zinc, Swift Meat Packing, and others have been receiving tax write-offs to develop cattle ranches, while the indigenous people are written off in the process by their government.

The military dictatorship also pleased its US backers by violently cracking down on movements for social justice, and in particular on the upstart Liberation Church and its demands to take care of the poor and oppressed. Again, Chomsky and Herman:

> Efforts to organize the peasantry, even for limited self-help activities, have been viewed with the deepest suspicion by the leaders of subfascism, and this form of subversion has led to the arrest, harassment and exile of numerous clergy in Brazil and elsewhere in the empire.
>
> Bishop Casadaliga was the first of many Brazilian bishops to be subject to military interrogation. Many have suffered more severely. Dom Adriano Hipolito, the Bishop of Nova Iguazu, who has often denounced the Brazilian Anti-Communist Alliance (AAB) as a "bunch of thugs directed and protected by the police" was kidnapped by the AAB, beaten, stripped, painted red, and left lying on a deserted road. And, in October 1976, Father Joao Brunier, who had gone to the police station with Bishop Casadaliga to protest the torture of two peasant women, was simply shot dead by a policeman. . . . Hundreds of priests and higher officials of the Latin American churches have been tortured, murdered or driven into exile [by

US-backed client states]. Six aides of Archbishop [Dom Helder] Camara have been murdered, and he is quite aware that only his international reputation has so far saved him from a similar fate.

The US State Department was well aware of such persecution as recently-declassified documents show. For example, a memo from the American Consulate dated December 10, 1969, describes seven Dominican seminarians who were arrested on "terrorism" charges because of their advocacy for "social and economic justice."[49] Another memo dated March 6, 1972, describes a meeting between a number of US officials and Dom Benedito Ulboa Viera, the auxiliary bishop of Sao Paulo.[50] This memo describes Bishop Ulboa's thoughts about Church-State relations after four years of military dictatorship:

> The Bishop said that, rather than diminishing, political repression and torture were increasing in Brazil. Even the techniques of torture had been refined and had become more scientific. The security forces were controlled by men who believed that the end of maintaining a communist-free Brazil justified any means; they looked upon the church as a defender of communism, hence an enemy of national security. He had recently gained confidential access to a "lengthy secret report" on the church prepared by the Second Army and initialed on each page [by] the Commanding General, Humberto Souza e Mello. The burden of the report was that the church was aiding and abetting communism.
>
> The "fascist" attitudes of those in power prevented any kind of acceptable relationship between the regime and the church. . . . The church must look upon the present government as a "threat" and within the clergy and among the bishops there was great solidarity in facing this threat.

The memo goes on to describe particular instances in which Catholic students were arrested and tortured by the regime.

I had the honor of hearing Brazilian archbishop Dom Helder Camara speak at the University of Dayton in the late 1980s. Archbishop Camara was one of the intellectual founders of liberation theology and famously said, "When I give food to the poor, they call me a saint. When I ask why they are poor, they call me a communist." In this short statement, Camara summed up the problem the US had with the Liberation Church, and why it had to snuff it out—because it asked pesky questions about the unjust economic order which benefits the US to the detriment of everyone else.

Curiously, the US Embassy in Brazil wrote a memo to the US Department of State in Washington in December of 1977 in which it goes into great detail about a speech given by Archbishop Camara at that time to 700 law students in Brasilia.[51] The memo notes that Camara was critical of then-president Jimmy Carter for claiming to be interested in human rights when he was turning a blind eye to the massive human rights abuses going on in Brazil at that time. Camara took Carter to task for overlooking human rights in countries in which the US had a strategic interest, such as Brazil.

As noted above, the US was largely successful in ridding the world of this philosophy, with the US Army School of the Americas bragging that it helped to defeat liberation theology.[52]

Chile

On Sept. 11, 1973, General Augusto Pinochet led a violent coup against the elected government of President (and medical doctor) Salvador Allende, bringing an end to democratic rule in that country for the next sixteen-plus years. Many refer to this as the "First 9/11," and it would be much more devastating than the 9/11 the US suffered in 2001 in terms of its body count and historical significance for a number of countries.

At the time of the coup, Chile had been the longest-standing constitutional democracy in Latin America—something the United States would generally claim to support. However, because the United States did not like the left-leaning (but not Communist) Dr. Allende, it chose to help foment the coup that toppled his government and then continue to support the Pinochet dictatorship even as its human rights crimes became apparent. General Pinochet's regime ultimately was responsible for the murder of at least 3,197 individuals and the torture of over 30,000.[53]

The CIA had been intervening in Chile for years, and was indeed successful in blocking the earlier election bid of Salvador Allende back in 1964. As Peter Kornbluh, in his book *The Pinochet Files*, based on declassified CIA documents, explains, the US spent billions of dollars, starting in 1961, to try to prevent Salvador Allende and his Popular Unity coalition from being elected.

This included $2.6 million in funds to directly bankroll the 1964 election campaign of Eduardo Frei and his Christian Democratic Party, and $3 million in anti-Allende black ops during this same campaign. Quoting the (Senator Frank) Church Committee which investigated CIA wrongdoing in the early 70s, the CIA's black ops included the following:

> Extensive use was made of the press, radio, films, pamphlets, posters, leaflets, direct mailing, paper streamers and wall paintings. It was a "scare campaign" that relied heavily on images of Soviet tanks and Cuban firing squads and was directed especially to women. Hundreds of thousands of copies of the anticommunist pastoral letter of Pope Pius XI were distributed by Christian Democratic organizations. . . . "Disinformation" and "black propaganda"—material which purported to originate from another source, such as the Chilean Communist Party—were used as well.[54]

And when these CIA efforts propelled Eduardo Frei to the presidency, the US really turned on the spigot. Thus, to make sure Frei stayed in power, the US provided "over 1.2 billion in economic grants and loans—an astronomical amount for that era."[55] That is almost $9 billion in today's dollars. In addition, "[a]lthough Chile faced no internal or external security threat," the US provided $91 million in military assistance to Chile between 1962 and 1970. As Kornbluh notes, this military assistance had one goal in mind—"to establish closer ties to the Chilean generals" in case later elections produced undesired results. And indeed, that insurance plan would soon be needed.

Thus, despite the expenditure of another $2 million in covert funds to influence the 1970 elections, Salvador Allende came out on top. In response, the CIA then moved to try to prevent Allende from ever taking office. Thus, a Sept. 19, 2000, document released by the CIA revealed that the CIA "sought to instigate a [military] coup" against Mr. Allende even before he took office in 1970.[56] And the decision to prevent the inauguration of Allende came from the president of the United States himself, Richard Nixon.

The notes of Nixon's directive, taken by the director of the CIA, Richard Helms, state:[57]

- 1 in 10 chance perhaps, but save Chile!
- worth spending
- not concerned risks involved
- no involvement of embassy
- $10,000,000 available, more if necessary
- full-time job—best men we have
- game plan
- make economy scream
- 48 hours for plan of action

As declassified documents show, "[t]he CIA pursued a basic three-step plan: (1) identify, contact, and collect intelligence on coup-minded officers; (2) inform them that the US was committed to 'full support in coup' short of sending the marines; (3) foster the creation of 'a coup

climate by propaganda, disinformation, and terrorist activities' to provide a stimulus and pretext for the military to move.'"[58]

However, all of these steps combined were to add up to one thing:
chaos. As a chilling, Top Secret CIA cable from Santiago, Chile, on
October 10, 1970, sums it all up: "'*Carnage could be considerable and
prolonged, i.e., civil war. . . . You have asked us to provoke chaos in Chile . . .
we provide you with formula for chaos which is unlikely to be bloodless.*'"
(emphasis in text).[59] This goal of creating chaos in an otherwise peaceful, democratic and hitherto allied nation can only be viewed as evil;
as the very worst fate one country could attempt to visit upon another.
But this was not only the goal of the US in Chile; it was and remains
the goal of the US in many other targeted countries, as this book
attempts to detail.

Meanwhile, as the CIA relates, it "was working with three different
groups of plotters," all of which "made it clear that any coup would
require the kidnapping of army Cmdr. Rene Schneider, who felt deeply
that the constitution required that the army allow Allende to assume
power."[60]

The CIA, not having any qualms about constitutionality or civilian rule, admits that it agreed with the assessment that the kidnapping
(though it claims not killing) of Schneider was necessary, and so it
provided weapons and $50,000 in cash for the kidnapping operation.[61]
The plan was to raise a "false flag" by then blaming the kidnapping on
the Communists. Not surprisingly, the kidnapping operation ended in
the killing of Schneider when he tried to defend himself. The path was
now being paved for the military overthrow of Allende.

The CIA continued to assist the coup-plotters through the time Dr.
Allende was overthrown. The overthrow of Allende was particularly
brutal, and laden with symbolism, with air force planes bombing the
Presidential Palace and killing Allende in the process. The message
was clear—democracy itself was under attack on that day.

The *Washington Post* would later explain the series of events in
which the CIA was a key player:

In Chile, the United States prevented Allende from winning an election in 1964. "A total of nearly four million dollars was spent on some fifteen covert action projects, ranging from organizing slum dwellers to passing funds to political parties," detailed a Senate inquiry in the mid-1970s that started to expose the role of the CIA in overseas elections. When it couldn't defeat Allende at the ballot box in 1970, Washington decided to remove him anyway.

"I don't see why we need to stand by and watch a country go communist due to the irresponsibility of its own people," Kissinger is said to have quipped. Pinochet's regime presided over years of torture, disappearances and targeted assassinations.[62]

As another *Washington Post* story summarized, in September of 1973, "the Chilean military, aided by training and financing from the US Central Intelligence Agency, gained absolute control of the country in less than a week. The new regime waged raids, executions, 'disappearances' and the arrest and torture of thousands of Chilean citizens—establishing a climate of fear and intimidation that would remain for years to come."[63]

In addition to the CIA, another key actor in the coup was the International Telephone and Telegraph Company (ITT), which wanted Allende gone for fear that he might be a threat to their interests in Chile. ITT, which was also involved in the military coup in Brazil in 1964 and which owned 70% of the Chilean Telephone Company as well as The Sheraton Hotel at the time, backed Allende's opponents in the 1970 elections and provided crucial financial support to the coup plotters against Allende.[64]

Shortly before the coup in which he would die, Dr. Allende gave an impassioned speech at the UN decrying the interference of ITT, as well as Kennecott Copper, in his country:

Two firms that are part of the central nucleus of the large transnational companies that sunk their claws into my country, the

International Telegraph and Telephone Company and the Kennecott Copper Corporation, tried to run our political life.

ITT, a huge corporation whose capital is greater than the budget of several Latin American nations put together and greater than that of some industrialized countries, began, from the very moment that the people's movement was victorious in the elections of September 1970, a sinister action to keep me from taking office as President.

With the urging of the CIA, the plan that ITT put into place, along with corporations like Anaconda and Kennecott copper companies, was to strangle the Chilean economy—in the words of Nixon himself, to "make [the] economy scream." As left-wing economist Zoltan Zigedy recently wrote upon the 45th anniversary of the 1973 coup against Allende:

> Credits and loans were denied. The global price of copper (70–80% of Chilean exports) was manipulated downward to deny Chile's government essential revenue for the country's social programs (salaries rose between 35% and 66% in 1971) and industrial development.
>
> Without hard currency, outside loans or revenue from trade, hyperinflation eventually plagued Chile, reaching 163% in 1973.
>
> "The US credit and trade squeeze was designed for a political purpose . . .: to promote the political demise of a democratic socialist government. Economic pressures led to economic dislocations (scarcities), which generated the social basis (discontent among the middle class) that created the political context for a military coup."
>
> Funding middle class truck-owners' "strikes" through the CIA and AIFLD [the AFL-CIO's international wing] further fueled middle class alienation. . . .[65]

The combined efforts of the CIA and transnational corporations worked, and Allende was violently overthrown and killed. And, once the coup in Chile took place, the United States continued to support the Pinochet regime, including Manuel Contereras, who served as an agent of the CIA from 1974 to 1977, and went on to head Chile's intelligence agency, known as the DINA, which played the key role in the human rights abuses carried out in Chile.[66] The CIA concedes that its friend Contereras "became notorious for his involvement in human rights abuses," and had a key role in the car-bombing of former Chilean ambassador to Washington Orlando Letelier and his young American assistant Ronnie Moffitt in the middle of Washington, DC, in 1976.

As Eduardo Galeano wrote of Letelier in his later edition of *Open Veins of Latin America*—a book originally published in 1970 on the hopeful note of Allende's election in Chile:

> In August of 1976, Orlando Letelier published an article describing the terror of the Pinochet dictatorship and the "economic liberty" of small privileged groups as two sides of the same coin. Letelier, who had been a minister in Salvador Allende's government, was exiled in the United States. There he was blown to pieces shortly afterwards. . . . Letelier described the massive destruction of gains made by the Chilean people during the Popular Unity government [of Salvador Allende]. The dictatorship had returned to their former owners half of the industrial monopolies and oligopolies which Allende nationalized, and put the other half up for sale. Firestone had bought the national tire factory, Parsons and Whittemore, a big paper plant. The Chilean economy, wrote Letelier, is more concentrated and monopolized now than on the eve of the Allende government. *Business free as never before, people in jail as never before; in Latin America free enterprise is incompatible with civil liberties. . . .*
>
> Infant mortality, substantially reduced during the Popular Unity regime, rose dramatically with Pinochet. When Letelier was assassinated in a Washington street, one quarter of Chile's population was getting no income and survived thanks to foreign charity or their own stubbornness and guile (emphasis in text).[67]

The Chilean coup had dire reverberations throughout the Southern Cone of South America, as the CIA itself recognizes. As it relates, "[w]ithin a year after the coup, the CIA and other US Government agencies were aware of bilateral cooperation among regional intelligence services to track the activities of and, in at least a few cases, kill political opponents. This was the precursor to Operation Condor, an intelligence-sharing arrangement among Chile, Argentina, Brazil, Paraguay and Uruguay established in 1975."

More than a "few" political opponents were killed by these regimes under Operation Condor, some of them, as in the case of Argentina, openly Nazi. As journalist Ben Norton explains, anywhere between 60,000 to 80,000 people were either killed or disappeared in Operation Condor, which grew out of the Chilean coup.[68]

THE 2002 COUP, THE REGIME CHANGE THAT ALREADY WAS

ANOTHER INSTANCE OF REGIME CHANGE WHICH is quite instructive is that which already took place in Venezuela in 2002 with the instigation, support and recognition of the United States.

Referencing the US's successful CIA-orchestrated coup in Iran in 1953 against the democratically-elected prime minister, Mohammad Mossadegh, former "economic hitman" John Perkins sets the stage for the replay of this coup in Venezuela in 2002. Perkins explains that, just as CIA bureau chief Kermit Roosevelt had undermined Mossadegh by intentionally undermining the Iranian economy and provoking numerous acts of violent street protests, the US ran a similar gambit in Venezuela. As Perkins relates in his best-selling *New Confessions of an Economic Hitman*[1]:

In Venezuela, the Bush Administration was bringing Kermit Roosevelt's Iranian model into play. As the *New York Times* reported,

Hundreds of thousands of Venezuelans filled the streets here today to declare their commitment to a national strike, now in its 28th day, to force the ouster of President Hugo Chavez.

The strike, joined by an estimated 30,000 oil workers, threatened to wreak havoc on this nation, the world's fifth-largest oil producer, for months to come. . . .

In recent days, the strike has reached a kind of stalemate. Mr. Chavez is using non-striking workers to try to normalize operations at the state-owned oil company. His opponents, led by a coalition of business and labor leaders, contend, though that their strike will push the company, and thus the Chavez government, to collapse.

Note the curious fact that "a coalition of business and labor leaders" were uniting to try to overthrow the Chavez government. These may seem like strange bedfellows until one understands that, as it was revealed later, US forces, including in the US trade union movement, were working behind the scenes to organize this anti-Chavez coalition for the purpose of regime change.

Again, John Perkins explains:

This was exactly how the CIA brought down Mossadegh and replaced him with the shah. The analogy could not have been stronger. It seemed history was uncannily repeating itself, fifty years later. Five decades, and still oil was the driving force.

Chavez's supporters continued to clash with his opponents. Several people, it was reported, were shot to death, and dozens more were wounded. The next day, I talked with an old friend who for many years had been involved with the jackals. . . . He told me that a private contractor had approached him to foment strikes in Caracas and to bribe military officers—many of whom had been trained at the School of the Americas—to turn against their elected president. He had rejected the offer, but he confided, "The man who took the job knows what he's doing."

When Perkins refers here to the "jackals," he is referring to CIA-backed groups who attempt to instigate coups and counter-revolutions through tactics including kidnapping and murder. As Perkins explains, if the "jackals" cannot get the job done, US military invasion follows. In terms of Venezuela, we are currently in the time of the jackals, with military intervention possibly in the near offing.

Perkins also refers here to the US Army School of the Americas (SOA), now based in Columbus, Georgia, which has been training Latin American military personnel in counter-insurgency techniques for decades and which has trained a number of top military leaders who have gone on to overthrow their elected governments. Indeed, Father Roy Bourgeois, the Maryknoll founder of the School of Americas Watch, an activist organization dedicated to trying to shut down the SOA, would later refer to the SOA as the "School of Coups."

Father Bourgeois referred to as such in the summer of 2009 when two Honduran generals trained at the SOA kidnapped their elected president, Manual Zelaya, an ally of Chavez and other left-wing Latin American leaders, in the middle of the night and flew him out of the country into forced exile. As Hillary Clinton would later admit in the hardcover version of her book *Hard Choices* (the admission would be expunged from her paperback version), she worked behind the scenes to make sure that Zelaya never returned to power.

Meanwhile, Perkins explains that "[o]il company executives and Wall Street feared a rise in oil prices and a decline in American inventories. Given the Middle East situation [after 9/11], I knew the Bush Administration was doing everything in its power to overthrow Chavez. Then came the news that they had succeeded; Chavez had been ousted."

Indeed, on April 11, 2002, Hugo Chavez was kidnapped by rogue members of the military and flown to a military base on a remote island as part of a coup which was well-orchestrated and directed from Washington, DC. As one can witness in the wonderful film, *The Revolution Will Not Be Televised*, the opposition, once in power after this kidnapping, showed its true, anti-democratic nature. Thus, the new, self-proclaimed president, Pedro Carmona—who up to that time was the president of the Venezuelan Chamber of Commerce (FEDCAMARAS)—immediately invalidated the Venezuelan Constitution which had been democratically approved in 1999; disbanded the National Assembly; ordered the Supreme Court shuttered; and fired the attorney general and all state governors and mayors elected during Chavez's tenure.

Very few world governments recognized this illegal coup government. The US was one of these few, and it recognized this coup government immediately, with the US press corps cheering it on. Indeed, our paper of record, the *New York Times*, celebrated with an editorial lauding the coup d'état. Referring to Chavez's alleged resignation—one which never in fact happened—the *Times* editorial board wrote, "[w]ith yesterday's resignation of President Hugo Chávez, Venezuelan democracy is no longer threatened by a would-be dictator. Mr. Chávez, a ruinous demagogue, stepped down after the military intervened and handed power to a respected business leader, Pedro Carmona."[2]

These lines should always be remembered when one reads the *Times* now for news on Venezuela or any other Latin American country. The fact that, in the view of the *Times*, democracy can be advanced in Latin America through a military coup which forcibly seizes power from a president elected twice (in 1998 and 2000) in the preceding four years and then hands it to a business leader who never even stood for election should make one quite skeptical of anything this paper writes about events in that region.

As became a matter of public record, the US had been behind this coup from the very beginning. As the US State Department would later admit, the US "provided training, institution building and other support to individuals and organizations understood to be actively involved in the brief ouster" of President Hugo Chávez and his government, according to the US State Department.[3]

Even the *Times* would later have to acknowledge the US's active role in the coup. According to the *New York Times*,[4]

In the past year, the United States channeled hundreds of thousands of dollars in grants to American and Venezuelan groups opposed to

President Hugo Chávez, including the labor group whose protests led to the Venezuelan president's brief ouster this month.

The funds were provided by the National Endowment for Democracy, a nonprofit agency created and financed by Congress. As conditions deteriorated in Venezuela and Mr. Chávez clashed with various business, labor and media groups, the endowment stepped up its assistance, quadrupling its budget for Venezuela to more than $877,000.

While the endowment's expressed goal is to promote democracy around the world, the State Department's human rights bureau is examining whether one or more recipients of the money may have actively plotted against Mr. Chávez.

But of course, that is the whole point of the so-called "democracy promotion" efforts of the National Endowment for Democracy (NED)—to support regime change throughout the world. And, that is a job it has been doing since the 1980s.

As F. William Engdahl, geopolitical analyst, risk consultant and author explains,[5]

During the Reagan Presidency very damaging scandals were becoming public about CIA dirty operations around the world. Chile, Iran, Guatemala, the top secret MK-Ultra project, the student movement during the Vietnam War to name just a few. To take the spotlight away from them, CIA Director Bill Casey proposed to Reagan creating a "private" NGO, a kind of cut-out that would pose as private, but in reality, as one of its founders the late Allen Weinstein said in a later interview to the *Washington Post*, "doing what the CIA did, but privately." This was the creation of the NGO named National Endowment for Democracy in 1983. Soon other Washington-steered NGOs were added like the Freedom House or the Soros Open Society Foundations, the United States Institute of Peace and so forth.

The money was often channeled via USAID of the State Department to hide its origin. Every major regime attack by the US Government since then including the Solidarnosc in Poland, the Yeltsin CIA-backed Russia coup, the 2004 Ukraine Orange Revolution, the 2008 Tibet riots, the Arab Spring of 2011 to today—all have been done by this group of very select "democracy" NGOs. Little wonder that countries like Russia and China or Hungary act to ban them as "undesirable NGOs."

One might be surprised to learn that one of the three main pillars of the NED's regime change operations, in addition to the International Democratic Institute (IDI) and the International Republican Institute (IRI), is the AFL-CIO's international division now known as the Solidarity Center.

Before it was known as the Solidarity Center, the AFL-CIO's international division was known as the American Institute for Free Labor Development (AIFLD). AIFLD had worked intimately with the CIA's regime change operations since the very beginning of the CIA itself, earning the AFL-CIO the derisive moniker, "AFL-CIA." And so, AIFLD had helped the CIA in regime change operations in Guatemala (1954), Brazil (1964) and Chile (1973), just to name a few.[6] Indeed, my former boss at the United Steelworkers (USW) international union, George Becker, who was president of the union at the time, confided to me on an elevator one day that he himself had been part of the 1954 coup in Guatemala, and that he felt bad about this ever since.

In addition, I was privy to an email between Becker's successor, current USW president Leo Gerard, and the USW's head of international affairs, Gerald Fernandez, which was sent in relation to calls for the AFL-CIO to come clean about its many years of involvement with CIA-led coups in the Third World. According to Fernandez, who himself had worked for AIFLD and who bragged to me once about hosting Elliott Abrams at his place in Costa Rica during the Contra War:

In reality the AFL-CIO has a lot to hide about the late 70's and 80's in relation to their international institutes. . . . The AFL always fared better in getting grants from republican presidents during this period because of communist insurgencies around the world or, at least, perceived communist insurgencies. As you are aware, I was part of the most active period for three years in Central America and the Caribbean. Some things I can relate and some things I can't because of the potential for prosecution. I can say that there is a lot of dirty laundry. Some of the funding was related to what I would call covert operations though this was a very small part of the total operation globally. Most of the activity was related to telling embassies and the State Department what they wanted to hear and that was the labor unions in all developing economies were under threat of communist and extreme left subversion even though in most instances it was nothing more that [sic] extreme nationalism and not communist inspired. In any event, that was how you got operating program grants and that is how the institutes built their power, with money and staff. Each country program director did the same thing, money, prestige, power, influence mover and shaker.

There is [sic] obvious reasons for not dealing with the past, classified information, loss of grants and, some people are still on staff though most were cleaned out. . . .

Belatedly, in 1995, four years after the collapse of the Soviet Union, the AFL-CIO announced that it was giving up its Cold War shenanigans, and starting afresh with the newly-christened Solidarity Center.[7] But, as we would learn later, this was not entirely true. Thus, in 2002, the AFL-CIO's Solidarity Center was greatly embarrassed when it came to light that it had been supporting actors in Venezuela who participated in the short-lived coup against President Hugo Chavez. As a number of authors and publications noted at the time, the Solidarity Center, with money donated from the National Endowment for Democracy (NED), gave support to the Confederation of Venezuelan Workers

(CTV) which in turn was instrumental in the coup against Chavez which, as the reader may recall, involved the kidnapping of Hugo Chavez.[8]

For example, the *New York Times* explained in an article entitled, "US Bankrolling Is Under Scrutiny for Ties to Chavez Ouster," that "[o]f particular concern is $154,377 given by the endowment to the American Center for International Labor Solidarity, the international arm of the AFL-CIO, to assist the main Venezuelan labor union in advancing labor rights." As the *Times* noted, "The Venezuelan union, the Confederation of Venezuelan Workers, led the work stoppages that galvanized the opposition to Mr. Chavez. The union's leader, Carlos Ortega, worked closely with Pedro Carmona Estanga, the business-man who briefly took over from Mr. Chavez, in challenging the government."

And what's more, it turns out that the Solidarity Center played a critical role, just before the coup, in bringing the CTV together with FEDECAMARAS (the Venezuelan chamber of commerce). This is important because the CTV and FEDECAMARAS went on to plan and carry out the coup together. However, quite curiously, the Solidarity Center did not stick around long enough to see how the coup ended up. This is because it moved its office (which is in charge of the entire Andean Region) from Caracas, Venezuela, to Bogota, Colombia, just three weeks before the coup took place. I know this because I was doing a lot of international work for the USW in Colombia at the time and knew about the transfer of the offices, and of the head of the office, Rhett Doumitt, shortly thereafter. It was Doumitt who was instrumental in bringing the CTV together with FEDECAMARAS before the coup.

The Solidarity Center attempted to defend itself against charges that it was up to its old Cold War tricks of working with the US government to overthrow progressive, nationalist governments in the Third World by denying that the CTV, which it supported up to and indeed through the time of the coup, had anything to do with the coup. As the *Boston Globe* later noted in an article entitled, "US Tax Dollars Helped Finance Some Chavez Foes, Review Finds," this was demonstrably untrue as proven by the fact that "the Venezuelan media broadcast a recorded telephone conversation between [exiled former president Carlos Andres] Perez and Carlos Ortega, president of the Confederation of Venezuelan Workers [CTV], in which the pair plotted against Chavez."[9]

In the end, the AFL-CIO later privately conceded that the CTV leadership did actively participate in the coup against Chavez. The same *Boston Globe* story concluded that the Solidarity Center's other defense—that it was merely helping the CTV with matters of internal democratization—was also proven to be false.

Again, Gerry Fernandez explained in his email to Leo Gerard what happened with John Sweeney and his attempt to move the AFL-CIO past its Cold War history. As Fernandez explained, "[s]ome people at the AFL were co-opted by the process" of receiving rich government grants and going on fancy government-funded trips. As Fernandez related, "John Sweeney was one of the favorites for being on these high-level delegations that participated in fact finding and solidarity missions all over the world. And, I might add, stayed in the best hotels and it was sort of like a high class tour group. . . . The positions themselves though can corrupt and are high profile internationally."

Questions remain about the AFL-CIO's continued activities in Venezuela, still under the leadership of Rhett Doumitt.

Meanwhile, another organization that played a treacherous role during the 2002 coup was the Organization of American States (OAS)—a regional organization created pursuant to Chapter VIII of the UN Charter ostensibly to help maintain peace and security in the Western Hemisphere and advance human rights and the rule of law— which stayed silent for the duration of the coup, refusing to issue any statement condemning it.[10] This is an important fact, for the OAS, and its secretary-general Luis Leonardo Almagro, has been a key player these past years calling for regime change in Venezuela. Thus, Almagro recently called for an emergency meeting to consider whether Venezuela should be kicked out of the OAS, explicitly stating that "the institutional crisis in Venezuela demands immediate changes to the Executive power."

None of this should be too surprising given the fact that, since its very inception, the OAS has been accused, quite rightly, of being a tool for US intervention in Latin America. In this excerpt from a three-part piece on the OAS in Cuba's *Granma* newspaper,[11] the OAS is condemned, in quite colorful terms as

[t]he organization that backed the 1952 coup d'état [of General Batista] in Cuba; that was so inert in the face of the military action against the constitutionally-elected government of Jacobo Arbenz in Guatemala; that backed the satrap [Nicaraguan dictator] Anastasio Somoza, and in 1961 failed to condemn the mercenary [Bay of Pigs] invasion of Cuba, just as it avoided any criticism of the coup d'état against Velazco Ibarra, the elected president of Ecuador, remained the same as the one that had indulgently sponsored the military invasion of the Dominican Republic in 1965, the shipment of Green Berets and weapons to Guatemala in 1966, and to Bolivia in 1967, while it applauded the graduation of hundreds of torturers and repressors from the Panama Canal School of the Americas.

It contemplated US government-sponsored coups in Uruguay, Argentina and Chile. It was silent in the face of the death of Salvador Allende, in the face of the murder and forced disappearance of tens of thousands of South Americans during the sinister Operation Condor. It failed to promote peace in Central America during the 1980s, in a conflict that cost nearly 100,000 human lives. It did not back any investigation into the suspicious death of General Torrijos in Panama, nor did its ambassadors stop drinking their coffee during the inglorious invasions of Grenada in 1983, and of Panama itself in 1989.

And so, the OAS was simply acting true-to-form in remaining silent for the duration of the short-lived coup against democratically-elected Venezuelan president Hugo Chavez in 2002. It did so for the same reason that it is now calling for President Maduro to be removed: because it is siding, as it has always done, with the US's campaign against left-leaning governments of Latin America.

One might wonder what Hugo Chavez's response was to those who had kidnapped him, usurped his presidential powers and attempted to wipe out the entire constitutional order of Venezuela. We can certainly be sure that any group who successfully kidnapped a US president, took him to a military base and then purported to throw out the US Constitution would be treated as traitors and possibly executed after trial, if they even made it that far without being gunned down. But this was not how Chavez responded at all.

Rather, as Reuters noted, "in a conciliatory move," Chavez ultimately granted a general amnesty to all those involved in the 2002 coup against him.[12] He also ceased wearing his trademark fatigues and red beret, opting instead for civilian clothes, and gave up his more fiery rhetoric—all moves intended to show conciliation with and make peace with the opposition.

Two individuals given such amnesty were Henrique Capriles, who would later run for president against Nicolas Maduro in 2013, and opposition darling and Kenyon College graduate, Leopoldo Lopez. Ultimately, Capriles only "served a few months in prison for participating in the coup, while Lopez avoided doing any time, thanks to . . . [the] general amnesty granted by Chávez."[13] That Capriles and Lopez received amnesty is quite notable given that they together led the kidnapping of a government minister during the 2002 coup.[14] For his part, Lopez would later boast "to local TV that the dictator installed by the coup (whom Lopez called 'President Carmona') was 'updated' on the kidnapping."[15] Again, imagine how such people would be treated for similar crimes in the United States.

Indeed, Hugo Chavez, moved by the Christian attributes of

forgiveness and mercy, was quite restrained in his response to the terrible events of April, 2002. A conversation he had with Fidel Castro right after these events also reveals his restraint as well as his humanity.

In 2014, Fidel Castro released the full transcript[16] of the phone call he had with then-president of Venezuela, Hugo Chavez, just after the coup failed. The transcript is both entertaining and illuminating, as it shows these two leaders, and very close friends, conversing freely and uninhibitedly about what Fidel refers to in the conversation as the greatest event he had ever witnessed.

The call opens with shared laughter between the two leaders, and with Fidel confessing that he had been unable to sleep because of the excitement of events. Chavez then quickly jumps to the story of what happened.

First, he talks about how he was kidnapped by the coup leaders and led away to five different locations until finally being brought to La Orchila, an island and military base off the coast of Venezuela. Chavez explains that he was able to talk to some of his loyal soldiers, who he refers to affectionately as "muchachos," and how they informed him that there were troops ready to mobilize with tanks and air support to try to save him. However, as Chavez explains to Fidel, he ordered these troops to stand down and to "Hold your position." Fidel interrupts him, finishing his thought, saying, that this was the right call "because a battle or even a civil war" could have broken out if such action were taken. Chavez confirms that this was his rationale, and explains that, in the end, "I decided to give myself up."

To get a good glimpse of Chavez being led away from the presidential palace, Miraflores, to the helicopter which would take him away to places he knew not where, one should watch the film, *The Revolution Will Not Be Televised*. This film shows Chavez being taken away to the tears, chants and songs of his supporters and Cabinet members. Chavez gently tells them that they should not worry because he will be back.

Meanwhile, as Chavez later explains in the conversation with Fidel, the coup leaders tried to force Chavez to resign his presidency at various times during the short-lived coup, including before they led him away from Miraflores, but that he had refused. While not discussed in this conversation, some accounts have it that Fidel had actually managed to call into Miraflores around midnight of April 11 to urge Chavez not to resign, but also to guard his life. Then—minister of defense, Jose Vicente Rangel, has been quoted as saying that "the call from Fidel was decisive so that there was no self-immolation. It was the determinant factor. His advice allowed us to see better in the darkness."

Despite the fact that Chavez refused to resign, the coup leaders, which had taken over all the media outlets, attempted to sew confusion amongst the Venezuelan population by claiming that he had in fact done so. Recall the *New York Times* editorial which mentions the alleged resignation as fact.

Chavez recounts that, when things looked very bleak, a "soldier boy" named Rodriquez entered his small cell where he was being held prisoner, and asked him: "Look, my Commander, did you quit?" "No," Chavez answered, "nor will I give up." "Well, okay," Rodriquez replied, "I have two minutes here. I'm going to ask a favor." The favor he asked was that Chavez jot down a note explaining that he had not resigned, and to leave the note in the garbage. Chavez agreed, writing a note to "All the Venezuelan people and to whom it may concern, I have not given up, ever!" Chavez explains that this young soldier then took that note out of the garbage and faxed it far and wide. This became critical in galvanizing his supporters inside and outside Miraflores to successfully demand his return.

Chavez explains to Fidel that he ended up enjoying his stay in the military base in La Orchila because he was able to talk to the rank-in-file soldiers and to learn about their struggles. As Chavez related, "Ah, that's another thing that helped me a lot, Fidel: conversations with the soldiers, you hear their complaints. . . . So much complaining about their bosses. . . . [T]hey had been forgotten, fuck, they have economic problems, there are very old facilities, they lack resources for training, for maintenance of weapons. Then I began to get all of those things for them, right? And that's a lesson. . . . You have to get down, and hear them, their problems."

It was indeed Chavez's rapport with the low-ranking soldiers that probably saved his life, for while the coup leaders, having failed to convince Chavez to leave the country aboard an airplane with US serial numbers, ordered that Chavez be killed. However, they could never find a soldier who was willing to carry out this order.

Indeed, in the end, Chavez was returned to power because of his rapport with the people, especially the poor of Venezuela who gathered in the tens of thousands to demand his return. Again, the film *The Revolution Will Not Be Televised* portrays this very well.

Fidel released this transcript when he did to show the benevolent nature of Chavez and the Bolivarian Revolution, as compared to the coup leaders, many of whom continue to lead the violent protests against the government now. During their conversation, both Fidel and Chavez explain that the coup leader who assumed leadership very briefly, Pedro Carmona, reminded them of Mussolini in that he quickly dissolved the National Assembly, the Supreme Court and declared the nationally-approved Constitution of 1999 null and void—not exactly the act of a democrat.

* * *

In the end, the 2002 coup is quite instructive about the key actors in the drama being played out in Venezuela. First, it shows the true undemocratic intentions of both the US and key sectors of the opposition forces which were behind that coup. In addition, the forces that forced the restoration of Chavez to office—the poor who live in the barrios of Caracas and beyond—are the same forces who support the ruling PSUV (United Socialist Party of Venezuela) now. It is the fact that the poor, through the PSUV, are governing Venezuela which is the real issue galling both the US and the opposition.

The US and opposition forces would prefer what they view as the natural state of things in which—as in the current US oligarchical system and as in Venezuela prior to the election of Hugo Chavez in 1999—the few rich govern the masses of poor and working people. Venezuela has a very different notion of what democracy should look like—one which is actually more authentically democratic—and that is why that country and its people are being put under a microscope, criticized and punished.

THE US TAKES DOWN VENEZUELA'S ALLIES ONE AT A TIME

FOR YEARS, THE US HAS BEEN systematically dismantling the Bolivarian Alliance for the People of Our America (ALBA) that Chavez had been so instrumental in building up. The US did so by toppling one ALBA government at a time, isolating Venezuela and making it ripe for its own regime change.

Haiti

The first Chavez ally to be toppled was Father Jean Bertrand Aristide, a liberation theologian and three-time elected president of Haiti. The toppling of Aristide, however, was simply another episode in the US's long war against that Caribbean nation.

The US has never allowed Haiti to govern itself. Thus, after the US Marines invaded Haiti and occupied it from 1915 to 1934, the US finally left after creating "a modern army, one that would continue the US occupation long after US troops were gone," functioning on behalf of the Haitian elite and their American counterparts. . . . "The US occupation wedded the country's future to North American business interests."[1]

Then, from 1957 to 1986, the US would economically and

militarily support the brutal dictatorships of Francois "Papa Doc" Duvalier and his son Jean-Claude "Baby Doc" Duvalier. To help "Papa Doc" stay in power, "US Marines trained the dictator's Tonton Macoutes paramilitary force, known for 'leaving bodies of their victims hanging in public, a clear warning to anyone stepping out of line, most especially leftists, socialists and pro-democracy activists.'"[2] US Marine instructors, "who were working through a company . . . under contract with the CIA and signed off by the US State Department'" then trained the paramilitary group known as the Leopards for "Baby Doc" Duvalier.[3]

Just after the fall of the "Baby Doc" dictatorship, the CIA helped to create the appropriately named S.I.N., short for the National Intelligence Service of Haiti. As the *New York Times*, referring to the S.I.N., would later explain, "[t]he Central Intelligence Agency created an intelligence service in Haiti in the mid-1980's to fight the cocaine trade, but the unit evolved into an instrument of political terror whose officers at times engaged in drug trafficking. . . ."[4] The depths of S.I.N.'s corruption was staggering. As the *Times* wrote,

> The Haitian intelligence service provided little information on drug trafficking and some of its members themselves became enmeshed in the drug trade, American officials said. A United States official who worked at the American Embassy in Haiti in 1991 and 1992 said he took a dim view of S.I.N.
>
> "It was a military organization that distributed drugs in Haiti," said the official, who spoke on condition of anonymity. "It never produced drug intelligence. The agency gave them money under counter-narcotics and they used their training to do other things in the political arena."

Still, the CIA support kept coming. Thus, the "S.I.N. received $500,000 to $1 million a year in equipment, training and financial support from the C.I.A.," and it received this assistance to and through the time the

S.I.N. engaged in its most notorious act "in the political arena"—the successful overthrow of the democratically-elected president, Father Jean-Bertrand Aristide, on September 30, 1991. Moreover, the US Drug Enforcement Agency said of the S.I.N. as late as 1992 that it "'works in unison with the C.I.A. at post.'"

That Father Aristide was overthrown by CIA-backed forces came as little surprise to most observers. Aristide has always been seen as a problem for the US in the region given his advocacy of liberation theology. Even worse, Aristide tried hard to put this philosophy into practice as president. As one commentator wrote:

> Aristide's coup-inducing crimes included inviting street children and homeless persons to breakfast at the National Palace and endeavouring to raise the daily minimum wage from $1.76 to $2.94. As Joanne Landy wrote in the *New York Times* in 1994, the latter effort was "vigorously opposed by the US Agency for International Development because of the threat such an increase would pose to the 'business climate', particularly to American companies paying rock-bottom wages to workers in Haiti".[5]

Even after the coup against Aristide, the CIA, along with the US Defense Intelligence Agency (DIA), continued to organize and work with repressive forces to ensure that Haiti would be a safe haven for sweatshops. One such force was the euphemistically-named Front for the Advancement and Progress of Haiti (FRAPH), a paramilitary organization intimately linked to the Haitian military that assumed the task of terrorizing the non-elite masses under the military junta which ruled after the coup.[6]

Again, the *New York Times*, invariably writing well after the fact, explained that Emmanuel Constant, "[t]he leader of one of Haiti's most infamous paramilitary groups [FRAPH] was a paid informer of the Central Intelligence Agency for two years and was receiving money from the United States while his associates committed political murders and other acts of repression. . . ."[7] The FRAPH chief was even on the CIA payroll, the *Times* explains, at the time the FRAPH was organizing violent protests to try to prevent the return to office of Father Aristide in 1994.

President Bill Clinton actually assisted Aristide in returning to office in 1994, even as his own CIA was working against these plans. However, Clinton's intervention in this regard was not altruistic—far from it. Rather, Clinton paved the way for Aristide's return on the express condition that Aristide make drastic changes to Haiti's agricultural system in order to benefit US, and in particular, Arkansas farmers. These changes, which required Haiti to import thousands of tons of rice, would be ruinous to the country, undercutting Haiti's ability to feed itself and resulting in millions of Haitians starving.[8] Clinton himself would later admit to this. As *Foreign Policy* explained:

> In the wake of Haiti's devastating 7.0-magnitude earthquake exactly three years ago, former US President Bill Clinton issued an unusual and now infamous apology. Calling his subsidies to American rice farmers in the 1990s a mistake because it undercut rice production in Haiti, Clinton said he had struck a "devil's bargain" that ultimately resulted in greater poverty and food insecurity in Haiti.
>
> "It may have been good for some of my farmers in Arkansas, but it has not worked," he said. "I have to live every day with the consequences of the lost capacity to produce a rice crop in Haiti to feed those people, because of what I did."[9]

Shortly after his re-election in 2001, Aristide disbanded the Haitian military—the military the US had helped create and that the US had used for decades to enforce its will upon the Haiti people. *In retaliation for this unforgivable offense, the US began to destabilize Haiti, to publicly vilify Aristide, and to pave the way for his ouster.*

First, "[i]n 2002, the US stopped hundreds of millions of dollars in loans to Haiti which were to be used for, among other public projects like education, roads."[10] And then, in early 2003, the US encouraged paramilitary incursions into Haiti from the neighboring Dominican Republic which ultimately led to the toppling of Aristide again. These paramilitaries were led by Andre Apaid, who "was in touch with US Secretary of State Colin Powell in the weeks leading up to Aristide's overthrow," and by Guy Phillippe and former FRAPH leader Emmanuel Constant, both who "had ties to the CIA, and were in touch with US officials" during this time.[11]

In 2004, the US then moved in, along with France and Canada, to remove Aristide in the name of restoring peace and order to Haiti—the peace and order which the US had helped to destroy in the first place. As one commentator put it succinctly, Aristide's "inability to maintain order in an atmosphere of US-backed destabilization had provided an excellent pretext for another exercise in 'regime change.'" Aristide was "kidnapped at gunpoint" by the joint US, France and Canadian forces, and "flown without his knowledge to the Central African Republic" on a US military aircraft.[12]

As the *Huffington Post* explained in a post mortem of the coup, "[i]n 2004, the US again destroyed democracy in Haiti. . . ."[13] Between 2004 and 2006, Haiti was ruled by Gerard Latortue. And during these two years, with Aristide gone, and peace and order restored, "Haiti experienced some 4,000 political murders, according to the *Lancet*— while hundreds of Fanmi Lavalas members, Aristide supporters, and social movement leaders were locked up—usually on bogus charges. Latortue's friends in Washington looked the other way"[14] (emphasis added). Haiti's democracy has not recovered. Indeed, "Haiti has remained rocked by political turmoil in the years since. . . ."[15]

Honduras

Another brazen coup of an ALBA nation came in 2009 in Honduras, which deposed democratically-elected Honduran president Manuel Zelaya. As the AP reported at the time, "Honduran President Manuel Zelaya was ousted in a military coup after betraying his own kind: a small clique of families that dominates the economy."[16] Zelaya's biggest sin was to have raised the minimum wage by 60%, infuriating business elites, both domestic and foreign (including, of course, Chiquita Banana).

Given such audacious crimes, Zelaya had to be gotten rid of. And so, the Honduran military took the direct route, kidnapping Zelaya at gun-point in the middle of the night and flying him out of the country to Costa Rica while he was still in his pajamas.

Not surprisingly, the two key military generals who carried out this coup were trained by the US at its infamous US Army School of the Americas (SOA), now located in Columbus, Georgia, and now known as the Western Hemisphere Institute for Security Cooperation (WHINSEC). WHINSEC trained over 500 Honduran officers from 2001 through 2009, and the general who violently kidnapped Zelaya (Romeo Orlando Vásquez Velásquez) is a two-time graduate.[17] Gen. Luis Javier Prince Suazo, the head of the Honduran Air Force, who arranged to have Zelaya flown into exile, was also trained at the School of the Americas.

I say it is not surprising that the coup leaders were trained by the US, for as an "academic named Jonathan Caverley, an associate professor at the Naval War College," concluded in a 2015 working paper, there is a direct link between US military training of foreign troops and "an increased likelihood of military coups."[18]

Meanwhile, more details have recently emerged that show an even closer connection between the US and the coup than once previously known. As a 2017 exposé in the *Intercept* explains, "[h]idden actors during the crisis tilted Honduras toward chaos, undermined official US policy after the coup, and ushered in a new era of militarization that has left a trail of violence and repression in its wake."[19]

In the words of Martin Edwin Andersen—former communications director for the Center for Hemispheric Defense Studies (CHDS) at the US Southern Command, who later turned whistleblower—"some of my senior colleagues at US Southern Command should have been punished for their hands-on role in the coup. To the best of my knowledge none were, even as Honduras now crashes and burns as the most violent country in the Western Hemisphere."[20] Andersen goes on to state that, "[i]n fact, perhaps still unbeknownst to the State Department, part of the real-time coup quarterbacking occurred just blocks from Capitol Hill."

What we now know is that the US and Honduran military officers and diplomats, who generally tend to be thick as thieves, partied together the night before the coup at the house of the US Embassy's defense attaché, Andrew Papp. The very next morning, soldiers kidnapped President Zelaya, took him to Soto Cano, the huge military base that is shared jointly by US and Honduran forces, and then flew him from there out of the country to Costa Rica. While the US military officials at the base claim that they never knew Zelaya was there or that he was flown out of the base, this seems highly unlikely given the fact that (1) the US ambassador was fully aware of the coup by this time; and (2) the Honduran military does not do anything without US approval, especially at the Soto Cano base—the biggest US military base in the region.

In addition, in the months leading up to the coup, the NED—the Reagan-era organization created to use "soft power" to meddle in other country's affairs and even help foment regime change—provided $1.2 million to the International Republican Institute to organize against Zelaya and his reforms, and to support the opposition groups which ended up toppling him.[21]

And, once Zelaya was successfully ousted, the US, and in particular the Pentagon and then–secretary of state Hillary Clinton, made sure that he stayed gone. The Center for Economic and Policy Research explains,[22] "the Pentagon's main interest was in maintaining relations with a close military ally, rather than in overturning the coup. Though the battle over Honduras appeared to be fought along partisan lines, in the end it was the Obama administration's State Department that sabotaged efforts to have Zelaya restored to the presidency, as statements by former Secretary Clinton and other high-level officials admit."

For example, as the *National Catholic Reporter* wrote at the time, while "[t]he Foreign Operations Appropriations Act requires that US military aid and training be suspended when a country undergoes a military coup, and the Obama administration has indicated those steps have been taken," those steps in fact were never taken.

Indeed, as the *NCR* article points out, I, along with Father Roy Bourgeois and other supporters of SOA Watch, personally would witness firsthand the falsehood of Obama's claim when we travelled to Honduras days after the coup.

Our first stop on this trip was to visit the US's Soto Cano Air Base where the US Southern Command's Joint Task Force–Bravo is stationed. The base was humming with activity, seemingly unaffected by the coup which had just happened, and we asked a Sgt. Reyes at the base point blank whether it was true that the US military had halted its joint operations with the Colombian military post-coup. Reyes responded, and I took notes of this at the time, that the US relationship with the Honduran military after the coup was "stable. Nothing has changed. That's just something they're telling the press." In addition, Lee Rials, public affairs officer for WHINSEC, confirmed post-coup that Honduran officers were still being trained at WHINSEC.

As diplomatic cables later obtained through a FOIA request revealed, it turns out that while the US announced on July 1, 2009 that it had "'cut off contact with those who have conducted the coup,'" Secretary of State Clinton secretly countermanded that order the very next day by writing to the US Embassy and "giving approval to 'engage elements of the Honduran Armed Forces and de facto regime'. . . ."[23]

Meanwhile, Col. Andrew Papp, the defense attaché who hosted the party the night before the coup, made it clear to the Honduran military that "we still wanted a relationship when this was all done with" regardless of whether the coup were reversed or not.[24]

For its part, the CHDS in Washington, DC, met with Honduran

military leaders shortly after the coup and apparently gave them a pat on the back for their overthrow of Zelaya on the basis that, in its view, "they prevented socialism from coming 'to the borders of the United States.'" Whistleblower Martin Edwin Andersen explains, in quite colorful terms: "Within days I found that another senior (and far-right) CHDS staff member, a vicious and vocal critic of Obama, and his minions had coordinated meetings for uniformed Honduran coup representatives on Capitol Hill, including the office of at least one now-retired Senator, and other places in our nation's capital, even as deadly 'mop up' operations took place in Tegucigalpa and in the countryside."

In addition, CHDS director Richard Downie later sent a memo to the Department of Defense and State Department saying, in effect, "that the US wouldn't want to push Zelaya back into office and so it would give the coup government some time to set things up before moving on to elections."

Downie later explained, "'that's what ended up happening'"— that is, the coup government moved on with elections without Zelaya having been returned to power and without Zelaya on the ballot. And it was discovered later how this came to be. Thus, recently declassified US military intelligence documents show that while the official position of the US government had been that no elections should go forward without Zelaya, US SOUTHCOM was actually encouraging the coup government to do just that—to hold on until new elections were held in the absence of Zelaya. The coup government took this as its cue and ran with it.

As we would find out later in Hillary Clinton's vanity book, *Hard Choices*, she too had proudly worked behind the scenes to ensure that elections would go forward in Honduras after the coup swiftly, without Zelaya, and in such a way as to "render the question of Zelaya moot." Quite tellingly, Clinton would later excise the above-quoted passage from her book when the paperback edition came out,[25] after she was shocked to realize that people were inexplicably upset by her cynical maneuvers to undermine democracy in Honduras.

One way that the Clinton State Department maneuvered to keep Zelaya from regaining office was to declare in September of 2009 that his ouster from power did not constitute a coup requiring the cutting off of military assistance.[26] This declaration was made against all evidence to the contrary and in contradiction of the US Embassy's earlier conclusion in June that it was an "'open and shut'" case that what happened was an "'illegal and unconstitutional coup.'"[27]

In addition, the State Department went ahead and announced even before elections were held that the US would recognize them even without Zelaya.[28] As the *Intercept* notes, US officials even went so far as to block a resolution at the Organization of American States that called for the restoration of Zelaya to office before elections were held.

The reader might also recall that a key public relations spokesman for the new coup regime was none other than Clinton campaign team member Lanny Davis.[29]

Ultimately, the US stood nearly alone in the Western Hemisphere in recognizing the election of President Porfirio Lobo Sosa that followed the coup, though this election took place in the absence of Zelaya being returned to Honduras and able to participate in the election. Dana Frank, writing in the *New York Times*, explained the significance of this:

> President Obama quickly recognized Mr. Lobo's victory, even when most of Latin America would not. Mr. Lobo's government is, in fact, a child of the coup. It retains most of the military figures who perpetrated the coup, and no one has gone to jail for starting it.
>
> This chain of events—a coup that the United States didn't stop, a fraudulent election that it accepted—has now allowed corruption to mushroom. The judicial system hardly functions. Impunity reigns. At least 34 members of the opposition have disappeared or been killed, and more than 300 people have been killed by state security forces since the coup, according to the leading human rights

organization COFADEH. At least 13 journalists have been killed since Mr. Lobo took office, according to the Committee to Protect Journalists.

Frank, citing a report by the Fellowship of Reconciliation, noted that, "[s]ince the coup the United States has maintained and in some areas increased military and police financing for Honduras and has been enlarging its military bases there. . . ."[30]

One individual who took umbrage at the pro-coup machinations of people like Hillary Clinton was Honduran Berta Cáceras, the acclaimed environmental and human rights activist, who was murdered by members of the Honduran Special Forces in 2016. As Berta was quoted as saying shortly before her death, "We're coming out of a coup that we can't put behind us. We can't reverse it. It just kept going. And after, there was the issue of the elections. The same Hillary Clinton, in her book, *Hard Choices*, practically said what was going to happen in Honduras. This demonstrates the meddling of North Americans in our country."[31]

Clinton was responsible for Berta's plight in one other significant way. Clinton's State Department year-after-year certified that the Honduras military was in compliance with US human rights criteria, despite its violent persecution of activists, thereby allowing military aid to be freed up for Honduras. The State Department did so even the year that Berta was murdered.[32]

And, it has been revealed that, not too surprisingly, the Special Forces who actually killed Berta were themselves trained by the US. As the *Guardian* recently reported:

Leaked court documents raise concerns that the murder of the Honduran environmentalist Berta Cáceres was an extrajudicial killing planned by military intelligence specialists linked to the country's US–trained special forces, a Guardian investigation can reveal.

A legal source close to the investigation told the Guardian: "The murder of Berta Cáceres has all the characteristics of a well-planned operation designed by military intelligence, where it is absolutely normal to contract civilians as assassins."[33]

To this day, the US remains closely allied to Honduras, continuing to use it as a giant military base from which to project its power throughout the region. Indeed, Honduras has once been described as "USS Honduras"—"a stationary, unsinkable aircraft carrier, strategically anchored" in the middle of Latin America.[34] And, the terrible repression unleashed by the 2009 coup continues at the hands of a military the US continues to support. Indeed, as CEPR explains, "[s]ince the coup, the militarization of Honduras has increased. While human rights abuses continue to shock the public, US security assistance and military training continue unabated."

As Latin American specialist Greg Grandin recently explained, "hundreds of peasant activists and indigenous activists have been killed. Scores of gay rights activists have been killed. . . . [I]t's just a nightmare in Honduras. . . . And Berta Cáceres, in that interview, says what was installed after the coup was something like a permanent counterinsurgency on behalf of transnational capital. And that was— that wouldn't have been possible if it were not for Hillary Clinton's normalization of that election, or legitimacy."[35]

In addition, Honduras is the most dangerous country in the hemisphere to be a journalist, with scores of journalists killed since the 2009 coup.[36] Moreover, as has recently been reported, the Garifunas— Hondurans of African descent who have been there for centuries—are being subjected to intense discrimination and are being forced off their land in large numbers by real estate developers and others who covet their land, with many being forced to leave Honduras altogether.[37]

And all of this post-coup repression was not accidental, but was in fact part of the plan for those in Washington who supported the coup. As whistleblower Martin Edwin Andersen explained in a sworn affidavit, there was not only "involvement in the Honduran coup" by senior colleagues at Southern Command Key, but also "behind the scenes advocacy of death squads by people who literally met privately with hundreds of active-duty Latin American military officers each year. . . ." He goes on to explain that this revelation "was accompanied by my discovery that another CHDS colleague had worked for [Chilean dictator Augusto] Pinochet's DINA death squad operation. It was DINA that had killed an exiled foreign minister, Orlando Letelier, and his American assistant, Ronni Moffitt, in a car bombing near the White House, one of the gravest terrorist attacks in our nation's capital before 9/11."

Andersen ends his affidavit with the following question: "Are not the clandestine and unpunished involvement in the Honduran coup, as well as the promotion of torture and murder, challenges to the rule of law as well as fundamental American values?" Sadly, history has shown that the answer to this question is a resounding no.

Nicaragua

Against great odds and the will of the US, the Sandinistas would be voted back into power in 2006 after 16 years in the wilderness, and they remain the governing party to this day, with Daniel Ortega as president. However, the US has been working hard to oust Ortega since the day he was elected in 2006, and the US came very close to doing so in the summer of 2018.

With the 2006 election of Ortega came great social advances for Nicaragua. Luca Di Fabio, writing quite recently for the anti-poverty NGO, The Borgen Project, explained that "[t]he amount of economic growth in Nicaragua is an unusual and unprecedented phenomenon in the Central American peninsula," and that "[e]xperts argue that such improvements in economic growth in Nicaragua are largely attributable to the re-election of President Daniel Ortega" who led the country to annual economic growth of nearly 5% every year since 2011, and who helped reduce poverty in Nicaragua by 30%.[38]

The independent Latin American Geopolitical Strategic Center

(CELAG) further explains how Ortega successfully took Nicaragua down a different path than his neighbors, leading to a more prosperous, stable and peaceful country. As CELAG concludes:

> It should be said that Nicaragua has important differences with neighbors such as Honduras, Guatemala and even El Salvador, countries that after the Peace Accords were prosecuted towards violent neoliberalism through various initiatives, mostly sponsored by the US government-private sector (read, for example, the Initiative for the Security of Central America and the Alliance for Prosperity). Within the framework of these plans, there has been a growing militarization and an upsurge of violence, in the style of Plan Colombia.
>
> Unlike these trajectories, Nicaragua shows (with the limitations and contradictions that must be pointed out) economic growth and poverty reduction, its security indices are infinitely greater than those of the countries of the Northern Triangle and its residents have not had to flee to the US border in search of better lives in the same proportion as Salvadorans, Guatemalans and Hondurans have done it. . . .[39]

And so again, we see Ortega continuing to bring peace and stability to Nicaragua. The result was that, as of October of 2017, he had nearly an 80% approval rating.[40] Moreover, in 2017, Nicaragua polled the highest in all of Latin America on the issue of whether the government was leading in the interests of all of the people, and it polled second on the overall evaluation of the functioning of its democracy.[41]

Finally, and most incredibly, in 2018 Nicaragua was ranked number 5 in the world for gender equality by the World Economic Forum (WEF).[42] The only four countries ranked higher were the usual suspects—Iceland, Norway, Sweden and Finland. Meanwhile, Nicaragua ranked above every other nation in the Americas, including the United States. Not too shabby. As one article summarized the WEF report[43],

The WEF annual reports, this year based on information from 149 countries, are a benchmark for capturing the magnitude of gender based disparities and tracking their progress. Countries are ranked according to economic participation and opportunity; educational attainment; health and survival; and political empowerment.

. . . Particularly noteworthy is Nicaragua's second position on political empowerment, and first position in terms of the ratio of women in ministerial positions. This is a result of a 50–50 law that mandates gender equality in party candidate lists for elections.

Nicaragua is ranked first on the criteria of health and survival, a testimony to the success of government health care programmes.

The US could not sit idly by as a political movement it had spent millions to destroy was demonstrating such seemingly-impossible success. It had to destroy this "danger of a good example," in the words of Noam Chomsky. It seized upon the opportunity presented by demonstrations against Ortega's announcement of very modest social security reforms on April 16, 2018, to spring its forces into action. The US and its allies in Nicaragua would run the same game plan run in so many other attempts at regime change—to create violent provocations which would lead to a reaction by the state which then could be blamed for the ensuing chaos. The plan worked like a charm, at least for three terrifying months.

The independent Nicaraguan media collective, *Tortilla Con Sal*, summarized the initial moves of what the Nicaraguan government is now portraying as a "soft coup":

During the days 19, 20 and 21 of April the armed groups of the political opposition mixed with students and young people and also integrated hundreds of delinquents recruited of different cities with the purpose of intensifying the attacks. They attacked all kinds of infrastructure with firearms . . . and Molotov cocktails. Since its inception, the protests have been very violent. Nevertheless, an image of

disproportionate repression and even speech of "massacres" has been
projected by means of a tremendous machinery of disinformation in
the social networks and the news media of the private company and
its international allies. An important component of misinformation
has been the manipulation of the figures of the dead and wounded.[44]

And, as the days passed, the brutality and violence of the extreme
opposition groups only increased. This violence greatly resembled
that of the Contras in the 1980s. John Perry, an American living in
Masaya, Nicaragua—the eye of the storm during this period—detailed
the violence which he and his Nicaraguan wife witnessed first-hand:

> In the first [phase of the protests], barricades that had been removed
> were re-erected, again blocking streets, with Masaya again the most
> affected. The "peaceful" protesters armed themselves with home-
> made mortars, repelling attempts by the police or Sandinista sup-
> porters to regain control. Rival marches took place, in many cases
> without problems, but friends of mine took part in a "peace" march
> that was greeted by hails of stones and mortar fire. A wave of destruc-
> tion began, focusing first on Sandinista offices, then moving on to
> public buildings, including town halls and in some cases schools and
> health centers. Houses of some Sandinista supporters in Masaya
> were ransacked or burned down. According to neighbors who wit-
> nessed it, alongside genuine protesters were unemployed youths paid
> $10–15 per night, some brought in by lorry, defending the barricades,
> attacking the police, and ransacking shops.[45]

And, while the Nicaraguan government, the subject of one of the wildest and deceptive media campaigns ever waged against a government,
was being accused of using "genocidal" violence during this crisis, this
is a characterization more applicable to the extreme opposition. As the
Morning Star of the UK relates:

A source in the city of Esteli told the *Star*: "Here in Esteli now the opposition are marking the houses of people identified as Sandinista."

> We're all taking what precautions we can, but I don't think the opposition are in the least interested in dialogue. They are determined not just to oust the government but to destroy the FSLN [Sandinista National Liberation Front].[46]

I have heard such stories from a number of sources in Nicaragua who believe, as the witness does above, that the violent opposition is bent upon destroying the FSLN and indeed all memories of it, for example by destroying Sandinista memorials throughout Nicaragua.

Meanwhile, each Sandinista, government employee and police officer killed is manipulatively placed in the tally of dead allegedly killed by the state. George Orwell could not conjure up a more dastardly tale of media manipulation.

And, of course, in the background of all of this is the United States, which continues its efforts to unseat the Sandinistas who had the audacity to overthrow the US-backed dictator in 1979. As we learned from journalist Max Blumenthal, "a publication funded by the US government's regime change arm, the National Endowment for Democracy (NED), bluntly asserted that *organizations backed by the NED have spent years and millions of dollars 'laying the groundwork for insurrection' in Nicaragua*"[47] (emphasis added). And, that groundwork bore the desired, bad fruit.

Meanwhile, the United States continues to punish Nicaragua, the most stable and prosperous country in Central America after successfully breaking off from US domination, for its impertinence in overthrowing the Somoza dictatorship, having the audacity to survive the Contra War which claimed fifty thousand lives, voting back in the Sandinistas, and for now working with the Chinese to build the canal that the United States has coveted for so long. Thus, the US Congress has recently, and unanimously, passed the NICA Act, which will cut

Nicaragua off from multilateral loans (e.g., from the World Bank, IMF). This, apparently, will show Nicaragua and other countries what they get for deciding to go their own way.

I leave this discussion with the conclusory words of CELAG which, though clearly quite critical of Daniel Ortega, expresses the proper concerns about the current events in Nicaragua:

> What is happening in Nicaragua is of the utmost gravity. It is, together with Costa Rica, the only country in Central America that maintains political, economic, social and security lines that seek to go beyond neoliberal orthodoxy, albeit in a contradictory and ambivalent manner, in a region plunged in misery and violence. But, unlike Costa Rica, Nicaragua does it without bowing to the interests of US foreign policy. . . . [I]t is fundamental to consider the importance of Nicaragua in the regional geopolitics, the interests that may be at stake and the sectors that could be looking to destabilize the government of the day. This does not imply that there is no discontent in different sectors of society. But what is striking is the way in which this disagreement is channeled, the way in which it is being presented by the hegemonic press and the arguments that are raised as the main complaints or claims to the government. . . .
>
> It is important to visualize, keep in mind, what happened in the countries that enjoyed "democratic springs" in the last decades: Who took power? What transformations were there? In favor of what sectors? What role did the USA play? Maybe after each spring 2.0 what is anticipated, more than a summer, is another long neoliberal winter without any obstacle or claim on the part of the international community.[48]

Brazil

This biggest prize for the US was Brazil, a country with a larger land mass than the US, with one of the biggest economies in the Western Hemisphere, and with a long border with Venezuela.

To take down Brazil as a key ALBA nation and ally of Venezuela, the US would have to remove and sideline Luiz Inacio Lula da Silva (president 2003–2010) and Dilma Rousseff (president 2011–2016) of the PT (Workers Party), and the US did so through what has come to be called a "legal coup."

The US had a hand in the take-down of Lula and Dilma, and for the same reasons the US intervened to forcibly oust Brazil's president João Goulart through a brutal military coup in 1964. As the award-winning investigative online journal, *Consortium News*, has explained:

> The significance of this historical record is the demonstration that the last time Brazil had a "mildly social democratic" government [Goulart], the US cooperated in its removal. The next social democratic government would be the now removed PT government of Presidents Luiz Inacio Lula da Silva and Dilma Rousseff.
>
> Since Lula da Silva took office in 2003, government policies have been credited for lifting millions of Brazilians out of poverty and making Brazil a powerful independent player on the world stage.
>
> In 2009, Lula da Silva was a key figure in the creation of the BRICS organization of emerging economies (Brazil, Russia, India, China and South Africa), representing a challenge to the dominance of the US-based International Monetary Fund and the World Bank. Among other initiatives, BRICS has called for a new global reserve currency, a direct threat to the power of the US dollar.[49]

Such blatant support for the poor, coupled with an audacious assertion of independence in the US's own "backyard," is simply unacceptable. And so, the US, through its Department of Justice (DOJ), has worked hand-in-glove with Brazilian prosecutors in an "anti-corruption" crusade known as *Lava Jato* to target progressive leaders such as Lula and Dilma while ushering in the truly corrupt Brazilian politicians, and sympathizers with the military dictatorship, to power.

As an exposé in *Truthdig* explains,

Despite public ignorance and its root in the media blind spot on this matter, US involvement in Brazil's Anti-Corruption Operation Lava Jato, which has already resulted in $3bn payout to North American investors, is not some fringe theory, as some like to pretend—US Acting Attorney General Kenneth Blanco has publicly boasted about it himself:

"It is hard to imagine a better cooperative relationship in recent history than that of the United States Department of Justice and the Brazilian prosecutors. We have cooperated and substantially assisted one another on a number of public matters that have now been resolved, and are continuing to do so on a number of ongoing investigations.

The cooperation between the Department and Brazil has led to extraordinary results. . . . Indeed, just this past week, the prosecutors in Brazil won a guilty verdict against former President Lula da Silva. . . ."[50]

As noted in a recent letter to the *Guardian* by a number of noted British professors, "[t]here is overwhelming evidence of his [Lula's] innocence and that he has been tried unfairly and imprisoned so as to deny his legitimate right to stand in October's presidential elections, where he is currently leading in the polls. Legal experts in Brazil and around the world have pointed to the irregularities of his trial and the questionable circumstances of his imprisonment."[51] The United Nations Human Rights Committee has even ruled that Brazil must allow the imprisoned Lula to stand for re-election—an election he would be certain to win—but the current government is refusing to honor this demand.[52]

But this is all quite acceptable to the US, which has weaponized anti-corruption prosecutions to remove politicians it does not like from contention. Incredibly, the US DOJ is able to sideline such politicians even in other countries thousands of miles away. The reverse—for example, Russia helping prosecute and impeach politicians in the US—would simply be unthinkable, and quite rightly so.

The joint US-Brazil *Lavo Jato* program also led to the impeachment of President Dilma, whose personal phone conversations were intercepted and taped by the Obama Administration,[53] from office. The absurdity of her impeachment for alleged corruption was well-expressed by David Miranda in an opinion piece in London's the *Guardian* newspaper, entitled, "The Real Reason Dilma Rousseff's Enemies Want Her Impeached":

It is impossible to convincingly march behind a banner of "anti-corruption" and "democracy" when simultaneously working to install the country's most corruption-tainted and widely disliked political figures. . . .

A *New York Times* article last week reported that "60% of the 594 members of Brazil's Congress"—the ones voting to impeach Rousseff—"face serious charges like bribery, electoral fraud, illegal deforestation, kidnapping and homicide". By contrast, said the article, Rousseff "is something of a rarity among Brazil's major political figures: she has not been accused of stealing for herself".

Last Sunday's televised, raucous spectacle in the lower house received global attention because of some repellent (though revealing) remarks made by impeachment advocates. One of them, prominent right-wing congressman Jair Bolsonaro—widely expected to run for president and who a recent poll shows is the leading candidate among Brazil's richest—said he was casting his vote in honour of a human-rights-abusing colonel in Brazil's military dictatorship who was personally responsible for Rousseff's torture [while in jail for organizing against the dictatorship]. His son, Eduardo, proudly cast his vote in honour of "the military men of '64"—the ones who led the coup.[54]

In other words, in typical fashion, the US, in the name of "democracy promotion," is helping bring about a coup very like the one it helped give birth to in 1964, and with the same results—results which, while horrifying for the people of Brazil, are quite advantageous to the US's interest of maximizing its exploitation of Brazil.

Thus, the removal of Dilma from office paved the way for the privatization of the Brazil's national oil company, Petrobras, and its "being sold off for cents to foreign producers such as US Chevron & ExxonMobil, UK's BP & Shell, and Norway's Statoil, at an estimated loss of R$1 trillion—funds once earmarked by Dilma Rousseff for a revolution in public education & health investment," and to the "decimation of worker's rights and overhaul of the pension system, all demanded by Wall Street. . . ."[55] And the sidelining of Lula in prison guarantees that these processes will not be reversed.

At the same time, the ousting of Lula and Dilma has allowed for the security forces and paramilitary groups to wipe out land rights and indigenous activists through mass murder. In 2017 alone, 57 land rights activists were murdered throughout Brazil, and such slaughter was the direct consequence of the weakening of institutions which Lula and Dilma created to protect them. Thus, as the *LA Times* recently explained:

> According to Global Witness, a nongovernmental organization that tracks the exploitation of indigenous people and their resources, 2017 was not only the most lethal year on record for environmental activists in Brazil, but one of the deadliest in any country. Global Witness said its tally in Brazil is probably an undercount because its methodology requires that it identify each victim by name, which can be a challenge because some potential victims live in highly isolated areas.
>
> The peril for land defenders in Brazil is not expected to improve anytime soon, the group says.
>
> "On paper, Brazil has many of the policies and institutions that

could solve this problem and protect the rights and well-being of ordinary Brazilians, but this government is weakening those institutions in favor of facilitating big business," said Ben Leather, senior campaigner for Global Witness.

In 2017, state agency FUNAI, which is responsible for protecting indigenous peoples' rights in Brazil, had its budget slashed in half, forcing it to close several regional offices. INCRA, the state agency responsible for redistributing land to small-scale farmers and Afrodescendants who live on lands called *quilombos*, had its budget cut by 30%.[56]

The words of Chomsky and Herman about the aftermath of the 1964 military coup are just as applicable to the current situation post-"legal coup": "[t]he state functions to prevent by force any defense of the rural majority and to allow the powerful to violate the already feeble law with impunity." And, with the October 28, 2018 election of close US ally Jair Bolsonaro—an election made possible with the continued jailing of Lula de Silva on bogus charges—the state will play this role with a vengeance, for Bolsonaro has been very clear that one of his chief goals as president is to open up Brazil's rainforests even more dramatically for capital penetration and exploitation.[57]

As I write this chapter, I learn of another land rights activist and indigenous leader, Jorginho Guajajara, a leader of the Guajajara people, murdered in Brazil in retaliation for his anti-logging activism.[58] The Amazon he was fighting to protect is literally the lungs of this world which we depend upon to breathe and survive. His death, which can be attributed to the meddling of our own government in his country's domestic affairs, and other deaths like his may guarantee that humanity's days on this earth are numbered.

THE WAR FOR VENEZUELA'S OIL INTENSIFIES

One [goal of US regime change efforts] is to take control again over Venezuelan resources, especially the very large oil reserves. Washington has never forgiven Chavez for nationalizing the oil and using the revenues from the oil flows for Venezuela rather than for the profits of American firms. So it's aimed at installing an American puppet that Washington has selected as president, who will privatize the oil company and other resources so that Americans can renew the exploitation of the country.[59]

—Paul Craig Roberts, Assistant Treasury
Secretary for President Ronald Reagan

THE STRATEGY OF MAKING THE ECONOMY of a country targeted for regime "scream," and then blaming the targeted government for the resulting woes of the people, is a tried and true one of the US. And indeed, the US is doing the very same to Venezuela as it did to Chile, Iran, Cuba and Nicaragua.

Indeed, the US has been economically attacking Venezuela for nearly 20 years now in order to overturn the government of Hugo Chavez and his successor Nicolas Maduro. As UN Expert Alfred de Zayas explains, after his intensive study of the situation in Venezuela, the crisis in that country is not the result of failures of the Bolivarian Revolution, but rather, the many-years assault against it by the West. As de Zayas writes,[1] the crisis

> is the result of the cumulative impacts of 20 years of internal and external economic war, financial blockade, and sanctions. The main-stream narrative attributes the crisis to incompetence and corruption, but these also plague most Latin American countries. Besides, the level of corruption in Venezuela in the 1980's and 1990's was higher and Chavez won the 1998 elections on a wave of disgust at the corruption of the neo-liberal governments. I spent two hours with the current Attorney General in Caracas, from whom I received ample documentation on the government's vigorous anti-corruption campaign, investigations and on-going prosecutions.
>
> US efforts to topple Chavez started early, and the CIA cooperated with the Venezuelan oligarchy in the failed coup against Chavez on 11/12 April 2002. The 48-hour President Pedro Carmona had promptly issued a decree doing away with 49 pieces of social legislation, suspending the Supreme Court, the Chavez National Assembly, dismissing governors, etc. Although there is nothing more undemocratic than a coup—Carmona and the US media spoke of "restoring democracy" in Venezuela.

And, de Zayas is clear that this campaign against Venezuela has nothing to do with humanitarian concerns, but rather, to steal that country's vast resources. According to de Zayas, "'Human Rights' has nothing to do with the US Venezuela policy. As it was in Iraq 2003 and Libya 2011, it is OIL. The US covets the largest oil reserves in the world, as well as the third largest reserves in gold and coltan. If Maduro is toppled, it will be a bonanza for US investors and transnational corporations."

Dr. de Zayas concludes his piece with the following warning: "History shows us that sanctions kill, and when the level of killing reaches a certain threshold, sanctions become a crime against humanity. This is a worthy challenge for the International Criminal Court. What Venezuela needs is an end to sanctions and interference in its internal affairs," which, de Zayas notes, amount to "violations of Articles 1–2 of the UN Charter and of articles 3, 19 and 20 of the OAS Charter. . . ."

It is worthy to note here, that while there appears to be a large consensus about the legitimacy of using economic sanctions against a country like Venezuela to bend it to its will—with even human rights groups such as the Washington Office on Latin America (WOLA) supporting Trump's draconian sanctions of August, 2017[2]—such sanctions are not only illegal, but indeed quite violent and quite deadly.

As respected human rights professor and former board member of Amnesty International (AI), Francis A. Boyle, explains, human rights groups have sadly failed to understand this reality. In 2012, Professor Boyle explained, for example, how AI itself aided and abetted the economic campaign against Iraq waged by the West[3]:

> During the past eight years, about 1.5 million People in Iraq have died as a result of genocidal sanctions imposed upon them primarily at the behest of the United States and Britain, including in that number about 500,000 dead Iraqi children. While on the AIUSA Board of Directors, I tried to get them and AI/London to do something about this genocidal embargo against the People of Iraq, and especially against the Iraqi Children. Both AI/London and AIUSA adamantly refused to act. . . .

And, it should be kept in mind that, as devastating as the sanctions regime was to Iraq, "the Venezuelan people have been even more vulnerable to US economic sanctions than Iraqis were. Venezuela is dependent on oil exports for almost all of the dollars the economy needs to import necessities such as medicine and food. This means that anything that reduces oil production is primarily hitting the general population by cutting off the dollars that both the private sector and government use to import goods for people's basic needs, as well as for transport, spare parts, and most goods that the economy needs in order to function."[4]

Meanwhile, the biggest blows the US was able to levy against Venezuela commenced in 2014 with the attack against the price of its main revenue source—oil. It was then that the US, with the connivance of its good friend Saudi Arabia—not exactly the paragon of democracy and human rights in the world—worked together to artificially depress the price of oil with the express intention of undermining the economies of countries like Iran and Russia.[5] However, the country most damaged by this maneuver was Venezuela, whose economy was "destroyed" by it.[6] As the *Independent* explains:

> It seems, after some hesitation and discussions in the early part of 2014, Saudi Arabia launched this oil price war in tandem with the US. America supported the policy as it wanted to undermine the influence of oil-dependent Russia, something it apparently considered more important than supporting its own fracking sector, while access to cheap imported oil is good news for US consumers and industry in general. Whether or not there was a clearly planned and agreed strategy, there seems to be an unmistakable convergence of interests between the Saudi and US positions.
>
> This strategy of keeping the price of oil down has not necessarily destroyed either the Russian or Iranian economies however. Instead, the hardest hit oil-producing nations are in South America and Africa, where petro-states such as Libya, Angola, and Nigeria are suffering.
>
> But the worst affected country of all is Venezuela, the most disastrously oil-dependent state in the world. Oil accounts for 96 per cent of exports and more than 40 per cent of government revenues.[7]

If this were not bad enough, President Obama, smelling blood in the proverbial water, then began imposing sanctions against Venezuela in

2015. Obama did so, just as Trump recently did in his bid to build a border wall, by "'declaring a national emergency with respect to the unusual and extraordinary threat to the national security and foreign policy of the United States posed by the situation in Venezuela,' Obama put it in a letter to House Speaker John Boehner."[8] Obama would twice make the preposterous claim that Venezuela somehow presented an "unusual and extraordinary threat to national security,"[9] though such a claim does not even pass the laugh test.

Of course, it is the reverse which is undeniably true—that the US poses an extraordinary threat to Venezuela.

In declaring such a national emergency to justify his economic war against Venezuela, Obama was taking a page out of Ronald Reagan's playbook against Nicaragua. As economist and Latin American expert Mark Weisbrot explains, this was precisely

> the approach of President Ronald Reagan in 1985 when he made a similar declaration in order to impose sanctions—including an economic embargo—on Nicaragua. Like the White House today, he was trying to topple an elected government that Washington didn't like. He was able to use paramilitary and terrorist violence as well as an embargo in a successful effort to destroy the Nicaraguan economy and ultimately overturn its government.[10]

While the press has downplayed the effects of Obama's Venezuela sanctions, and certainly never questioned how Venezuela could possibly pose a threat to US national security, these sanctions were nonetheless devastating for Venezuela and the Venezuelan people. Again, Mark Weisbrot:

> The sanctions imposed by the Obama administration in March 2015 . . . also had a very serious impact. This is well-known in financial institutions, but generally not reported in the major media, which treat these sanctions as they are advertised by the US government, as

"sanctions against individuals." But when the individuals are high-level government officials, for example the finance minister, the sanctions cause enormous problems, as these officials are cut off from necessary transactions in most of the world financial system.

Financial institutions increasingly turned away from Venezuela after March 2015, as they saw the risks of lending to a government that the United States was increasingly determined to topple—and, as the economy worsened, looked more likely to succeed in doing so. The Venezuelan private sector was cut off from vital access to credit, which contributed to the unprecedented, indeed almost unbeliev-able, 80 percent drop in imports over the past six years, which has devastated this import-dependent economy.[11]

Obama's regime plans for Venezuela have only been accelerated with the presidency of Donald Trump. As one commentator sums it up:

Soon after Donald Trump assumed the Presidency, Senator Marco Rubio (R-FL) and Vice President Mike Pence began a concerted cam-paign to convince Trump to adopt a plan to oust elected Venezuelan President Nicolas Maduro. As the *New York Times* reported, "Mr. Rubio's approach has generated unusually bipartisan support, including from leading Democrats like Senators Richard J. Durbin of Illinois and Robert Menendez of New Jersey."[12]

Trump was brought on board quickly, upping the ante against Venezuela in August of 2017, by imposing heightened sanctions which made it impossible for Venezuela to obtain international financing. These sanctions, the most severe up to that point, when piled upon Obama's, crippled Venezuela's economy—an economy already reeling from the artificially-depressed oil prices. As Mark Weisbrot explains:

The Trump sanctions of August 2017 imposed a financial embargo that cut Venezuela off from most borrowing. This had an enormous impact on oil production, which had already been declining. The rate of decline accelerated rapidly; during the year following the sanctions, it would fall by 700,000 barrels a day, about three times as fast as it had fallen over the previous 20 months. This post-sanction acceleration in the loss of oil production amounts to the loss of more than $6 billion. For comparison, Venezuela, when the economy was growing, spent about $2 billion per year on medicines. Total goods imports for 2018 are estimated at $11.7 billion.

At the time of these sanctions, Venezuela was already suffering from a deep recession and balance-of-payments problems that necessitated a debt restructuring. To restructure the debt, the government has to be able to issue new bonds, but the US sanctions made this impossible.

The Trump sanctions—both the August 2017 sanctions and now the new oil embargo—also make it pretty near impossible for the government to take measures that would end the hyperinflation, currently estimated at 1.6 million percent annually. To stabilize hyperinflation, you have to restore faith in the domestic currency. This would very likely be done through creating a new exchange-rate system and other measures that would require access to the dollar-based international financial system—but the sanctions preclude that.[13]

The human toll of these Trump sanctions has been enormous. Thus, an April 25, 2019 report of the Center for Economic Policy Research produced by Mark Weisbrot and world-renowned economist Jeffrey Sachs demonstrates that over 40,000 Venezuelans have been killed so far as a result; specifically by preventing them from receiving food and life-saving medicine—including medicines for HIV, cancer, diabetes, hypertension, and kidney treatment.

In addition to the official sanctions, there have been numerous acts of economic sabotage being carried out by the private sector against Venezuela, and specifically against the Venezuelan people. As Dr. de Zayas explained in his official UN report of December, 2017,[14] international criminal groups are responsible for theft of public resources, food items and medicines, which have found their way into neighbouring countries, affecting the enjoyment of human rights by populations for whom these resources were originally intended. . . . In Venezuela there has been widespread sabotage of public property, arson against public buildings, hospitals and other institutions, destruction of electricity and telephone lines, etc., sometimes associated with electoral campaigns. I am concerned about reports I have received about these acts of sabotage, which could even be considered under the rubric "terrorism".

Dr. de Zayas also notes his concern about "hoarding, black market activities, induced inflation, and contraband in food and medicines."

Specific examples of attempts by private actors to increase misery in Venezuela include US-based Citibank's refusal to accept Venezuelan monies for the purchase of 300,000 doses of insulin;[15] Colombia firm BSN medical's refusal to send malaria medicine to Venezuela *after* accepting Venezuela's payment for it;[16] the Belgian financial services company Euroclear's blocking of "$450 million earmarked primarily for the purchase of drugs and food abroad"[17]; and numerous instances of large quantities of food, medicine and household items being hoarded, and in some cases, burned by opposition forces.[18]

Then, to try to influence the 2018 Venezuelan presidential elections—elections I observed in Caracas—President Trump threatened that he would impose more sanctions if Venezuela went to the polls and voted for Nicolas Maduro.[19] Even more concerning, Trump and other White House officials openly threatened a military invasion of Venezuela unless Maduro were removed.[20] As one commentator explains[21],

Last August [2017], President Trump casually mentioned a "military option" for Venezuela from his golf course in New Jersey, provoking an uproar in Latin America but barely a peep in Washington.

Similarly, Rex Tillerson, then-Secretary of State, spoke favorably about a possible military ouster of Venezuelan president Nicolás Maduro.

In recent months, opinion pieces suggesting that a coup or a foreign military intervention in Venezuela might be a good thing have dotted the US media landscape: from the *Washington Post* to Project Syndicate to *The New York Times*. Occasionally a pundit argues that a coup d'état could have undesirable consequences, for instance if a hypothetical coup regime should decide to deepen relations with Russia or China.

Rarely does anyone point out that this is an insane debate to be having in the first place, particularly regarding a country where elections occur frequently and are, with few exceptions, considered to be competitive and transparent. On Sunday, May 20th, Maduro will be up for reelection. Polls suggest that, if turnout is high, he could be voted out of office.

The fact that coups, not elections, are the hot topic is a sad reflection of the warped direction that the mainstream discussion on Venezuela has taken.

Threatening a country and its electorate with sanctions and invasion if they do not vote the "right" way is a form of extortion, pure and simple, and there can be no greater way of attempting to influence an election outcome. The threat of invasion, moreover, is clear violation of Article 2(4) of the UN Charter which explicitly forbids both the use and "threat of force." Again, there was certainly a rogue and lawless nation in action here, and it wasn't Venezuela.

In addition to his attempt to change the outcome of the 2018 presidential elections, Trump took actions to ensure that, whatever the outcome, he would be able to declare the elections illegitimate and a sham. Thus, as long-time Venezuela observer Alex Main explains, Trump first tried to coerce the opposition candidate, business leader Henri Falcon, from running at all in the election. And, when this didn't work, he urged Venezuelan voters to stay home. As Main relates,

> the Trump administration, after unsuccessfully threatening Falcón with individual financial sanctions if he didn't give up his candidacy, has supported the election boycott by more hardline opposition sectors that see Falcón, who was a Chávez ally until 2010, as too willing to compromise with *chavistas* if elected. The US administration has even threatened sanctions targeting Venezuelan oil if the elections are held. Sources indicate that when both Falcón and the Venezuelan government requested that the UN send an international observation team to monitor the elections, US officials intervened to ensure that no such monitoring effort would take place.
>
> With the US government and Venezuela's opposition doing their best to empower hard-liners' call for a boycott, there is a high probability that turnout from the opposition camp will be low and that Maduro will win the election by a strong margin. We can expect the administration to immediately denounce a "fraudulent" and "illegitimate" process and take further actions that will make life even more difficult for ordinary Venezuelans.[22]

And, of course, this is exactly what happened—there was a relatively low voter turnout, with about 47% of the electorate voting, and 68% of these voted for Nicolas Maduro. And so, Maduro was re-elected, and quite properly so, but Trump, with nearly unanimous media support, has successfully been able to paint these elections as somehow illegitimate because of the predictably low voter turnout and the resultant lopsided vote.

Meanwhile, Trump and his posse continued to double down on their regime change operations. One key piece of the plan was to find a leader amenable to US interests in Venezuela. And so, in late 2018, after some initial talks between Trump officials and rogue Venezuelan military officers about a military coup which never materialized,

[t]he focus shifted to finding some figurehead who could claim to be the "legitimate" Venezuelan ruler. After considering various opposition politicians, Rubio and Pence settled on the little-known engineer serving as president of the Venezuelan National Assembly, Juan Guaidó. According to AP and the *Washington Post*, the preparations for the current coup and secret meetings with Guaidó date back at least to December, 2018. "In mid-December, Guaido quietly traveled to Washington, Colombia and Brazil to brief officials on the opposition's strategy of mass demonstrations to coincide with Maduro's expected swearing-in for a second term on Jan 10 . . . "

On Tuesday, January 22, Trump, Pence and National Security Advisor John Bolton met to discuss options. According to the *Times*, Pence advised Trump to assure Guaidó that the US would recognize his bid for power if, by chance, he were to make such a claim. Trump agreed. Later that day, Pence called Guaidó to give him the good news. Pence then posted a video online asserting that elected President "Nicolas Maduro is a dictator with no legitimate claim to power." In the video, Pence went on to proclaim US support for Guaidó. Then, surprise, surprise: Guaidó claimed he was the rightful president the very next day. The Trump administration and US imperial allies around the world quickly endorsed Guaidó's claim.

Shortly after declaring himself "interim president," Guaidó moved to seize Venezuelan oil revenue held in the US so as to use those funds to finance his assault. As the *Washington Post* reported, "For now, the hope is to use the newly declared interim government as a tool to deny Maduro the oil revenue from the United States that provides Venezuela virtually all of its incoming cash, current and former US officials said."[23]

Guaido, who has "pledged mass privatizations and harsh rounds of austerity" if he takes power, was unknown to Venezuelans prior to being hand-chosen by the Trump Administration to lead Venezuela.[24] Indeed, at the time he declared himself president, one poll showed that 80% of Venezuelans had never heard of him before. But why should that be an impediment to the US's "democracy promotion" plans for the country?[25]

Meanwhile, Trump has just announced a new, and even more damaging round of sanctions. He is planning to sanction Venezuela's Social & Economic Development Bank (Bandes), and its subsidiaries located in neighboring countries, namely Banco Prodem in Bolivia and Banco Bandes Uruguay. As *Telesur* explains, "[t]he new sanctions on the financial sector intend to block the implementation of social and productive plans promoted by the public and private economic agents of Venezuela"; that is, it is aimed at the heart of Venezuela's ability to provide necessary social programs and services for the Venezuelan people.[26]

These sanctions will affect 23 million individuals. In addition, according to the Venezuelan government, "the Trump administration now vows to cripple other 'important Venezuelan financial institutions,' with an aim to curtail the Bolivarian Republic's 'right to its integral development and to the sustainability of its national and international financial system.'"[27]

While the US government and its captive media claim that this regime change operation is justified by the US's intentions to help the Venezuelan people, these types of sanctions prove that quite the opposite is true. And indeed, one need just scratch the surface to see what the true, primary purpose is: to control Venezuela's vast oil supplies.

* * *

A great, succinct summary of the CIA's operations in 1953 to make Iran's oil safe for Western exploitation, and the intense repression that followed, can be found in Dean Henderson's *Big Oil & Their Bankers in the Persian Gulf*:

> Wherever the Four Horsemen (Exxon Mobil, Chevron Texaco, BP Amoco & Royal Dutch/Shell) gallop the CIA is close behind. Iran

was no exception. By 1957 the Company, as intelligence insiders know the CIA, created one of its first Frankensteins—the Shah of Iran's brutal secret police known as SAVAK.

Kermit Roosevelt, the Mossadegh *coup*-master turned Northrop salesman, admitted in his memoirs that SAVAK was 100% created by the CIA and Mossad, the Israeli intelligence agency that acts as appendage of the CIA. For the next 20 years the CIA and SAVAK were joined at the hip when it came to matters of Persian Gulf security.

Three hundred fifty SAVAK agents were shuttled each year to CIA training facilities in McLean, Virginia, where they learned the finer arts of interrogation and torture. . . .

From 1957–79 Iran housed 125,000 political prisoners. SAVAK "disappeared" dissenters, a strategy replicated by CIA surrogate dictators in Argentina and Chile.

. . . In 1974 the director of Amnesty International declared that no country had a worse human rights record than Iran. The CIA responded by increasing its support for SAVAK.[28]

Of course, the battle the US is waging against Venezuela is, just as it was against Iran's Mossadegh, one for oil. And, the usual suspects are present for this struggle.

As the *Independent* explains, the US's hand-picked choice for Venezuelan president has already announced his plans to place Venezuela's oil into private US hands:[29]

Venezuela's government-in-waiting will allow foreign private oil companies a greater stake in joint ventures with its state-owned oil giant, Juan Guaido's envoy to the US has said.

Currently, Venezuela's socialist government has requirements that Petroleos de Venezuela (PDVSA) keep a controlling stake in any joint ventures with other energy companies.

But Carlos Vecchio, a representative for National Assembly

leader Mr Guaido, who has been recognised by the US as the interim leader of Venezuela, told *Bloomberg* Mr Guaido's government would look to open up the economy to increase oil production.

"The majority of the oil production that we want to increase will be with the private sector," he said on Monday.

Venezuelan-born sociologist María Páez Victor explains why Venezuelan oil, in particular, is so important to the US, and how the current government is such an impediment to the ability of private oil companies to get at it:

> Venezuela has the largest known oil reserves in the world in a highly strategic geographical location. It takes 43 days for an oil tanker to travel from the Middle East to the Texas refineries, while it only takes 4 days for one to go from Venezuela there. The oil companies, and governments they support, covet Venezuelan oil. If the country only produced mangos no one would care what happened there. The Venezuelan government took control of its oil company (PDVSA), opened up private/partnership contracts for oil exploitation but with the state owning the majority shares, made them pay taxes that had been at 1% for 60 years. The oil income—instead being distributed to elite businesses—has been used to fund the necessary public services that for decades had failed to meet the needs of the population.[30]

Meanwhile, talks are already underway to begin the process of the US corporate takeover of Venezuelan oil. Thus, Trump's national security adviser John Bolton openly said that "we're in conversation with major American companies now. . . . It would make a difference if we could have American companies produce the oil in Venezuela. We both have a lot at stake here."[31] Meanwhile, Juan Guaido has taken it upon himself to appoint a new Board of Citgo, Venezuela's state-owned oil company. Quite tellingly, all six board members he appointed live in the United States, and two of them are US-born citizens.[32]

Lest there be any doubt about what is going on here, the US and Western allies have already begun the fleecing of Venezuela, seizing key assets and designating them for Juan Guaido who, as a faithful steward of Western interests, will make sure they flow to private Western corporations.

Thus, for example, the Bank of England has taken Venezuela's gold deposits worth $1.2 billion and designated these for Guaido.[33]

The US, for its part, has already seized $7 billion in Venezuelan assets located in the US and has again earmarked these for Guaido who, in turn, has promised to begin allocating these to US and allied interests.[34] As *McClatchy News* explained, "[t]he State Department certified that Guaidó has authority to control all Venezuelan government bank accounts in the US financial system, giving him access to any cash or gold Venezuela may be holding in US banks."[35]

The plan is for Guaido to start distributing assets to North American oil interests immediately, including "two Canadian mining companies, Cristallex and Rusoro Mining, both of which have sought to auction off parts of Citgo, and ConocoPhillips, which has seized some PDVSA assets in the Caribbean as part of efforts to be repaid by Venezuela."[36]

As the Venezuelan government has also claimed, Guaido has been diverting some of these monies, totaling $1 billion, to organize terrorist activities within Venezuela.[37]

Meanwhile, of the $7 billion seized by the US, $5 billion had been earmarked by the Venezuelan government for purchase of medicines and raw materials for medicine production.[38] But now, the Venezuelan government, and those Venezuelans in need of the medicines, will never see those monies nor the medicine.

In other words, this "humanitarian intervention" of the US is nothing but an old-fashioned bank heist dressed up as something altruistic. And, it is not so humanitarian as even the *New York Times* has had to concede, explaining, as if it needed any explanation, that seizing Venezuela's national assets will cause immediate harm to the people of Venezuela. As the *Times* explains[39]:

Many Venezuelans worry that while the reduced revenue streams . . . will drastically worsen the already dire shortages of food and medicine and shutter the few remaining private businesses.

"If these sanctions don't force the endgame soon, they will cause a lot of pain for the people," said José Bodas, an anti-government oil union leader in Puerto La Cruz. "The rich will not stop getting richer, it's the workers who will shoulder the cost of these measures." . . .

. . . [I]n pharmacies across the Venezuelan capital, desperate patients searching for scarce medicine said they fear new sanctions could push the already collapsing health care system over the edge.

"If this gets worse this week because of the measures to pressure the government, I'm going to go crazy," said Juliana López, owner of a small pharmacy on the outskirts of the capital, as she turned away customer after customer. "We're already just barely surviving. To get worse we would have to be hit by a meteorite."

And, while the *Times* portrays the suffering of the Venezuelan people as somehow an unfortunate and unintended consequence of Western actions against Venezuela, this really misses the point. The whole point of these actions, beyond enriching Western companies, is to cause the suffering of the Venezuelan people so that they will rise up against Maduro and support Juan Guaido as their new leader. That is, these actions constitute the intentional infliction of pain and suffering on the Venezuelan people to cause a desired political outcome. This is the case text definition of terrorism. Such means to achieve the ends of regime change are simply unacceptable.

And as for the ends, it must be noted that it is some of the worst players in the gas and oil business who are leading the charge to grab Venezuela's oil and who stand to gain the most from this effort. Thus, as it was in the battle for Iran, Exxon is galloping in the war for Venezuela. Indeed, recall that Trump's first secretary of state, Rex Tillerson, was a former Exxon executive, showing how much a hold that company has over Trump's foreign policy. And alongside Exxon are the infamous Koch Brothers, the biggest bankrollers of right-wing political causes and of Donald Trump. As investigative journalist Greg Palast recently reported[40]:

> People don't know the Kochs have these giant refineries, some of the biggest in the world, on the Gulf Coast of Texas, in the middle of oilfields. They can't use Texas oil because it's not heavy and filthy enough, so they have to take almost all their oil from Venezuela, one of the only places where you get this super heavy oil. Normally it's discounted. But because they know the Kochs have to use their oil, Chavez, who was a really bright man, was squeezing the Kochs by the cojones and charging them a premium for his oil. The Kochs have been going crazy—they were losing money at their refinery because of the price.
>
> So they had two choices. Buy Tar Sands gunk from Canada, via the XL Pipeline, but it's taking too long. First they had to get Trump to come in as president and overcome all of the environmental objections to get the XL Pipeline approved. But it still ain't there. So what do you do? You better overthrow the government of Venezuela with some guy named Juan Guaido who said, and I quote, "I will open up the Venezuela oil fields to American companies." You have to understand, Exxon was basically thrown out of Venezuela. They've had lawsuits going against Venezuela. Guaido says he'll pay off Exxon and he will let Exxon take control again of the Venezuelan oil fields. That's what this game is about, it's about the oil.

It strains credulity to believe that anything good could come out of allowing the likes of the Koch Brothers and Exxon to get their hands on Venezuela's oil. And it is also impossible to believe that these forces would play fair in trying to achieve this end. Indeed, the Kochs and Exxon are the worst of the worst, having spent millions of dollars to suppress evidence of global climate change and the role that carbon-based fuels play in this phenomenon. Thus, an article in the *Huffington Post*[41] details,

> The Kochs have spent over $88 million in "traceable" funding to groups attacking climate change science, policy and regulation. Of that total, $21 million went to groups that recently bought a full page *New York Times* advertisement defending ExxonMobil from government investigations into its systematic misrepresentation of climate science. . . .
>
>   . . . Exxon itself spent half as much on the same people and groups, $10.1 million; money that the front groups spent on tactics like . . . a $100,000-or-so full page ad buy in the *New York Times!*

It is hard to believe that any of us can stomach another war for oil, and one which will benefit those who seem hell-bent upon destroying our planet. And yet, that is the war that is being fought in Venezuela, and the US is on the wrong side of it, as usual.

ELLIOTT ABRAMS, A WAR CRIMINAL RUNNING US POLICY TOWARDS VENEZUELA

APPARENTLY, EVEN FOR MANY LIBERALS, THE fact that the ultimate decision-maker behind Venezuela policy is Donald Trump—an individual many liberals believe (quite rightly) is a liar, racist and self-dealer—does not delegitimize this policy. Neither is the policy put into question, apparently, by the fact that it involves key support from the death squad state of Colombia and the government of Brazil's Jair Bolsonaro, whose family, as Glenn Greenwald of the *Intercept* recently detailed, has "direct, multilayered, and deeply personal ties to the paramilitary gangs and militias responsible for Brazil's most horrific violence," including the March 2018 assassination of the Rio City Council's Councilor Marielle Franco.[1]

However, there are even more nefarious characters (if that is possible) involved that should give people great pause, if not outright feelings of disgust.

In January of 2019, US Secretary of State Mike Pompeo appointed Elliott Abrams to the post of special envoy to Venezuela, putting Abrams in charge of US policy towards that country. There certainly is some logic to this choice given that Abrams was a key figure behind the push for the Iraq invasion in 2003—another war for oil, of course, and another war based on lies, specifically the lies about Weapons of Mass Destruction (WMDs).[2] And, Abrams pushed for this war despite the fact that, as declassified documents show, the Bush Administration was keenly aware that this would most likely lead to chaos throughout the Middle East.[3]

The choice of Abrams is quite telling and troubling given his long and checkered history in Latin America as well as his track record of lying, even under oath to Congress. I would submit that the fact that he is heading US policy towards Venezuela at this time guarantees that this policy will end very badly for the Venezuelan people, and that any claims he makes about this policy and its justifications must be treated with a great deal of suspicion.

The title of an article from the *Nation* magazine back in 2017 when Abrams was being considered for another post in the State Department says it all: "An Actual American War Criminal May Become Our Second-Ranking Diplomat, *Elliott Abrams spent the Reagan years abetting genocide....*"[4] As the article explains, while some past US leaders are accused of being war criminals, sometimes imprecisely and hyperbolically, Abrams is a real war criminal, and many times over.

While the article of course notes the well-known fact that "Abrams was forced to plead guilty to deliberately misleading Congress regarding his nefarious role in the Iran-contra scandal"—the operation through which the Reagan illegally funded the Nicaraguan Contras through illegal arms sales to Iran as well as sales of cocaine on US streets—"this is just the tip of a colossal iceberg."

Thus, the *Nation* article continues:

As a member of George W. Bush's National Security Council staff, Abrams encouraged, according to credible reports, a (briefly successful) military coup against the democratically elected government of

Venezuela in 2002, poisoning the US relationship with that government once it returned to power. . . .

As the *Guardian* reported shortly after the 2002 coup, which resulted in
the deaths of around 100 Venezuelans, several Bush officials were involved
in helping to spur on the effort to overthrow Chavez, "[b]ut the crucial
figure around the coup was Abrams, who operates in the White House as
senior director of the National Security Council for 'democracy, human
rights and international operations'."[5] As the *Guardian* notes, Abrams
"was a leading theoretician of the school known as 'Hemispherism', which
put a priority on combating Marxism in the Americas. It led to the coup
in Chile in 1973, and the sponsorship of regimes and death squads that
followed it in Argentina, El Salvador, Honduras, Guatemala and elsewhere. During the Contras' rampage in Nicaragua, he worked directly to
. . . [in] harvesting illegal funding for the rebellion."

Speaking of death squads in Guatemala and El Salvador, Abrams
had a role in those as well.

As assistant secretary of state for human rights, Abrams sought to
ensure that General Efraín Ríos Montt, Guatemala's then-dictator,
could carry out "acts of genocide"—those are the legally binding
words of Guatemala's United Nations–backed Commission for
Historical Clarification—against the indigenous people in the Ixil
region of the department of Quiché, without any pesky interference
from human-rights organizations, much less the US government.

As the mass killings were taking place, Abrams fought in
Congress for military aid to Ríos Montt's bloody regime. He credited
the murderous dictator with having "brought considerable progress"
on human-rights issues. Abrams even went so far as to insist that "the
amount of killing of innocent civilians is being reduced step by step"
before demanding that Congress provide the regime with advanced
arms because its alleged "progress need[ed] to be rewarded and
encouraged."

Promoted to assistant secretary of state for inter-American affairs, Abrams repeatedly denounced the continued protests by organizations seeking to call attention to the mass murders of both Ríos Montt and the no less bloodthirsty President Vinicio Cerezo Arévalo, who came to power fewer than three years later. In one village during the latter's reign, "the army herded the entire population into the courthouse, raped the women, beheaded the men, and took the children outside to smash them to death against rocks," according to *Inevitable Revolutions*, Walter LaFeber's classic history of the United States in Central America. At the time, a leader of the Guatemalan Mutual Support Group (an organization of mothers of the disappeared), her brother, and her 3-year-old son were found dead in their wrecked car. Abrams not only supported the nonsensical official explanation (there was "no evidence indicating other than that the deaths were due to an accident"), he also denounced a spokeswoman for the group who demanded an investigation, insisting that she had "no right to call herself a human rights worker." When *The New York Times* published an op-ed challenging the official State Department count of the mass murders under way—by a woman who had witnessed a death-squad-style assassination in broad daylight in Guatemala City without ever seeing it mentioned in the press—Abrams lied outright in a letter to the editor, even citing an imaginary story in a nonexistent newspaper to insist that the man's murder had, in fact, been reported.[6]

All told, about 200,000 Guatemalans were killed in this genocidal war which Elliott Abrams aided and abetted. But this too is not the end of the story of Abrams' crimes. Other sources tell of Abrams' similar aiding and abetting of grave crimes in El Salvador at the same time he was running cover for the genociders in Guatemala. To wit, Abrams

sought to discredit witness accounts of a massacre in the indigenous El Salvador community of El Mozote and surrounding villages, in which Salvadoran troops rounded up men, women and children, gunned them down and set their homes on fire. Some 1,000 people were killed by soldiers of the Atlacatl Battalion, who had recently been trained by the US. During the country's 12-year civil war, the US also sent billions of dollars to the Salvadoran government.

According to Human Rights Watch, Abrams "artfully distorted several issues in order to discredit the public accounts of the massacre" during a Senate hearing on the massacre.

The rights organisation said this included his insistence that the casualty figures couldn't have been as high because only 300 people were living in El Mozote at the time. His comments came despite witness accounts that said about 500 people were living in El Mozote and reports that the massacre occurred in the community and surrounding villages.[7]

The El Mozote massacre, that took place in December of 1981 and was denied by the Reagan Administration, including Elliott Abrams, is considered "the worst massacre in modern Latin American history,"[8] which is saying quite a lot. The murders carried out by the US-trained and backed soldiers—the US was sending the Salvadoran military a million dollars a day at this point—were cold, calculated and clinical, taking place systematically over many hours.[9] Mostly women, children and the elderly were killed.[10]

A journalist writing for the *New Yorker*, Mark Danner, would show years later, in 1993, not only that the massacre took place, but that the Reagan Administration was well aware of the fact that it had but denied it just the same.[11] In Danner's piece, "The Truth of El Mozote"[12] (annoyingly, my computer does not recognize "Mozote," of course), he details how the soldiers, ordered to kill each and every person in the village and outlying area, killed the men first, decapitating many of them and placing their heads in the church. They then killed the women whose children they separated from them. They left the children for last.

Here is one account of the murder of the children:

[T]he youngest children, most below the age of twelve—the soldiers herded from the house of Alfredo Márquez across the street to the sacristy, pushing them, crying and screaming, into the dark tiny room. There the soldiers raised their M16s and emptied their magazines into the roomful of children.

Not all the children of El Mozote died at the sacristy. A young man now known as Chepe Mozote told me that when the townspeople were forced to assemble on the plaza that evening he and his little brother had been left behind in their house, on the outskirts of the hamlet, near the school. By the next morning, Chepe had heard plenty of shooting; his mother had not returned. "About six o'clock, around ten soldiers in camouflage uniforms came to the house," Chepe says. "They asked me where my mother was. I told them she had gone to the plaza the night before. I asked them if I could see my mother, and they said I couldn't but I should come with them to the playing field"—near the school. "They said when we got there they would explain where my mother was."

Carrying his little brother, Chepe went with the soldiers and walked along with them as they searched house to house. "We found maybe fifteen kids," he says, "and then they took us all to the playing field. On the way, I heard shooting and I saw some dead bodies, maybe five old people." When they reached the playing field, "there were maybe thirty children," he says. "The soldiers were putting ropes on the trees. I was seven years old, and I didn't really understand what was happening until I saw one of the soldiers take a kid he had been carrying—the kid was maybe three years old—throw him in the air, and stab him with a bayonet.

This is Reagan's "war against Communism" in bold relief—the grisly murder of women and babies. And Abrams was a key henchman of Reagan in helping cover up such crimes of this dirty war. And now, we are to believe that Abrams has come to bring democracy and human rights to Venezuela. Of all the lies being told about US designs upon and operations against Venezuela, this may very well be the biggest and wildest.

TRUMP DOUBLES DOWN ON REGIME CHANGE, EXACERBATING THE US'S HUMANITARIAN CRISIS

Never Send To Know For Whom The Bell Tolls; It Tolls For Thee.
—John Donne

AS THE WHITE HOUSE CONTINUES ITS quest for oil and dominance in Venezuela, US citizens should think about what this means for them. It is no coincidence that Trump is attempting to delegitimize and crush socialism in Venezuela at the very same time that Americans are beginning to seriously talk about socialism, "Medicare for all," and "Green New Deals." While the US government wants to show other developing nations that resistance to the capitalist norms is futile, it equally wants to teach the American public this lesson so that they don't maintain any "crazy" ideas of social change. This has been a lesson the US has been aggressively promoting for many decades.

As researcher and author William Blum put it so well,

Imagine that the Wright brothers' first experiments with flying machines all failed because the automobile interests sabotaged each and every test flight. And then the good and god-fearing folk of the world looked upon this, took notice of the consequences, nodded their collective heads wisely, and intoned solemnly: Humans shall never fly.

Fact: Virtually every socialist experiment of any significance in the twentieth century has been either overthrown, invaded, or bombed . . . corrupted, perverted, or subverted . . . sanctioned, embargoed, or destabilized . . . or otherwise had life made impossible for it, by the United States. Not one of these socialist governments or movements—from the Russian Revolution to Fidel Castro in Cuba, from Communist China to the Sandinistas in Nicaragua—not one was permitted to rise or fall solely on its own merits; not one was left secure enough to drop its guard against the all-powerful enemy abroad and freely and fully relax control at home.[1]

The very same can be said of the Bolivarian Revolution in the 21st century as well.

And, beyond undermining the American people's belief that a better, more equitable world is possible, the other trope of the US government has been to focus their attention elsewhere and away from their own pressing needs. This has always been the trope of the US, certainly since the dawn of US imperial adventures beginning in 1898—focus Americans' concerns on problems happening in far-away lands rather than on their own; put them in fear of these other lands; and fleece them of their hard-earned tax dollars for wars in these foreign lands which could otherwise be used to alleviate dire social needs at home.

And so, Donald Trump is presently asking for $500 million for regime change efforts in Venezuela as part of his giant welfare package for the military-industrial complex.[2] In total, Trump is asking for a military budget of unheard of proportions while he proposes to slash all programs benefitting human beings in this country. As The Real News Network put it:

> Trump's budget dropped on the doorstep of Congress. It's the largest budget in American history, with increased military budget making for a record breaking $4.75 trillion; all of this built on the backs of working people, families mired in poverty, by hacking away at Medicare, Medicaid; through student loan forgiveness, ending that; work requirements for the poor; slashing important programs and budgets for education and environmental regulation. This is a budget around which Trump will build his presidential campaign.[3]

Trump may indeed be able to pull off this feat, with complicity of the mainstream media, by convincing the American people that Venezuela, and other like countries, is in dire need of "saving" from a humanitarian disaster, without explaining, of course, that the US is behind much of Venezuela's woes to begin with. The reality is that Venezuela is not so much in need of "saving" as it is of being left alone to sort out its own problems without constant meddling by the United States. This is a lesson we should have learned so many times from US interference abroad, particularly in Latin America, and yet it's a lesson we seem to constantly forget.

Meanwhile, the US itself is in desperate need of saving, of an inward focus to fix the real problems that plague this country and which have transformed the US, despite its vast wealth, into a Third World country. It is the United States that suffers from a fatal amount of corruption which we accuse other, lesser developed countries (like Venezuela) of having.

Even *Bloomberg* news, not exactly a liberal media outlet, was forced to acknowledge what so many of us already know, even if we are loath to admit it:

> [A]cross the country, construction costs for both the public and

private sectors have swelled as productivity has stagnated or fallen. It costs much more to build each mile of train in the US than in heavily unionized France. No one seems to be able to put their finger on the reason—instead, the US simply seems riddled with corruption, inefficient bidding, high land-acquisition costs, overstaffing, regulatory barriers, poor maintenance, excessive reliance on consultants and other problems. These seemingly minor inefficiencies add up to a country that has forgotten how to build. Unsurprisingly, much of the country's infrastructure remains in a state of disrepair.[4]

As *Bloomberg* explains, there is no justification for this state of affairs; for the fact that while "[t]he US is still a very rich nation—richer than countries such as Germany, Sweden, Japan, Canada or Denmark . . . that wealth masks a number of glaring areas where the US looks more dysfunctional than its peers." Thus, the US, while spending more on health care than any nation on earth, has some of the worst outcomes in terms of declining life expectancies and rising maternal mortality. The US is also facing a dire housing crisis, which few of us frankly need to be told as we see the tent cities lining most major cities.

As *Bloomberg* sums up, the US

also has a tragic opioid epidemic. Suicide rates have risen substantially. Whole cities have had their drinking water contaminated with lead. Measures of corruption are rising. The list goes on. Other dysfunctions are more long-standing. The US has an incredibly large prison population [actually, the largest on earth by far at over 2 million], and a violent crime rate much higher than other developed nations. It also has more poverty and hunger.

This is a crisis which will not be solved by throwing more money at another foreign intervention which will most certainly, judging from nearly all past ones, wreak more havoc than it will prevent.

Indeed, a successful intervention in Venezuela will only exacerbate the problems of Americans and humanity in general, for it will only lead to the further engorging of the superrich who are destroying this planet and who have given up on trying to save it.

And so, what do they want all this wealth for? Not to alleviate human need and suffering, but to escape humanity and the earth upon which humanity lives—this is the dirty little secret behind both the interventions, like that in Venezuela, and the failure (really refusal) to rebuild America—the superrich intend to take as much wealth as they can out of countries like Venezuela and the US and skip town, in ways they never could before.

If one wants proof of this assertion, look at who strangely popped up to organize a bizarre, over-priced "benefit concert" for Venezuela on the Colombia/Venezuela border, timed for the very day that the US was attempting its Trojan Horse "aid" delivery to Venezuela—British entrepreneur Richard Branson of the Virgin Group which includes Virgin Galactic. Virgin Galactic is Branson's company offering to take the very rich, including himself, to space for $250,000 a pop.[5] While these initial space flights, and those of other like companies, may be for mere amusement, there are clearly other plans afoot. As an interesting piece in the *Guardian* discusses:

> Amazon founder Jeff Bezos is the latest tech billionaire to invest his money in spaceships: on Tuesday, he debuted his space travel company Blue Origin's newest rocket. Now, those who want to cruise the galaxy can choose between the sleek new rocket and the stubbier model Bezos announced in April—or they can opt to ride with Tesla founder Elon Musk on a SpaceX ship, or hop on Richard Branson's Virgin Galactic. . . .
>
> Of course, uber-wealthy tech entrepreneurs aren't just buying rockets for their personal amusement. They're founding or investing in space travel—they want to get you off-planet, too. Well, not you-you, but someone like you with much, much, much more money. . . .

Companies like Blue Origin are using money and resources to push outwards, to expand the worlds of their rich customers all the way into space. But those same customers—and some of the owners—are making their terrestrial money in the classic capitalist terrestrial way: by working around any obstacle to profit, including environmental regulations and conservation efforts. . . .

The *Guardian* piece then raises the sixty-four-thousand-dollar question: are these superrich such Richard Branson "just gearing up to wash their hands of the planet and leave the rest of us to clean up? By pushing outward while ignoring the problems it causes back on the home turf, are they effectively creating a galactic upper class that rests on the backs of the earthbound? Even if that's not literally the plan, it may be the ultimate outcome."

Branson is a perfect face of the "humanitarian interventionist" program for Venezuela. Branson and his ilk need Venezuela's oil more than anyone in order to feed their voracious spaceships. The Bolivarian government of Venezuela, which has nationalized the oil for the benefit of the people, is standing in the way; indeed, this government is an affront to people like Branson who believe themselves entitled to take whatever they want, and as much of it, whenever they want.

This is why it makes total sense that Branson would participate in the Venezuela regime change project, a project which also includes Brazilian president Jair Bolsonaro, who was recently elected on a platform of opening up Brazil's vast rainforests to private, mostly foreign penetration and exploitation. And the Bolsonaro administration has wasted no time in beginning to violently remove indigenous peoples from the rainforests to accomplish this end.[6] Bolsonaro is the perfect ally of people like Branson in their bid to engage in the super-exploitation of the earth.

But for those of us who care about our earth, about the environment, the future of humanity, about indigenous rights, Branson and Bolsonaro are not our friends—they are objectively our enemies; as are the climate change denying Koch Brothers and Exxon, and Trump and Elliott Abrams, the *genocidaire*. Their goals are not the goals of humanity, for they are truly enemies of humanity.

Rather, the goals of humanity are better represented by the government in Venezuela they wish to overthrow—a government that is trying to prevent people like them from exploiting Venezuela's precious resources, which wants to use Venezuela's resources to meet human needs, and which is attempting to protect indigenous peoples and their land.

Finally, those pushing for the regime change in Venezuela appear willing to risk a possible world war in order to pull it off. And this is so given the fact that Russia now has an increasing presence in Venezuela in order to deter an armed intervention. Rhetoric on both sides is becoming increasingly bellicose, with John Bolton calling the Russian presence in Venezuela "a direct threat to international peace and security in the region"—a direct reference to language in the UN Charter which can be the basis for the use of armed force.[7] In return, Russia's foreign minister Sergei Lavrov has called such remarks "insolent," and has pointed to the US's over 800 military bases around the globe as a justification for Russia to maintain a military presence in Venezuela.[8]

If either the US or Russia calls the other's bluff, there is the real possibility that a war between the US and Russia, one which could involve the use of nuclear weapons, will result. Indeed, we have seen this scenario played out before in the Cuban Missile Crisis of 1962 in which the world came within a hair's breadth from nuclear conflagration as the US and Russia confronted each other over Soviet missiles in Cuba. This all makes the conflict with Venezuela even more urgent for all of us.

In short, the battle for Venezuela, which is well underway, has huge implications for all of humanity. None of us can stay neutral on this issue. And given the nefarious designs of the US upon Venezuela, the suffering the US is already bringing to the Venezuelan people through its regime change operations, and the threat of global conflagration, it is incumbent upon us to resist this latest US intervention.

ENDNOTES

Foreword

1   Mora, Frank O. "What a Military Intervention in Venezuela Would Look Like." *Foreign Affairs*. March 26, 2019. https://www.foreignaffairs.com /articles/venezuela/2019-03-19/what-military-intervention-venezuela -would-look.

Preface

1   Sequera, Vivian, and Tibisay Romero. "Venezuela Blackout Drags into Third Day, Maduro Announces 'Load Management.'" Reuters. March 28, 2019. https://af.reuters.com/article/worldNews/idAFKCN1R81JU.

2   Sanchez, Maria Isabel, and Marc Burleigh. "Venezuela Accuses US of 'Terrorist Attack' on Oil Facility." Yahoo! News. March 14, 2019. https: //news.yahoo.com/venezuela-accuses-us-terrorist-attack-oil-facility -160528169.html.

3   Vaz, Ricardo. "Venezuela: New Power Outage As Oil Output Plummets." Venezuelanalysis.com. April 11, 2019. https://venezuelanalysis.com/news /14425.

4   Walsh, Nick Paton, Natalie Gallón, and Evan Perez. "The August Plot to Kill Maduro with Drones." CNN. March 14, 2019. https://www.cnn.com /2019/03/14/americas/venezuela-drone-maduro-intl/index.html.

5   *See,* tweet and video here: https://twitter.com/camilatelesur/status /1115449883442413568?s=21.

6   "De Zayas: There Was Also a Blackout in Chile Before the Coup Against Allende." *Orinoco Tribune.* March 16, 2019. https://orinocotribune.com /de-zayas-there-was-also-a-blackout-in-chile-before-the-coup-against -allende.

7   Leetaru, Kalev. "Could Venezuela's Power Outage Really Be a Cyber Attack?" *Forbes.* March 9, 2019. https://www.forbes.com/sites /kalevleetaru/2019/03/09/could-venezuelas-power-outage-really-be-a -cyber-attack/#16d90a31607c.

8   "Maduro's Claim That Washington Has Used Cyberwarfare to Bring Down Venezuela's Power Grid Cannot Be So Easily Dismissed." What's Left. March 10, 2019. https://gowans.wordpress.com/2019/03/10/maduros -claim-that-washington-has-used-cyberwarfare-to-bring-down-venezuelas -power-grid-cannot-be-so-easily-dismissed/.

9   Blumenthal, Max. "US Regime Change Blueprint Proposed Venezuelan Electricity Blackouts As 'Watershed Event' For 'Galvanizing Public Unrest'." PopularResistance.Org. March 12, 2019. https://popularresis- tance.org/us-regime-change-blueprint-proposed-venezuelan-electricity -blackouts-as-watershed-event-for-galvanizing-public-unrest/.

10   Daugherty, Alex. "Marco Rubio's Inaccurate Tweets on Venezuela Embolden Liberal Critics." *Miami Herald.* March 13, 2019. https://www .miamiherald.com/news/nation-world/world/americas/venezuela/article 227462709.html.

11   Dobson, Paul. "Red Cross, UN Slam 'Politicised' USAID Humanitarian Assistance to Venezuela." Venezuelanalysis.com. Feb. 22, 2019. https: //venezuelanalysis.com/news/14316.

12   "NYT's Exposé on the Lies About Burning Aid Trucks in Venezuela Shows How US Government and Media Spread Pro-War Propaganda." *The Intercept.* March 10, 2019. https://theintercept.com/2019/03/10/ nyts-expose-on-the-lies-about-burning-humanitarian-trucks-in-venezuela -shows-how-us-govt-and-media-spread-fake-news/.

13   "Did President Maduro, Plop Down Giant Shipping Containers to Prevent Truckloads of US 'Humanitarian Aid' from Entering Venezuela?" Telesur English. Feb. 22, 2019. https://www.facebook.com/teleSUR English/posts/258617538187003/.

14   Kurmanaev, Anatoly, Isayen Herrera, and Clifford Krauss. "Venezuela
      Blackout, in 2nd Day, Threatens Food Supplies and Patient Lives." *New
      York Times*. March 8, 2019. https://www.nytimes.com/2019/03/08/world
      /americas/venezuela-blackout-power.html.

15   Johnson, Tim. "The Lights Are Back On, but After $3.2B Will Puerto
      Rico's Grid Survive Another Storm?" Mcclatchydc, as reprinted in the
      Miami Herald. Nov. 29, 2018. https://www.mcclatchydc.com/news/nation
      -world/national/hurricane/article217480370.html.

16   "US-Led Coalition Bomb Kills 50 Syrian Women, Children." News |
      TeleSUR English. March 11, 2019. https://www.telesurenglish.net/news
      /US-led-Coalition-Bomb-Syrian-Killing-50-Women-Children-20190311
      -0005.html.

Introduction

1   "5 Major Atrocities in US Military History." Public Radio International.
      March 12, 2012. https://www.pri.org/stories/2012-03-12/5-major-atrocities
      -us-military-history.

2   Tillerson, Rex W., "Remarks at the Global Coalition Against ISIS"
      (speech, Washington, DC, March 22, 2017). https://bh.usembassy.gov
      /tillerson-addresses-coalition-68-nations-defeat-isis/.

3   Dong-Choon Kim. "Forgotten War, Forgotten Massacres—the Korean
      War (1950–1953) As Licensed Mass Killings." *Journal of Genocide Research*.
      https://www.academia.edu/6417696/Forgotten_war_forgotten
      _massacres—the_Korean_War_1950-1953_as_licensed_mass_killings.

4   "Prevent the Crime of Silence." Reports from the Sessions of the
      International War Crimes Tribunal (founded by Bertrand Russell) at
      LONDON, STOCKHOLM, & ROSKILDE (1967). http://raetowest
      .org/vietnam-war-crimes/russell-vietnam-war-crimes-tribunal-1967
      .html#v1217-Sartre-on-genocide.

5   Memo by George Kennan, Head of the US State Department Policy
      Planning Staff. Written February 28, 1948, Declassified June 17, 1974.
      George Kennan, "Review of Current Trends, US Foreign Policy, Policy
      Planning Staff, PPS No. 23. Top Secret. Included in the US Department
      of State, Foreign Relations of the United States, 1948, volume 1, part 2

(Washington DC: Government Printing Office, 1976), 509–29. https://en.wikisource.org/wiki/Memo_PPS23_by_George_Kennan.

6 "Use It and Lose It: The Outsize Effect of US Consumption on the Environment." *Scientific American*. https://www.scientificamerican.com/article/american-consumption-habits/.

7 Hersh, Seymour M. "The Redirection." *New Yorker*. June 19, 2017. http://www.newyorker.com/magazine/2007/03/05/the-redirection.

8 Hennigan, W.J., Brian Bennett, and Patrick J. McDonnell. "In Syria, Militias Armed by the Pentagon Fight Those Armed by the CIA." *Los Angeles Times*. March 27, 2016. http://www.latimes.com/world/middleeast/la-fg-cia-pentagon-isis-20160327-story.html.

9 Power, Samantha. *"A Problem from Hell": America and the Age of Genocide*. Basic Books, 2013.

10 Oakford, Samuel. "As Saudis Block a Human Rights Inquiry in Yemen, America Stays Quiet." VICE News. Oct. 2, 2015. https://news.vice.com/en_us/article/xw3yjn/as-saudis-block-a-human-rights-inquiry-in-yemen-the-us-stays-quiet. *See also*, Oakford, Samuel, Lance Williams, Jeff Greenfield, Tamara Cofman Wittes, and Ilan Goldenberg. "As the Saudis Covered Up Abuses in Yemen, America Stood By." *POLITICO* Magazine. July 30, 2016. https://www.politico.com/magazine/story/2016/07/saudi-arabia-yemen-russia-syria-foreign-policy-united-nations-blackmail-214124.

11 "'Good for Business': Trump Adviser Bolton Admits US Interest in Venezuela's 'Oil Capabilities'." RT International. https://www.rt.com/usa/449982-john-bolton-oil-venezuela/.

12 Vyas, Kejal, and Juan Forero. "Venezuela's Maduro Wins Re-Election Amid Opposition Boycott." *Wall Street Journal*. May 21, 2018. https://www.wsj.com/articles/venezuela-votes-as-oil-rich-nation-reels-from-economic-crisis-1526835058.

13 Bulent Gokay, "In Saudi Arabia's Quest to Debilitate the Iranian Economy, They Destroyed Venezuela." *The Independent* (Aug. 9, 2017). https://www.independent.co.uk/voices/venezuela-saudi-arabia-oil-prices-iran-price-war-inflation-destabilisation-a7883846.html.

14 "Venezuelan Housing Plan Passes 'Milestone' with 2.5M Homes." News | TeleSUR English. Dec. 26, 2018. https://www.telesurenglish.net/news

/Venezuelan-Housing-Plan-Passes-Milestone-with-2.5M-Homes-20181226-0023.html.

15   Kokalitcheva, Kia. "Red Cross Spent Half a Billion Dollars to Build Six Homes in Haiti." *Time*. June 4, 2015. http://time.com/3908457/red-cross-six-homes-haiti/.

16   Archibold, Randal C. "In Haiti's Cholera Fight, Cuba Takes Lead Role." *New York Times*. Nov. 7, 2011. https://www.nytimes.com/2011/11/08/world/americas/in-haitis-cholera-fight-cuba-takes-lead-role.html.

17   "Cholera in Haiti, an End in Sight." United Nations. http://www.un.org/News/dh/infocus/haiti/CholeraHaitiAnEndInSight.pdf.

18   Campbell, Duncan. "Bush Rejects Chávez Aid." *The Guardian*. Sept. 6, 2005. https://www.theguardian.com/world/2005/sep/07/venezuela.hurricanekatrina.

19   "Reality Check. When Venezuela and Cuba Offered Aid to the Victims of Hurricane Katrina." Tony Seed's Weblog. March 20, 2019. https://tonyseed.wordpress.com/2019/03/02/reality-check-when-venezuela-and-cuba-offered-aid-to-the-victims-of-hurricane-katrina/.

20   "Why Did Bush Reject Aid Offers from Cuba After Hurricane Katrina?" MintPress News. Sept. 5, 2017. https://www.mintpressnews.com/bush-reject-aid-offers-cuba-hurricane-katrina/231566/.

21   "Hurricane Katrina Statistics Fast Facts." CNN. Aug. 30, 2018. https://www.cnn.com/2013/08/23/us/hurricane-katrina-statistics-fast-facts/index.html.

22   Dodd, Paisley. "UN Peacekeepers in Haiti Ran Child Sex Rings, Raped Women: AP Investigation." Global News. April 14, 2017. https://globalnews.ca/news/3380202/un-peacekeepers-child-sex-haiti/.

23   "Protests, Violence in Haiti Prompts International Call for 'Realistic and Lasting Solutions' to Crisis | UN News." United Nations. https://news.un.org/en/story/2019/02/1032441.

24   "In Yemen, World's Worst Cholera Outbreak Traced to Eastern Africa." Reuters. Jan. 2, 2019. https://www.reuters.com/article/us-yemen-cholera/in-yemen-worlds-worst-cholera-outbreak-traced-to-eastern-africa-id USKCN1OW1EA.

Chapter 1

1   Taylor, Adam. "What Is the Monroe Doctrine? John Bolton's Justification for Trump's Push against Maduro." *Washington Post*. March 4, 2019. https://www.washingtonpost.com/world/2019/03/04/what-is-monroe -doctrine-john-boltons-justification-trumps-push-against-maduro/?

2   Gunther, John. *Inside Latin America*. Harper & Bros., 1941, 183.

3   US State Department. "Venezuela—Human Rights Report." Nov. 27, 1978. https://wikileaks.org/plusd/cables/1978STATE300219_d.html.

4   Amnesty International. "Venezuela: Eclipse of Human Rights." July 1993. https://www.amnesty.org/download/Documents/188000 /amr530071993en.pdf.

5   *Id.*

Chapter 2

1   *Id.*

2   Ciccariello-Maher, George. "The Fourth World War Started in Venezuela." Counterpunch. March 3, 2007. https://www.counterpunch.org /2007/03/03/the-fourth-world-war-started-in-venezuela/.

3   *Id.*

4   *Id.*

5   Webb, Whitney. "Leaked Wikileaks Document Reveals How US Military Uses IMF, World Bank as Unconventional Weapons." Mint Press. Feb. 7, 2019. https://www.mintpressnews.com/leaked-wikileaks-doc-reveals-how-us -military-uses-of-imf-world-bank-as-unconventional-weapons/254708/.

6   Hardy, Charles. *Cowboy in Caracas: A North American's Memoir of Venezuela's Democratic Revolution*. Curbstone Books, 2007.

7   "Number of Victims of US Invasion of Panama Unknown 27 Years On." Telesur. Dec. 20, 2016. https://www.telesurenglish.net/news/Number-of -Victims-of-US-Invasion-of-Panama-Unknown-27-Years-On -20161220-0011.html.

8   Peppe, Matt. "The Invasion of Panama." Counterpunch. Dec. 15, 2014. https://www.counterpunch.org/2014/12/15/the-invasion-of-panama/.

9   The Center for Justice & Accountability. "The Jesuits Massacre Case." https://cja.org/what-we-do/litigation/the-jesuits-massacre-case/.

10   Kovalik, Dan. "Extradition Order Forces US to Confront Its Role in Persecuting the Latin American Church." Huffington Post. Feb. 10, 2017. https://www.huffingtonpost.com/dan-kovalik/extradition-order-forces_b_9201076.html.

11   Herman, Edward and Noam Chomsky. *Manufacturing Consent: The Political Economy of the Mass Media*. Pantheon, 1988.

12   Cooper, Linda and James Hodge. "Extradition Order in Jesuit Priest Killings Could Lead to More Arrests." *National Catholic Reporter*. Feb. 8, 2016. https://www.ncronline.org/news/justice/extradition-order-jesuit-priest-killings-could-lead-more-arrests.

13   *Id.*

14   "On Religion and Politics." Noam Chomsky interviewed by Amina Chaudary. *Islamica Magazine*, Issue 19, April-May 2007. https://chomsky.info/200704___/.

15   Nelson-Pallmeyer, Jack. *School of Assassins: Guns, Greed, and Globalization*. Orbis Books, 2001.

16   Cooper, Linda and James Hodge, *id.*

17   "El Salvador: The Declining Influence of the Roman Catholic Church." US Embassy. Sept. 5, 2009. http://wikileaks.org/cable/2005/09/05SAN SALVADOR2679.html.

Chapter 3

1   Chomsky, Noam. *Year 501: The Conquest Continues*. London: Pluto Press, 2015, 235–36.

2   Branford, Sue. "Hugo Chavez Fails to Overthrow Venezuela's Government: Archive, 5 February 1992." *The Guardian*. Feb. 5, 2016. https://www.theguardian.com/world/2016/feb/05/hugo-chavez-venezuela-failed-coup-1992.

3   *Id.*

4   Amnesty International. "Venezuela: Eclipse of Human Rights." July 1993. https://www.amnesty.org/download/Documents/188000/amr530071993en.pdf.

5   Chomsky, Noam. *Year 501*, *id.*

6   Branford, Sue, *id.*

7   Staff, NPR. "Enshrined and Oft-Invoked, Simon Bolivar Lives On." NPR. April 10, 2013. https://www.npr.org/2013/04/13/176783269/enshrined -and-oft-invoked-simon-bolivar-lives-on.

8   Masur, Gerhard Straussmann. "Simón Bolívar." Encyclopædia Britannica. Jan. 30, 2019. https://www.britannica.com/biography/Simon-Bolivar.

9   Staff, NPR, *id.*

10   Bulmer-Thomas, Victor. "Analysis: How Hugo Chavez Changed Venezuela." BBC News. March 6, 2013. https://www.bbc.com/news/world -latin-america-15240081.

11   "How the US Is Strangling Haiti As It Attempts Regime Change in Venezuela." *Haitian Times*. Feb. 20, 2019. https://haitiantimes.com/2019 /02/20/how-the-u-s-is-strangling-haiti-as-it-attempts-regime-change-in-venezuela/.

12   Bulmer-Thomas, Victor, *id.*

13   W. T. Whitney Jr. "Cuba's 'Operation Miracle' Celebrated throughout Latin America." People's World. July 21, 2014. https://www.peoplesworld .org/article/cuba-s-operation-miracle-celebrated-throughout-latin-america/.

14   Kebede, Rebekah. "Venezuela Brings Free Heating Oil to Poor in NY." Reuters. Dec. 14, 2007. https://www.reuters.com/article/citgo-energy -bronx-assistance/venezuela-brings-free-heating-oil-to-poor-in-ny -idUSN1425588920071214.

15   Chomsky, Noam. "Hugo Chavez's Death and Legacy." Venezuelanalysis .com. April 19, 2013. http://venezuelanalysis.com/video/8695.

16   Wilpert, Gregory. "Venezuela's Mission to Fight Poverty." Venezuelanalysis. com. Nov. 11, 2003. https://venezuelanalysis.com/analysis/213.

17   Kovalik, Dan. "Legislative Victory of US-Backed Counter-Revolution in Venezuela No Cause for Joy." Huffington Post. Dec. 17, 2016. https://www.huffingtonpost.com/dan-kovalik/us-gloating-about -venezue_b_8830928.html.

18   Shupak, Gregory. "US Media Erase Years of Chavismo's Gains." Venezuelanalysis.com. March 15, 2019. https://venezuelanalysis.com /analysis/14376.

19   *Id.*; citing, Forero, Juan, and David Luhnow. "Paradise Lost: Venezuela's Path from Riches to Ruin." *Wall Street Journal*. Feb. 7, 2019. https://www

.wsj.com/articles/paradise-lost-venezuelas-path-from-riches-to-ruin
-11549570900.

20   *See*, Mallett-Outtrim, Ryan. "'Part of the Transition to Socialism':
Venezuela's Labour Law Comes into Effect." Venezuelanalysis.com. May
10, 2013. https://venezuelanalysis.com/news/9202.

21   "Venezuela Says Taking Over Halted Kimberly-Clark Plant." Reuters.
July 12, 2016. https://www.reuters.com/article/us-venezuela-kimberlyclark
-idUSKCN0ZR2JT.

22   Perry, John. "Lessons from Latin America: The Case for Public Investment
in Housing." *The Guardian*. June 6, 2013. http://www.guardian.co.uk
/housing-network/2013/jun/06/public-investment-housing-venezuela?
INTCMP=SRCH.

23   UN Development Programme. "Human Development Report 2013, The
Rise of the South: Human Progress in a Diverse World." http://hdr.undp
.org/sites/default/files/reports/14/hdr2013_en_complete.pdf.

24   Casselman, Ben. "Katrina Washed Away New Orleans's Black Middle
Class." FiveThirtyEight. Aug. 24, 2015. https://fivethirtyeight.com/features
/katrina-washed-away-new-orleanss-black-middle-class/.

25   *Id.*

26   Gokay, Bulent. "In Saudi Arabia's Quest to Debilitate the Iranian
Economy, They Destroyed Venezuela." *The Independent*. Aug. 9, 2017.
https://www.independent.co.uk/voices/venezuela-saudi-arabia-oil
-prices-iran-price-war-inflation-destabilisation-a7883846.html.

27   De Zayas, Dr. Alfred. "Report of the Independent Expert on the Promotion
of a Democratic and Equitable International Order: Visit to Venezuela and
Ecuador," Sept. 10, 2018. https://dezayasalfred.wordpress.com/2018/09/10
/report-of-the-independent-expert-on-the-promotion-of-a-democratic
-and-equitable-international-order-visit-to-venezuela-and-ecuador/.

28   Shupak, Gregory, *id.*

29   *Id.*

30   Watson, Katy. "Venezuela Crisis: Why Chavez's Followers Are Standing
by Maduro." BBC News. March 4, 2019. https://www.bbc.com/news
/world-latin-america-47441642.

31   Chengu, Garikai. "Libya: From Africa's Richest State Under Gaddafi, to
Failed State After NATO Intervention." Global Research. March 9,

2018. https://www.globalresearch.ca/libya-from-africas-richest-state-under
-gaddafi-to-failed-state-after-nato-intervention/5408740.

32   *Id.*

33   Gilmour, Jared. "Rubio Tweets Bloodied Gaddafi Photo As He Calls for
Maduro to Step down in Venezuela." *Miami Herald.* Feb. 24, 2019. https://
www.miamiherald.com/news/nation-world/world/article
226732089.html.

34   Rebelion, Pedro Santander. "Dialogue or Coups." Venezuelanalysis.com.
Feb. 19, 2014. https://venezuelanalysis.com/analysis/10369.

35   Beeton, Dan. "Statistical Study Shows That First Audit of Venezuelan
Election Is Decisive | Press Releases." CEPR. http://cepr.net/press
-center/press-releases//statistical-study-shows-that-first-audit-of
-venezuelan-election-is-decisive.

36   Weisbrot, Mark. "Why the US Demonizes Venezuela's Democracy | Mark
Weisbrot." *The Guardian.* Oct. 3, 2012. https://www.theguardian.com
/commentisfree/2012/oct/03/why-us-dcemonises-venezuelas
-democracy.

37   Riva, Alberto. "Jimmy Carter: US 'Has No Functioning Democracy'."
Salon. July 18, 2013. https://www.salon.com/2013/07/18/jimmy_carter_us_has
_no_functioning_democracy_partner/.

38   *Id.*

39   Emersberger, Joe. "Western Media Shorthand on Venezuela Conveys
and Conceals So Much." FAIR. Aug. 27, 2018. https://fair.org/home
/western-media-shorthand-on-venezuela-conveys-and-conceals-so-much/.

40   *Id.*

41   Kurmanaev, Anatoly, and Clifford Krauss. "US Sanctions Are Aimed at
Venezuela's Oil. Its Citizens May Suffer First." *New York Times.* Feb. 8,
2019. https://www.nytimes.com/2019/02/08/world/americas/venezuela
-sanctions-maduro.html.

42   John Pilger. "The War on Venezuela Is Built on Lies." Consortiumnews.
Feb. 23, 2019. https://consortiumnews.com/2019/02/22/john-pilger-the
-war-on-venezuela-is-built-on-lies/.

43   Murray, Craig. "The Vultures of Caracas." Jan. 26, 2019. https:
//www.craigmurray.org.uk/archives/2019/01/the-vultures-of-caracas
/comment-page-4/.

44   Palast, Greg. "Venezuela: The Trump Coup and Our Next Oil War."
     March 15, 2019. https://www.gregpalast.com/venezuela-the-trump-coup
     -and-our-next-oil-war/.

45   Lockhart, P.R. "Trump Is Ignoring One Huge Factor in the Current
     Status of Haiti: US Foreign Policy." *Vox.* Jan. 12, 2018. https://www.vox.com
     /policy-and-politics/2018/1/12/16883224/trump-shithole-foreign
     -policy-haiti.

46   *Id.*

47   Buschschluter, Vanessa. "The Long History of Troubled Ties between
     Haiti and the US." BBC. Jan. 16, 2010. http://news.bbc.co.uk/2/hi/americas
     /8460185.stm; *see also*, Makandal, Kiki. "100 Years of Imperialist
     Domination: The US Occupation of Haiti (1915–34) and Its Current
     Consequences." *Idées Nouvelles/Idées Prolétarienes.* July 28, 2015. http:
     //koleksyon-inip.org/100-years/.

48   Makandal, Kiki, *id.*

49   "Hurricane Maria Caused an Estimated 2,975 Deaths in Puerto Rico,
     New Study Finds." CBS News. https://www.cbsnews.com/news/hurricane
     -maria-death-toll-puerto-rico-2975-killed-by-storm-study-finds/.

50   Voz, Jesús Chucho García-La. "Why Are There No Barricades in Afro-
     Descendant Communities?" Venezuelanalysis.com. April 23, 2014. https:
     //venezuelanalysis.com/analysis/10637.

51   Kovalik, Dan. "The Venezuelan Revolution & the Indigenous Struggle."
     Huffington Post. Dec. 7, 2017. https://www.huffingtonpost.com/dan
     -kovalik/the-venezuelan-revolution_b_5989882.html.

52   *Id.*

53   Van Cott, Donna Lee. "Andean Indigenous Movements and Constitutional
     Transformation: Venezuela in Comparative Perspective." Sept. 2001.
     http://lasa.international.pitt.edu/Lasa2001/VanCottDonna.pdf.

54   Fischer-Hoffman, Cory. "Honoring Indigenous Resistance Day in
     Venezuela, the Struggle Continues." Venezuelanalysis.com. Oct. 25,
     2018. https://venezuelanalysis.com/news/10959.

55   "Venezuela: The Disturbing Message of Robert Serra's Murder." *The
     Guardian.* Oct. 9, 2014. https://www.theguardian.com/world/2014/oct
     /09/venezuela-disturbing-message-robert-serra-murder.

56   Fischer-Hoffman, Cory, *id.*

57   "Venezuela: The Disturbing Message of Robert Serra's Murder," *id.*

58   Shupak, Gregory. "US Media Erase Years of Chavismo's Gains." Venezuelanalysis.com. March 15, 2019. https://venezuelanalysis.com/analysis /14376.

59   *See,* https://twitter.com/ajitxsingh/status/1114836468667703296?s=21.

60   "Venezuela: The Disturbing Message of Robert Serra's Murder," *The Guardian.* Oct. 9, 2014. https://www.theguardian.com/world/2014/oct /09/venezuela-disturbing-message-robert-serra-murder.

Chapter 4

1   "Colombia Has Highest Number of Internally Displaced People." Colombia News | Colombia Reports. June 19, 2018. https://colombiareports .com/colombia-has-highest-number-of-internally-displaced-people/.

2   "15 Facts About Colombia's Land Restitution Process." Amnesty International. https://www.amnesty.org/en/latest/news/2014/11/facts-about -colombia-s-land-restitution-process/.

3   "Why Do Colombians Continue Migrating to Venezuela?" TeleSUR English. Sept. 10, 2015. https://www.telesurenglish.net/analysis/Why-Do -Colombians-Continue-Migrating-to-Venezuela—20150910-0028.html.

4   *Id.*

5   "Despite Challenges, Venezuelan Migration into Colombia Can Boost Its Growth." World Bank. Nov. 6, 2018. https://www.worldbank.org/en /news/feature/2018/11/06/despite-challenges-venezuelan-migration -into-colombia-can-boost-its-growth.

6   Moloney, Anastasia. "Silence Surrounds Colombia's 92,000 Disappeared: ICRC." Reuters. Aug. 29, 2014. https://www.reuters.com/article/us -foundation-colombia-missing/silence-surrounds-colombias-92000 -disappeared-icrc-idUSKBN0GT22520140829?feedName=worldNews.

7   Daniels, Joe Parkin. "Colombian Army Killed Thousands More Civilians Than Reported, Study Claims." *The Guardian.* May 8, 2018. https: //www.theguardian.com/world/2018/may/08/colombia-false -positives-scandal-casualties-higher-thought-study.

8   "Colombia's 'False Positives' Scandal." Colombia Reports Data. July 24, 2018. https://data.colombiareports.com/false-positives/.

9   "Colombian Priest Killed in Continuing Trend of Violence." Catholic
      News Agency. Accessed March 24, 2019. https://www.catholicnewsagency
      .com/news/colombian-priest-killed-in-continuing-trend-of-violence.

10   "ICC to Be Asked to Investigate Mass Killing of Colombia's Social
      Leaders." Colombia News | Colombia Reports. March 21, 2019. https:
      //colombiareports.com/icc-to-be-asked-to-investigate-mass-killing
      -of-colombias-social-leaders/.

11   *Id.*

12   Colombia, 2018 Report. Frontline Defenders. https://www.frontlinede
      fenders.org/sites/default/files/stk_-_colombia_0.pdf.

13   "Colombia's Killer Networks: The Military—Paramilitary Partnership
      and the United States." Human Rights Watch. 1996. https://www.hrw
      .org/reports/1996/killer2.htm.

14   *Id.*

15   "Colombia Denies UN Claim of Paramilitary-Linked Violence." News |
      TeleSUR English. May 2, 2017. https://www.telesurenglish.net/news
      /Colombia-Denies-UN-Claim-of-Paramilitary-Linked-Violence
      -20170502-0038.html.

16   Sontag, Deborah. "The Secret History of Colombia's Paramilitaries and
      the US War on Drugs." *New York Times.* Jan. 20, 2018. http://www
      .nytimes.com/2016/09/11/world/americas/colombia-cocaine-human
      -rights.html?_r=0.

17   "UN: Mexico's Violent Death Rate Resembles 'Country at War'." News |
      TeleSUR English. April 11, 2019. https://www.telesurenglish.net/news
      /UN-Mexicos-Violent-Death-Rate-Resembles-Country-at-War
      -20190411-0010.html.

18   ZNet Commentary: Noam Chomsky on Colombia. http://colombiasupport
      .net/archive/200004/znet-chomsky-0424.html.

19   "Chiquita, Dole and Del Monte Financed Murderous Militias." Daily
      Kos. May 19, 2007. http://www.dailykos.com/story/2007/5/19/336518/-.

20   Frontline Defenders, 2018 Global Analysis. https://www.frontlinedefenders
      .org/sites/default/files/global_analysis_2018.pdf.

21   *Id.*

22   Vaz, Ricardo. "Venezuela: Communist Campesino Leaders Assassinated

As Land Struggles Continue." Venezuelanalysis.com. Jan. 15, 2019. https://venezuelanalysis.com/news/14128.

23   "US Military Assistance and Latin America." WOLA. https://www .wola.org/analysis/u-s-military-assistance-latin-america/.

24   *Id.*

25   Chomsky, Noam. "The United States and the 'Challenge of Relativity'." https://chomsky.info/199811___/.

26   Frontline Defenders, 2018 Global Analysis, *id.*

27   Chomsky, Noam. "The United States and the 'Challenge of Relativity'." https://chomsky.info/199811___/.

28   "At Least 13 Human Rights, Social Leaders Killed in Colombia So Far in 2019." WOLA. Feb. 7, 2019. https://www.wola.org/2019/02/human -rights-social-leaders-killed-colombia-january-2019/.

29   Colombia, 2018 Report. Frontline Defenders. https://www.frontlinede fenders.org/sites/default/files/stk_-_colombia_0.pdf.

30   "Over 40 of Colombia's Indigenous Groups Close to Extinction Due to Mining: UN." Colombia News | Colombia Reports. Feb. 26, 2015. https://colombiareports.com/40-indigenous-populations-risk -extinction-colombia-due-mining-operations-un/.

31   Balch, Oliver. "Cerrejón Mine in Colombia: Can It Address Its Human Rights Risks?" *The Guardian.* July 25, 2013. https://www.theguardian .com/sustainable-business/cerrejon-mine-colombia-human-rights.

32   "Over 40 of Colombia's Indigenous Groups Close to Extinction Due to Mining: UN," *id.*

33   Balch, Oliver, *id.*

34   "Stop Forced Displacements by Cerrejon Coal in Colombia!" *The Ecologist.* Nov. 17, 2017. https://theecologist.org/2014/dec/03/stop-forced -displacements-cerrejon-coal-colombia.

35   "Human Rights Group Demands Colombia Protect Indigenous Children." News | TeleSUR English. Dec. 18, 2015. https://www .telesurenglish.net/news/Human-Rights-Group-Demands-Colombia -Protect-Indigenous-Children-20151218-0037.html.

36   A copy of our full delegation report can be found here: https://www .usw.org/act/activism/civil-rights/resources/FINALCBTUdelreport.pdf.

37   *Id.*

38   Moloney, Anastasia. "Death Threats Won't Stop Colombian Anti-Mining Activist." Reuters. April 28, 2018. https://www.reuters.com/article/us -colombia-environment-rights/death-threats-wont-stop-colombian -anti-mining-activist-idUSKBN1HY2O2.

39   *Id.*

40   "Colombia: New Killings, Disappearances in Pacific Port." Human Rights Watch. March 4, 2015. https://www.hrw.org/news/2015/03/04 /colombia-new-killings-disappearances-pacific-port.

41   Frontline Defenders, #Colombia. https://www.frontlinedefenders.org /en/location/colombia.

42   Parkinson, Charles. "Colombian Paramilitary Paid US$250,000 for Murder of Robert Serra." News | TeleSUR English. Oct. 17, 2014. https: //www.telesurenglish.net/news/Colombian-Paramilitary-Paid -US250000-for-Murder-of-Robert-Serra-20141017-0052.html.

Chapter 5

1   "Venezuelan FM Blasts US for 'Celebrating' Amid Power Outage in Venezuela." *Orinoco Tribune*. March 9, 2019. https://orinocotribune .com/venezuelan-fm-blasts-us-for-celebrating-amid-power-outage -in-venezuela.

2   Lamrani, Salim, Paul Estrade, Wayne S. Smith, and Larry Oberg. *The Economic War Against Cuba: A Historical and Legal Perspective on the US Blockade.* New York: Monthly Review Press, 2013.

3   Noam Chomsky. "Cuba in the Cross-Hairs: A Near Half-Century of Terror." (Excerpted from *Hegemony or Survival*). https://chomsky.info /hegemony02/.

4   *Id.*

5   *Id.*

6   *Id.*

7   *Id.*

8   "US and Puppet Guaido Implicated in Terrorism Plot." Popular Resistance.org. March 24, 2019. https://popularresistance.org/us-and -puppet-guaido-implicated-in-terrorism-plot/.

9   *Id.*

10   *Id.*

11   Karni, Annie, and Nicholas Casey. "New US Sanctions Seek to Block Venezuelan Oil Shipments to Cuba." *New York Times.* April 6, 2019. https://www.nytimes.com/2019/04/05/us/politics/trump-sanctions -venezuela-cuba.html.

12   "How the US Is Strangling Haiti As It Attempts Regime Change in Venezuela." *Haitian Times.* Feb. 20, 2019. https://haitiantimes.com /2019/02/20/how-the-u-s-is-strangling-haiti-as-it-attempts-regime-change -in-venezuela/.

13   International Court of Justice. *Nicaragua v. United States* (Case Concerning Military and Paramilitary Activities in and Against Nicaragua), Judgment, 1986. https://www.icj-cij.org/files/case-related/70/070-19860627 -JUD-01-00-EN.pdf.

14   "Samuel Moncada: The US Is Organizing an Insurgent Army in Colombia (Contras?)." *Orinoco Tribune* (March 1, 2019). Retrieved at: https://orinocotribune.com/samuel-moncada-the-us-is-organizing-an -insurgent-army-in-colombia-contras.

15   Parry, Robert, "Contras, Dirty Money and CIA." *Consortium News.* Dec. 19, 2013. https://consortiumnews.com/2013/12/19/contras-dirty-money -and-cia/.

16   Perez, Ricardo. "Cimientos de Democracia." Redvolucion.net. June 25, 2018. http://www.redvolucion.net/2018/06/25/cimientos-de-la-democracia/.

17   Litkey, Charles, et al. "US Waged 'Low-Intensity' Warfare in Nicaragua." Dec. 1, 1989. http://www.brianwillson.com/u-s-waged-low-intensity-warfare -in-nicaragua/.

18   Willson, Brian S. "How the US Purchased the 1990 Nicaraguan Elections." July 1, 1990. http://www.brianwillson.com/how-the-u-s-purchased -the-1990-nicaragua-elections/.

19   Perez, Ricardo, *id.*

20   Baizerman, Paul. "The Nicaraguan Elections: US Government Promotes Fear and Divisiveness to Ensure Right-wing Victory." US International Election Observation Delegation. https://www.yachana.org/reports/nica2001 /baizerman.html.

21   Blum, William. "The Anti-Empire Report, #156." March 15, 2018. https: //williamblum.org/aer/read/156.

22   *Id.*

23   Kinzer, Stephen. *All the Shah's Men.* Hoboken: John Wiley & Sons, Inc., 2008, 115.

24   Kinzer, Stephen, *ibid.*

25   2017 CIA Release, 578–79, "Memorandum of Conversation." May 30, 1953. https://history.state.gov/historicaldocuments/frus1951-54Iran/d212.

26   *Id.*

27   2017 CIA Release, 595–96, "Memorandum of Conversation." June 19, 1953. https://history.state.gov/historicaldocuments/frus1951-54Iran/d220.

28   2017 CIA Release, 472–74, "Memorandum Prepared in the Directorate of Plans, Central Intelligence Agency." March 3, 1953. https://history.state.gov/historicaldocuments/frus1951-54Iran/d170.

29   2017 CIA Release, 536, "Memorandum from the Chief of the Iran Branch, Near East and Africa Division (Waller) to the Chief of the Near East and Africa Division, Directorate of Plans, Central Intelligence Agency (Roosevelt)." April 16, 1953. https://history.state.gov/historical documents/frus1951-54Iran/d192.

30   Wilayto, Phil. *In Defense of Iran.* Defender's Publications. 2008.

31   2017 CIA Release, 685–86, "Telegram from the Embassy in Iran to the Department of State." Aug. 18, 1953. https://history.state.gov/historical documents/frus1951-54Iran/d280.

32   2017 CIA Release, 699, "Telegram from the Station in Iran to the Central Intelligence Agency." Aug. 19, 1953. https://history.state.gov/historical documents/frus1951-54Iran/d286.

33   2017 CIA Release, 701, "Telegram from the Station in Iran to the Central Intelligence Agency." Aug. 20, 1953. https://history.state.gov/historical documents/frus1951-54Iran/d289.

34   Kinzer, Stephen, *ibid.*

35   2017 CIA Release, 950, Appendix, Summary of the Terms of the Oil Agreement between the International Oil Consortium and the Government of Iran, Signed 30 October 1954." https://history.state.gov/historicaldocuments/frus1951-54Iran/d375.

36   Bengali, Shashank, and Ramin Mostaghimm. "The Return of U.S. Sanctions Is Expected to Sow Misery in Iran." *LA Times.* May 29, 2018. http://www.latimes.com/world/middleeast/la-fg-iran-economy-2018 -story.html#.

37 Chomsky, Noam, and Edward S. Herman. *The Washington Connection and Third World Fascism*. Chicago: Haymarket Books, 2014.

38 "1964: Brasil & CIA." CounterSpy, April-May 1979, 4–23, reprinted in Brasil Wire (March 13, 2016). Retrieved at: http://www.brasilwire.com/1964-brasil-cia/.

39 *Id.*

40 *Id.*

41 *Id.*

42 Black, Jan Knippers. "The US and Brazil: On Reaping What You Sow." *NACLA*. March 6, 2015.

43 CounterSpy, *id.*

44 *Id.*

45 Pereira, Anthony W. "The US Role in the 1964 Coup in Brazil: A Reassessment." *Bulletin of Latin American Research—Wiley Online Library*. Retrieved at: https://onlinelibrary.wiley.com/doi/full/10.1111/blar.12518.

46 *Id.*

47 Black, Jan Knippers *id.*

48 Department of State briefing on "The Esquadrão da Morte (Death Squad)." June 8, 1971. Retrieved at: http://cnv.memoriasreveladas.gov.br/images/pdf/docs/Doc11_53384-6-002.pdf.

49 Memorandum of Conversation, Re: "Dominican Involvement in Terror." Dec. 10, 1969. Retrieved at: http://cnv.memoriasreveladas.gov.br/images/pdf/docs/Doc04_53384-4-001.pdf.

50 Memorandum of Conversation, Re: "Church-State Relations." March 6, 1972. Retrieved at: http://cnv.memoriasreveladas.gov.br/images/pdf/docs/Doc14_53384-6-005.pdf.

51 Message Text, from US Embassy in Brasilia to US Department of State, Re: "Dom Helder Camara Condemns Obsession with National Security and Defends Human Rights." Dec. 1977. Retrieved at: http://cnv.memorias reveladas.gov.br/images/pdf/docs/Doc41_CFPF.1977BRASILIA10229.pdf.

52 "On Religion and Politics." Noam Chomsky interviewed by Amina Chaudary. *Islamica Magazine*, Issue 19, April-May 2007. Retrieved at: https://chomsky.info/200704___/.

53 Reel, Monte, and J.Y. Smith. "A Chilean Dictator's Dark Legacy."

Washington Post. Dec. 11, 2006. http://www.washingtonpost.com/wpdyn /content/article/2006/12/10/AR2006121000302.html.

54   Kornbluh, Peter. *The Pinochet File, a Declassified Dossier on Atrocity and Accountability.* The New Press, 2004, 4.

55   *Id.,* 5

56   "CIA Activities in Chile." Sept. 18, 2000. https://www.cia.gov/library /reports/general-reports-1/chile/.

57   Kornbluh, *id.,* 1–2.

58   *Id.,* 14.

59   *Id.,* 1.

60   "CIA Activities in Chile," *id.*

61   *Id.*; and Kornbluh, *id.,* 22–29.

62   Thorer, Ishan. "The Long History of US Interfering with Elections Elsewhere." *Washington Post.* Oct. 13, 2016. https://www.washingtonpost .com/news/worldviews/wp/2016/10/13/the-long-history-of-the-u-s-interfering -with-elections-elsewhere/?noredirect=on&utm_term=.afc98b76b313.

63   "Pinochet's Chile." *Washington Post.* http://www.washingtonpost.com /wp-srv/inatl/longterm/pinochet/overview.htm.

64   Garces, Juan, and Peter Kornbluh. "The Pinochet File: How US Politicians, Bankers and Corporations Aided Chilean Coup, Dictatorship." *Democracy Now!* Sept. 10, 2013. http://m.democracynow .org/web_exclusives/1883.

65   Zigedy, Zoltan. "Remembering Chile." *ZZ's Blog,* Sept. 7, 2018. http://zzs -blg.blogspot.com/, citing, Petras, James, and Morris Morley. *The United States and Chile: Imperialism and the Overthrow of the Allende Government.* New York: Monthly Review Press, 1975.

66   "CIA Activities in Chile," *id.*

67   Galeano, *id.,* 270–71.

68   Norton, Ben. "Victims of Operation Condor by Country." BenNorton. com. May 28, 2015. http://bennorton.com/victims-of-operation-condor -by-country/.

Chapter 6

1   Perkins, John. *New Tales of an Economic Hitman.* Oakland: Berret-Koehler Publishers, 2016, 209–12.

2   "Hugo Chávez Departs." *New York Times.* April 13, 2002. https://www.nytimes.com/2002/04/13/opinion/hugo-chavez-departs.html.

3   Weisbrot, Mark, and Al Jazeera America. "Obama Absurdly Declares Venezuela a Security Threat." Venezuelanalysis.com. March 6, 2019. https://venezuelanalysis.com/analysis/11262.

4   Marquis, Christopher. "US Bankrolling Is Under Scrutiny for Ties to Chávez Ouster." *New York Times.* April 25, 2002. https://www.nytimes.com/2002/04/25/international/americas/us-bankrolling-is-under-scrutiny-for-ties-to-chvez.html.

5   "The US Empire, the CIA, and the NGOs." *American Herald Tribune.* https://ahtribune.com/in-depth/1789-william-engdahl-cia-ngos.html.

6   Shorrock, Tim. "Labor's Cold War." *The Nation.* Jan. 27, 2017. https://www.thenation.com/article/labors-cold-war/.

7   *Id.*

8   *Id.*

9   "US Tax Dollars Helped Finance Some Chavez Foes, Review Finds." Other News and *Boston Globe.* http://www.other-news.info/2004/02/us-tax-dollars-helped-finance-some-chavez-foes-review-finds/.

10   "THE OAS: Its Shameful History." Haiti-cuba-venezuela. March 7, 2010. https://hcvanalysis.wordpress.com/the-oas-its-shameful-history-parts-i-ii-and-iii/.

11   *Id.*

12   "Venezuela's Chavez Grants Amnesty in Coup." Reuters. Jan. 1, 2008. https://www.reuters.com/article/us-venezuela-chavez-idUSN3159004020080101.

13   Emersberger, Joe. "Western Media Shorthand on Venezuela Conveys and Conceals So Much." FAIR. Aug. 27, 2018. https://fair.org/home/western-media-shorthand-on-venezuela-conveys-and-conceals-so-much/. As this article notes, Lopez was ultimately arrested in 2014 for leading another violent effort to overthrow the government.

14   *Id.*

15   *Id.*

16   Rebelion. *Conversacion Indita Entre Chavez Y Fidel Tras Golpe De Abril En 2002.* http://rebelion.org/noticia.php?id=182710.

Chapter 7

1   Fernandez, Belen. "Paramilitarism and the Assault on Democracy in Haiti." Al Jazeera (Oct. 4, 2012) (citing, Jeb Sprague, *Paramilitarism and the Assault on Democracy in Haiti* (Monthly Review Press, 2012). Retrieved at: https://www.aljazeera.com/indepth/opinion/2012/09/201293072613719320.html.

2   *Id.*

3   *Id.*

4   Engelberg, Stephen, Howard W. French, and Tim Weiner. "C.I.A. Formed Haitian Unit Later Tied to Narcotics Trade." *New York Times* (1993). Retrieved at: https://www.nytimes.com/1993/11/14/world/cia-formed-haitian-unit-later-tied-to-narcotics-trade.html.

5   Fernandez, Belen, *id.*

6   *Id.*

7   Engelberg, Stephen. "A Haitian Leader of Paramilitaries Was Paid By C.I.A.," *New York Times* (1994). Retrieved at: https://www.nytimes.com/1994/10/08/world/a-haitian-leader-of-paramilitaries-was-paid-by-cia.html.

8   O'Connor, Maura R. "Subsidizing Starvation, How American Tax Dollars Are Keeping Arkansas Rice Growers Fat on the Farm and Starving Millions of Haitians." *Foreign Policy* (Jan. 11, 2013). Retrieved at: https://foreignpolicy.com/2013/01/11/subsidizing-starvation/.

9   *Id.*

10   Quigley, Bill. "Why the US Owes Haiti Billions—the Briefest History." Huffington Post, (May 25, 2001). Retrieved at: https://www.huffingtonpost.com/bill-quigley/why-the-us-owes-haiti-bil_b_426260.html.

11   Guma, Greg. "US Imperial Ways in Haiti. A History of Regime Change." *Global Research* (Jan. 30, 2017). Retrieved at: https://www.globalresearch.ca/u-s-imperial-ways-in-haiti-a-history-of-regime-change/5571770.

12   *Id.*; and Fernandez, Belen, *id.*

13   Quigley, Bill, *id.*

14   Fernandez, Belen, *id.* (quoting Greg Grandin).

15   Lockhart, P. R., *Id.*

16   Olson, Alexandra. "Honduran Coup Shows Business Elite Still in Charge" Associated Press (Aug. 2009). http://www.newsday.com/honduran-coup-shows-business-elite-still-in-charge-1.1353372.

17   Hodge, James, and Linda Cooper. "US Continues to Train Honduras Troops." *National Catholic Reporter.* July 14, 2009. https://www.ncronline .org/news/global/us-continues-train-honduran-soldiers.

18   Johnston, Jake. "How Pentagon Officials May Have Encouraged a 2009 Coup in Honduras." *The Intercept* (Aug. 29, 2017). https://theintercept .com/2017/08/29/honduras-coup-us-defense-departmetnt-center -hemispheric-defense-studies-chds/.

19   *Id.*

20   "Testimony That US Military Really Was Involved in the 2009 Honduras Coup: Statement of Martin Edwin Andersen to Department of Defense Inspector General Glenn Fine, on the Hands-On Role of Senior CHDS/ US Southern Command Staff in the 2009 Honduran Coup." May 23, 2016. https://www.facebook.com/crossbordernetwork/posts/testimony-that -us-military-really-was-involved-in-the-2009-honduras-coupstatemen /10153842910279440/.

21   Taliano, Mark. "What Happens When Empire Intervenes in the Affairs of Other Countries." Huffington Post. Dec. 19, 2014. http://www.huffing tonpost.ca/mark-taliano/canada-foreign-affairs_b_6011844.html.

22   Beeton, Dan. "Investigation Reveals New Details of US Role in 2009 Honduras Military Coup." CEPR online, http://cepr.net/press-center /press-releases/investigation-reveals-new-details-of-us-role-in-2009 -honduras-military-coup.

23   Johnston, Jake, *id.*

24   *Id.*

25   Planas, Roque. "Hillary Clinton's Response to Honduran Coup Was Scrubbed from Her Paperback Memoirs." Huffington Post. March 12, 2016. http://www.huffingtonpost.com/entry/hillary-clinton-honduras-coup -memoirs_us_56e34161e4b0b25c91820a08.

26   Johnston, Jake, *id.*

27   Naiman, Robert. "Wikileaks Honduras: State Dept. Busted on Support of Coup." Huffington Post. Nov. 29, 2010. https://www.huffingtonpost. com/robert-naiman/wikileaks-honduras-state_b_789282.html.

28   Johnston, Jake, *id.*

29   Fang, Lee. "During Honduras Crisis, Clinton Suggested Back Channel with Lobbyist Lanny Davis." *The Intercept.* July 6, 2015. https://theintercept .com/2015/07/06/clinton-honduras-coup/.

30   Frank, Dana. "In Honduras, a Mess Made in America." *New York Times*. Jan. 27, 2012. http://www.nytimes.com/2012/01/27/opinion/in-honduras -a-mess-helped-by-the-us.html.

31   "Before Her Assassination, Berta Cáceres Singled Out Hillary Clinton for Backing Honduran Coup." *DemocracyNow!* March 11, 2016. https: //www.democracynow.org/2016/3/11/before_her_assassination_berta _caceres_singled.

32   Johnston, Jake, *Id.*

33   Lakhani, Nina. "Berta Cáceres Court Papers Show Murder Suspects' Links to US-Trained Elite Troops." *The Guardian*. Feb. 28, 2017. https://www .theguardian.com/world/2017/feb/28/berta-caceres-honduras-military -intelligence-us-trained-special-forces.

34   Vine, David. *Base Nation: How US Military Bases Abroad Harm America and the World*. Metropolitan Books Henry Holt & Company, LLC, 2015.

35   *Democracy Now!, Id.*

36   Kane, Corey. "Honduras: the Most Deadly Place for Journalists in the Americas." Latin Correspondent. Nov. 5, 2015. http://latincorrespondent .com/2015/11/honduras-the-most-deadly-place-for-journalists -in-the-americas/#R5AuAP8me7A6WdAG.97.

37   Brigida, Anna Catherine. "Garifunas Flee Discrimination and Land Grabs in Record Numbers." Telesur. Feb. 23, 2017. http://www.telesurtv .net/english/news/Garifuna-Flee-Discrimination-and-Land-Grabs-in -Record-Numbers-20170223-0002.html.

38   di Fabio, Luca. "Economic Growth in Nicaragua Has Helped Reduce Poverty." The Borgen Project. April 2018. https://borgenproject.org /economic-growth-in-nicaragua-helped-reduce-poverty/.

39   CELAC, "*Primavera democrática en Nicaragua ¿anticipo del verano . . . o el invierno?*" May 12, 2018. http://www.celag.org/primavera-democratica -en-nicaragua-anticipo-del-verano-o-el-invierno/.

40   Prensa Latina, "Nicaraguan President Daniel Ortega at 80% Approval Rating." Telesur. Oct. 19, 2017. https://www.telesurtv.net/english/news /Nicaraguan-President-Daniel-Ortega-at-80-Aproval-Rating -Poll-20171019-0008.html.

41   Corporación Latinobarómetro, Informe 2017. https://t.co/lqTEHMGmki.

42   "The Global Gender Gap Report 2018." World Economic Forum. https:
      //www.weforum.org/reports/the-global-gender-gap-report-2018.

43   "NSCAG News: Nicaragua, 5th Place in the World in Gender Equality."
      Nicaragua Solidarity Campaign. http://www.nicaraguasc.org.uk/news
      /article/332/nicaragua,-5th-place-in-the-world-in-gender-equality.

44   Capelan, Jorge, and Stephen Sefto. "The Left Over Nicaragua: Between
      Pride and Ignorance." *Tortilla Con Sol* (May 16, 2018). Retrieved at: http:
      //www.tortillaconsal.com/tortilla/node/2807.

45   Perry, John. "After 2 Months of Unrest, Nicaragua Is at a Fateful
      Crossroads." *The Nation*. June 22, 2018. https://www.thenation.com/article
      /two-months-unrest-nicaragua-fateful-crossroad/.

46   Sweeney, Steve. "Right-Wing Militias Committing 'Acts of Terrorism' in
      an Attempt to Destabilize Nicaragua, Police Say." *Morning Star*. June 11,
      2018. https://www.morningstaronline.co.uk/article/f-lead-nicaraguan-acts
      -terrorism.

47   Blumenthal, Max. "US Gov. Meddling Machine Boasts of 'Laying the
      Groundwork for Insurrection' in Nicaragua." Grayzone Project. June 19,
      2018. https://grayzoneproject.com/2018/06/19/ned-nicaragua-protests-us
      -government/.

48   CELAG, *id.*

49   Snider, Ted. "A US Hand in Brazil's Coup?" *Consortium News*. June 1,
      2016. https://consortiumnews.com/2016/06/01/a-us-hand-in-brazils-coup/.

50   Brasil Wire Editors. "Hidden History: The US 'War on Corruption' in
      Brazil." Truthdig. Feb. 4, 2018. https://www.truthdig.com/articles
      /hidden-history-u-s-war-corruption-brazil/.

51   Treece, David, et al. "Brazil's Ex-President Lula Imprisoned to Keep Him
      Out of the Election." *The Guardian*. June 8, 2018. https://www.theguardian
      .com/world/2018/jun/08/brazils-ex-president-lula-imprisoned-to-keep-him
      -out-of-the-election-letters.

52   "UN: Brazil's Jailed Ex-President Lula Can't Be Disqualified from
      Election." *Agence France-Presse*. Aug. 17, 2018. https://www.theguardian
      .com/world/2018/aug/17/un-brazils-jailed-leader-lula-cant-be
      -disqualified-from-election.

53   Black, Jan Knippers. "The US and Brazil: On Reaping What You Sow."
      NACLA. March 6, 2015.

54   Miranda, David. "The Real Reason Dilma Rousseff's Enemies Want Her Impeached." *The Guardian.* April 21, 2016. https://goo.gl/ZZccDm.

55   Truthdig, *id.*

56   Langolis, Jill. "It's Been a Deadly Season for Environmental Activists and Land Defenders in Brazil." *LA Times.* Aug. 1, 2018. http://www .latimes.com/world/la-fg-brazil-environmentalists-killed-20180801-story .html.

57   Phillips, Dom. "Jair Bolsonaro Launches Assault on Amazon Rainforest Protections." *The Guardian.* Jan. 2, 2019. https://www.theguardian .com/world/2019/jan/02/brazil-jair-bolsonaro-amazon-rainforest -protections.

58   Milhorance, Flávia. "Brazil: Murder of Indigenous Leader Highlights Threat to Way of Life." *The Guardian.* Aug. 16, 2018. https://www.theguardian .com/environment/2018/aug/16/brazil-jorginho-guajajara-amazon -indigenous-leader.

59   "'Washington Has Never Forgiven Chavez for Nationalizing Oil'— Economist." *Orinoco Tribune.* March 13, 2019. https://orinocotribune .com/washington-has-never-forgiven-chavez-for-nationalizing-oil-economist.

Chapter 8

1   "The Crisis in Venezuela." Inter Press Service. March 2019. http://www .ipsnews.net/2019/03/the-crisis-in-venezuela/.

2   "Reactions to New US Economic Sanctions on Venezuela." Venezuelan Politics and Human Rights. Aug. 25, 2017. https://venezuelablog.org /reactions-new-us-economic-sanctions-venezuela/.

3   Boyle, Francis A. "Amnesty International: Imperialist Tool." *Counter Currents.* Oct. 23, 2012. https://www.countercurrents.org/boyle231012 .htm.

4   Weisbrot, Mark. "Trump's Other 'National Emergency': Sanctions That Kill Venezuelans." Op-Eds & Columns. CEPR. http://cepr.net/publica- tions/op-eds-columns/trump-s-other-national-emergency -in-the-americas-with-sanctions-that-kill.

5   Gokay, Bulent. "In Saudi Arabia's Quest to Debilitate the Iranian Economy, They Destroyed Venezuela." *The Independent.* Aug. 9, 2017.

https://www.independent.co.uk/voices/venezuela-saudi-arabia-oil
-prices-iran-price-war-inflation-destabilisation-a7883846.html.

6   Gokay, Bulent, *id.*

7   *Id.*

8   Weisbrot, Mark, and Al Jazeera America. "Obama Absurdly Declares
Venezuela a Security Threat." Venezuelanalysis.com. March 6, 2019.
https://venezuelanalysis.com/analysis/11262.

9   Boothroyd-Rojas, Rachael. "Obama Extends Executive Order Targeting
Venezuela for Second Time." Venezuelanalysis.com. March 5, 2018.
https://venezuelanalysis.com/news/12885.

10 Weisbrot, Mark, and Al Jazeera America, *id.*

11 Weisbrot, Mark. "Trump's Other 'National Emergency': Sanctions That
Kill Venezuelans," *id.*

12 Lesnick, Bruce. "Corporate Titans Target Venezuela." CounterPunch.
org. Feb. 6, 2019. Accessed March 25, 2019. https://www.counter punch.
org/2019/02/06/corporate-titans-target-venezuela/.

13 Weisbrot, Mark. "Trump's Other 'National Emergency': Sanctions That
Kill Venezuelans," *id; see also*, Jackson, Janine and Joe Emersberger.
"These Are Sanctions Directly Aimed at the Civilian Population." FAIR.
May 1, 2018. https://fair.org/home/these-are-sanctions-directly-aimed-at-the
-civilian-population/.

14 "End Mission Statement by the Independent Expert on the Promotion of
a Democratic and Equitable International Order to Venezuela and
Ecuador from 26 November to 9 December 2017." OHCHR. https:
//www.ohchr.org/EN/NewsEvents/Pages/DisplayNews.aspx?NewsID
=22530&LangID=E.

15 *Id.*

16 *Id.*

17 Boothroyd-Rojas, Rachael. "Venezuela's Maduro Blasts 'Kidnapping' of
Venezuelan Funds." Venezuelanalysis.com. March 21, 2019. https://vene
zuelanalysis.com/news/13519.

18 Mallett-Outtrim, Ryan. "Venezuela: "Terrorists" Torch 50 Tons of Food
as Ex-National Guard Chief Indicted." Venezuelanalysis.com. June 30,
2017. https://venezuelanalysis.com/news/13214.

19 Emersberger, Joe. "Western Media Shorthand on Venezuela Conveys

and Conceals So Much." FAIR. Aug. 27, 2018. https://fair.org/home
/western-media-shorthand-on-venezuela-conveys-and-conceals-so-much/.

20　*Id.*

21　"The United States' Hand in Undermining Democracy in Venezuela."
NACLA. https://nacla.org/news/2018/05/18/united-states'-hand-undermining
-democracy-venezuela.

22　*Id.*

23　Lesnick, Bruce. "Corporate Titans Target Venezuela." CounterPunch.
org. Feb. 6, 2019. https://www.counterpunch.org/2019/02/06/corporate
-titans-target-venezuela/.

24　MacLeod, Alan. "Everyone Washington Supports, by Definition, Is a
Moderate Centrist." FAIR. March 23, 2019. https://fair.org/home
/everyone-washington-supports-by-definition-is-a-moderate-centrist
/?awt_l=OLVK4&awt_m=gGEPWMXwp2R._TQ.

25　Ciccariello-Maher, George. "Venezuela: Call It What It Is—a Coup." *The
Nation*. Jan. 27, 2019. https://www.thenation.com/article/venezuela
-coup-guaido-maduro/.

26　"Venezuelan Government Slams New Trump Sanctions Imposed to
Cripple Economy." News | TeleSUR English. March 23, 2019. https:
//www.telesurenglish.net/news/Venezuelan-Government-Slams-New
-Trump-Sanctions-Imposed-to-Cripple-Economy-20190323-0001.html.

27　*Id.*

28　Henderson, Dean. *Big Oil & Their Bankers in the Persian Gulf, Four
Horsemen, Eight Families & Their Global Intelligence, Narcotics & Terror
Network*, 3rd Edition (Create Space 2010).

29　Embury-Dennis, Tom. "Guaido to Open Venezuela Oil Deals to Foreign
Private Companies, His US Envoy Says." *The Independent*. Feb. 5, 2019.
https://www.independent.co.uk/news/world/americas/juan-guaido
-will-open-up-oil-deals-to-foreign-private-companies-a8763821.html.

30　Páez Víctor, Dr. Maria: "The USA Has Opposed, Destabilized,
Overthrown on Assassinated Every Progressive Reformer That Has
Appeared on the Political Scene in the Region for More Than a Century."
American Herald Tribune. https://ahtribune.com/world/americas/2264-maria
-paez-victor.html.

31　"'Good for Business': Trump Adviser Bolton Admits US Interest in

Venezuela's 'Oil Capabilities'." RT International. https://www.rt.com /usa/449982-john-bolton-oil-venezuela/.

32 Midwest Communications Inc. "Exclusive: Venezuela's Self-Declared President Guaido to Nominate Own Citgo Board—Sources." 101 WIXX. Feb. 13, 2019. https://wixx.com/news/articles/2019/feb/12/exclusive -venezuelan-juan-guaidos-team-prepares-to-nominate-its-own-citgo -board-sources/.

33 Bloomberg.com. Jan. 25, 2019. https://www.bloomberg.com/news/articles /2019-01-25/u-k-said-to-deny-maduro-s-bid-to-pull-1-2-billion-of -gold.

34 Staff. "US Seizes $7 Billion in Venezuelan Oil Assets." PopularResistance. org. Jan. 30, 2019. https://popularresistance.org/us-seizes-7-billion-in -venezuelan-oil-assets/.

35 Johnson, Tim. "US Yanks Bank Assets from Venezuela, Lays Ground for Battle over Citgo." Mcclatchydc. Jan. 29, 2019. https://www.mcclatchydc .com/news/nation-world/world/latin-america/article225240320.html.

36 Id.

37 "US and Puppet Guaido Implicated in Terrorism Plot." Popular Resistance.org. March 24, 2019. https://popularresistance.org/us-and -puppet-guaido-implicated-in-terrorism-plot/.

38 Dobson, Paul. "Maduro: US Withholding $5bn of Medical Supplies in 'Criminal' Measure." Venezuelanalysis.com. March 22, 2019. https://venez uelanalysis.com/news/14397.

39 Kurmanaev, Anatoly, and Clifford Krauss. "US Sanctions Are Aimed at Venezuela's Oil. Its Citizens May Suffer First." *New York Times*. Feb. 8, 2019. https://www.nytimes.com/2019/02/08/world/americas/venezuela -sanctions-maduro.html.

40 Palast, Greg. "Venezuela: The Trump Coup and Our Next Oil War." March 15, 2019. https://www.gregpalast.com/venezuela-the-trump-coup -and-our-next-oil-war/.

41 Gibson, Connor. "Koch Brothers Gave $21 Million to Groups Defending ExxonMobil's Climate Cover-Up." Huffington Post. Dec. 7, 2017. https:// www.huffingtonpost.com/connor-gibson/koch-brothers-gave-21- mil_b_10602398.html.

Chapter 9

1   "Video: As Brazil's Jair Bolsonaro Prepares to Meet Donald Trump, His Family's Close Ties to Notorious Paramilitary Gangs Draw Scrutiny and Outrage." *The Intercept*. March 18, 2019. https://theintercept.com/2019 /03/18/jair-bolsonaro-family-militias-gangs-brazil/.

2   "Oil Greed? Bush Admin Knew Iraq Invasion Would Destabilize Entire Region: Classified Memo." News | TeleSUR English. March 14, 2019. https://www.telesurenglish.net/news/Oil-Greed-Bush-Admin-Knew -Iraq-Invasion-Would-Destabilize-Entire-Region-Classified -Memo-20190314-0021.html.

3   *Id.*

4   Alterman, Eric. "An Actual American War Criminal May Become Our Second-Ranking Diplomat." *The Nation*. Feb. 2, 2017. https://www .thenation.com/article/an-actual-american-war-criminal-may-become -our-second-ranking-diplomat/.

5   Vulliamy, Ed. "Venezuela Coup Linked to Bush Team." *The Guardian*. April 21, 2002. https://www.theguardian.com/world/2002/apr/21/usa .venezuela.

6   Alterman, Eric, *id.*

7   "Who Is Elliott Abrams, US Special Envoy for Venezuela?" Venezuela News | Al Jazeera. Feb. 12, 2019. https://www.aljazeera.com/news /2019/02/elliott-abrams-special-envoy-venezuela-190212012146896.html.

8   Brigida, Anna-Cat. "El Mozote Massacre: Waiting for Justice Nearly 40 Years Later." El Salvador News | Al Jazeera. Dec. 11, 2018. https: //www.aljazeera.com/news/2018/12/el-mozote-massacre-waiting -justice-40-years-181210151727647.html.

9   *Id.*

10 *Id.*

11 Danner, Mark. "The Truth of El Mozote." *New Yorker* and MarkDanner. com. 1993. http://www.markdanner.com/articles/the-truth-of-el-mozote.

12 *Id.*

Chapter 10

1   Blum, William. "Will Humans Ever Fly? Smashing Socialism in the 20th Century." https://williamblum.org/essays/read/will-humans-ever-fly -smashing-socialism-in-the-20th-century.

2   "Trump Admin Wants $500M to Fund Its Intervention in Venezuela." News | TeleSUR English. March 12, 2019. https://www.telesurenglish .net/news/Trump-Admin-Wants-500M-to-Fund-Its-Intervention-in -Venezuela-20190312-0007.html.

3   "Trump's Militarized Budget Slashes Medicare, Medicaid, and Clean Energy." The Real News Network. March 25, 2019. https://therealnews .com/stories/trumps-militarized-budget-slashes-medicare -medicaid-and-clean-energy.

4   Bloomberg.com. "US Is a Rich Country with Symptoms of a Developing Nation." Feb. 21, 2019. https://www.bloomberg.com/opinion/articles /2019-02-21/u-s-is-a-rich-country-with-symptoms-of-a-developing-nation.

5   "Virgin Galactic Founder Richard Branson Sets Date of First Trip into Space." NBCNews.com. https://www.nbcnews.com/mach/science/virgin -galactic-ceo-richard-branson-sets-date-first-trip-space-ncna969436.

6   "Jair Bolsonaro Praised the Genocide of Indigenous People. Now He's Emboldening Attackers of Brazil's Amazonian Communities." *The Intercept.* Feb. 16, 2019. https://theintercept.com/2019/02/16/brazil -bolsonaro-indigenous-land/.

7   Higgins, Eoin. "Rejecting Demand to Leave Venezuela, Russia's Lavrov Says 'Whole World Dotted' with US Soldiers." Common Dreams. April 4, 2019. https://www.commondreams.org/news/2019/04/04/rejecting -demand-leave-venezuela-russias-lavrov-says-whole-world-dotted-us -soldiers.

8   *Id.*